POLICEMAN'S LOT

ERICH HAR

THE AUTHOR IN NEW YORK, 1954.

Policeman's Lot

by HARRY SÖDERMAN

Funk & Wagnalls Company

New York

*A Criminologist's Gallery
of Friends and Felons*

2

Ah, take one consideration with another—
A policeman's lot is not a happy one!
　　—W. S. Gilbert: *The Pirates of Penzance*

This book is humbly dedicated to the two men who taught and inspired me most deeply: The late

CARL A. HAGGLUND, D.D.

in my day headmaster of the state high school and junior college at Ostersund, Sweden, who taught Lutheran divinity in the great tradition, who ran his school as a patriarch administers his family, and who by the simplicity of his thoughts and actions and the force of his strong personality instilled in those of us fortunate to sit under him a clear and solid sense of God and man, and

EDMOND LOCARD, D.M., M.J.

former director of the Police Laboratory at Lyons, France, a genius in criminology, a man of the world, and my fatherly friend whose quick and witty Gallic mind managed somehow to leaven my heavy Nordic brain, and by whose generosity of heart and mind an unknown Swedish youth was enabled to understand the police profession and to work his way up in it.

The cases told about in this book are all actual ones. Some have been discussed many times in the press. But as I don't believe in hurting people, and particularly so their innocent relatives, I have therefore changed sometimes names and places with the hope that no one will have old wounds reopened by my re-telling of tragic tales.

ACKNOWLEDGMENTS

In the writing of this book only a small number of other people have been implicated. To two of them, however, I feel a special sense of indebtedness: William Sloane, formerly editorial director of my publishers, who understood the problems confronting a man to whom English is only an acquired rather than a native language, and Sanford J. Greenburger, who proved both a friend and guide in the complexities of book authorship.

My thanks also go to Dr. Alphonse Morlet, of Vichy, France, who read and corrected the section on the Glozel mystery and lent some of the artifacts used to illustrate those pages. I am grateful also to M. Nepote, *Commissaire Principal* of the *Sûrete Nationale* and assistant to the Secretary General of the International Criminal Police Commission, who has both read the manuscript and given me valuable comments on it.

Whatever inspiration the reader may detect in the pages of this book I owe in good measure to my three children, Erik, aged eight, Karin, four, and small Michael, who was only nine months old when I began the writing. These pages were first drafted in a beautiful house on the west bank of the Hudson River, a house so modern in design that it had doors only for the bedrooms and baths. Thus, my literary labors in the drawing-room were punctuated by what Longfellow has called the patter of little feet. Some of the shortest sentences are perhaps the best the reader will find, and these I owe to my children.

Children seem able to take the strains of parental authorship in their stride. Erik has not neglected either me or the Lone

Ranger during these months. He has taken up the construction of space ships in his spare time, and, like his sister Karin, has played in comparative silence while his father paced the floor and fumbled for the words that follow. Little Michael, too, remained patient in his playpen even when certain of his personal needs were urgent. His blue eyes have been fixed on me day after day, but he has never lost his calm. Before such an audience a man can do only his best.

These three small lives have been an inspiration in the writing of this book. It has given me comfort to think that many years hence they may read this volume and learn what their foolish father did when he and the century alike were young.

HARRY SÖDERMAN

Rockland County, New York
August, 1954

PUBLISHERS' NOTE

While he was engaged in a final revision of the manuscript of this book, Dr. Söderman died unexpectedly of a heart attack at Tangier, North Africa. His publishers, however, had received most of his final emendations and thus the following pages are substantially in the form in which he would have wished to see them. Dr. Söderman had been also engaged in continuing these memoirs with a second volume narrating the events of his later years as an international criminologist and describing in detail a number of recent and famous cases with which he had been associated but which are not included in the present volume. He had also intended to continue to follow up the Glozel affair in the hope that modern scientific research might supply a final answer to that fascinating enigma.

CONTENTS

Contents

Policeman's World

Illustrations at pages 84, 116, 244, 276

The drawings of the Glozel artifacts in Chapter 17 were rendered especially for this book by Mamie Harmon.

LYONS AND EDMOND LOCARD

1

LITTLE GIRL LOST

This particular moment was a fragment of time which seemed to have no existence in the present. There were only the past with its burden of violent memories, and the future, which I knew already was destined to add another nearly intolerable entry to the catalog of deaths which I carried in my head. Death was, of course, a part of my profession: death and rape and larceny and swindle and arson and fraud and sadism and all the rest of the grim index of violences which man practices on man. Only this time it was not man on whom the violence had been visited. It was a little girl. A nine-year-old child. My mind almost refused to confront the starkness of that fact. Professional training is not a complete suit of armor against emotion, and even doctors never find death an easy thing to accept. The criminologist, the professionally-trained policeman, finds it no easier, and especially so in the case of a little girl destroyed by a maniacal impulse.

The cold, bitter rage which possessed me was nothing like the professional detachment which was theoretically the proper mood in which to approach the scene of a murder. It was so intense an emotion that I could imagine I tasted it on my tongue and felt it in the hairs at the back of my neck. I was hardly aware of the afternoon turning to evening, of the city's outskirts giving place to field and copse. Beyond the long sweep of the car's hood the headlights were making a broad cone of yellow on the black macadam, and the tires whined as the driver swung us round the curves.

My other two companions in the back seat, men with long experience under their belts, were as silent as I. Unquestionably they were gripped by the same rage as I was, and unquestionably, too, they also were being reminded of other instances of horror. Such memories do not fade; they merely accumulate.

All three of us were aware of the special importance of this case to which we were hurrying through the waning twilight. Behind us, in Stockholm, was the National Institute of Technical Police, an organization only recently established by the Swedish Government and still on trial as a new-fangled thing which cost money and was perhaps not at all necessary. As the Director of the new Institute, I was eager to justify its existence by our handling of this first major case. A detached segment of my mind informed me that the chances of failure were excellent. We had the barest minimum of information, knowing, indeed, only that the little girl's name was Gerd Andersson and that she was about nine—that she had been about nine, I corrected myself. She would never be any older. We also knew that her father was a workman, who lived with his wife in a modest residential district of the city.

A week before, Gerd had not returned from school. Mr. and Mrs. Andersson had telephoned neighbors and friends to inquire, but no one had seen the child. The panic of the parents began to mount. The father went out and combed every street in the neighborhood, but the dark Swedish night of early winter had already set in, and the girl was not to be seen anywhere. Then followed the usual pitiful steps—the telephone calls to hospitals and police precinct stations, all to no avail, the sending out of the missing-person alarm, the newspaper stories, the empty rumors and false reports, and the days of waiting, each a little more empty of hope than the one before. A whole week of that yielded no hint or sign of what had become of Gerd Andersson.

Now, on the eighth day, she had at last been found. Two hours earlier a couple of small boys, playing in the woods along a dirt road on the way home from their neighborhood school, had come upon her body where it lay on the ground, half covered with light snow. They had run to the house of a woman living not far away and told her, gasping and trembling, what they had come upon. The woman had notified the police, and the police in turn had telephoned to me in my capacity as the newly appointed Director of the Swedish National Institute of Technical Police. In a matter of minutes my men and I had loaded a staff car with our paraphernalia and were racing through the streets of Stockholm on our way to the scene.

The car began to slow for a turn.

"This is the place," the driver muttered, cutting into an unpaved track leading through woods.

As we jolted along the frozen ruts, the headlights picked out the trunks of trees and clumps of bushes. It was already very dark; I could see only a few distant house lights.

"This lane goes in to a dump," the driver told us. "Not many people live around a place like this."

None of us answered; the remark hardly needed making. After a quarter of a mile there was a cluster of lanterns and flashlights ahead. We pulled up to find two uniformed policemen, some local precinct detectives, and perhaps twenty onlookers gathered together. The sight reassured me slightly; I could now hope that nothing had been touched by the crowd, so that if there were any clues here we should have a chance to find them.

There was no need for me to issue any instructions. My two staff men, Carl Billsjö and Otto Wendell—men who never overlooked anything—were the best on the force. We had brought with us, in addition to the usual police equipment, the National Institute's most recent acquisition, a pair of portable floodlights bright enough to permit photographing the details of any "scene," as policemen call the physical setting of a crime. Billsjö and Wendell set to work, assembling the tripods for these lamps.

While they were putting up the standards, I took my flashlight and began to examine the scene. The general conditions were not encouraging. The ground had been frozen rock-hard for weeks, and I could find no trace of any struggle on its surface. There was a faint set of tire tracks leading toward where I knew the body was lying, but they were too blurred to provide any clue or identification. I could find nothing else; the thin, light snow of a few days before had not been sufficient to cover the ground, and the wind had already scoured it off the road and against the bushes and trees.

Suddenly the floodlights came on, and in their glare the setting took on almost the clarity of daylight. But even this fresh burst of light revealed nothing new. Several more cars drove up, adding their headlights to the general brightness. One was the old, black ambulance from the city morgue, and the others were police squad cars. The photographers were getting their cameras ready, the footprint and fingerprint men were preparing their kits, and the whole forgotten, desolate strip of road became suddenly populous and busy. I walked toward the body of Gerd Andersson.

It was lying about thirty feet to the right of the road, almost under a clump of bushes, and it looked like something thrown away. She was sprawled loosely on the ground, and something about the way she was lying made me guess at once that her body had been dumped there after the killing. She looked broken and pitifully small.

I could see strands of pale gold hair escaping from under the edges of the white aviator's cap she was wearing. She was fully clothed, and over her dress was the blue, belted trench coat that her parents had described in the first alarm. Blown snow had drifted into its folds, and the body itself was stiff with the angular rigidity of freezing. As I bent over her, forcing myself not to feel but merely to observe, I could see a line, dark by contrast with the stark whiteness of the rest of her skin, around her throat. Here was clearly the mark of strangulation.

The rest of my examination yielded nothing of use.

The sense of helpless fury which I had been suppressing went through me almost uncontrollably as I watched the photographers and police specialists go through their routines. Who would want to destroy a child like this, harmless, sweet, with her whole life still in front of her? Some kind of maniac, a sick mind and a sicker soul. And then to toss the body here, at the edge of a dump heap, and drive away! It simply did not bear thinking about. The other men must have felt much the same; they worked in almost absolute silence, and rapidly. In a short while the scene had been photographed, measured, and recorded.

The two small boys turned out to know nothing more than the fact of their discovery. The woman to whose house they had gone also knew nothing; she had never even seen Gerd Andersson. The bystanders could add nothing. The place itself was far from the Andersson home. It was impossible that the child could have walked there after school. No, I decided, if there were any clues, the girl's body would have to provide them. I issued a number of routine orders and then watched as the men from the morgue lifted the small, stiffened corpse into their ambulance and drove off, the motor coughing and spitting in the cold dark. Then the rest of us packed our things and returned silently to the city.

Back in my office I reviewed the general pattern of the case. Hard and careful detail work would reveal something on which we could go ahead: of that I felt confident. On the other hand, I felt almost equally sure that conventional police work on this case would lead nowhere.

It was fair to assume that the motivation had been purely sexual. The child could have had nothing of value on her. The autopsy would reveal whether she had been assaulted, or so I supposed. But even if there were no such evidence, the police would inevitably bring in all the known sex offenders and deviates in Stockholm and its surrounding area. In every police department there is a catalog of such persons, and they are generally easy to round up. Then would follow endless hours of questioning, endless checking of alibis, thousands of hours of painstaking work, with the strong probability that nothing would come of it all. Even in my apprentice years under a criminologist as great as Edmond Locard, and in a city like Lyons, this roundup procedure had never uncovered the offender, and here was a crime which might have been committed by anyone, likely somebody without a previous police record and wholly outside the catalog of known sex criminals.

This supposition was to be borne out in the ensuing days. The police rounded up dozens of men with past histories of rape, indecent exposure, and every sort of sex offense, but not one of them proved to be a logical suspect. Whoever had killed Gerd Andersson, it was not one of the cataloged offenders.

The report of the medical examination, which reached me later that same night, was not notably helpful. The girl's underwear had been ripped and rape attempted, but it had not been consummated, either before the strangulation or afterward. No conclusion, it seemed to me, could be drawn from these facts except the obvious one that the child had been killed while resisting a man. That was something, of course, but it was not much to go on. The problem was, which man?

I had decided to make the most meticulous examination of every single article of the girl's apparel, and to keep each piece of clothing in a separate bundle, so that if there were a clue on one it could not be accidentally transferred to a different article. On this scrutiny I based my hope for a successful solution of the case, so we awaited the arrival of the clothes from the morgue with the keenest anxiety. When they arrived about an hour later, we spread them out separately and went to work. I devoted my own primary attention to the girl's trench coat.

Together with my trusted Laboratory Director, Nils Landin, I examined the coat closely. Almost immediately we discovered that there were both fibers and hairs on it. As our examination proceeded, it became plain that almost all of the fibers were of the same kind, one which anyone could recognize: they were jute fibers, from sacking of the sort that potatoes and other vegetables are transported in. The hairs were almost equally unmistakable—rather short, stiff, and glistening. They had come from the coat of some dog. So—the body had then been lying in a place where there was, or had been, a dog, and where there were also vegetable sacks.

The rest of Gerd's clothes did not yield much in the way of information. The underwear had been ripped and there were fibers and hairs, though not many, adhering to the stockings. Well, those were the clues, and that was the evidence. Now, between us, Landin and I knew a good bit about hairs. In France, in my youth, I had helped to examine hairs in several murder cases. I knew how frail an item of evidence hairs are without some collaborating support such as dirt, some infection of the follicle, or other factors to support specific identification. But I was determined to follow this slender lead to its end. So I phoned Professor Axel Palmgren, an acquaintance of mine who held the chair of histology at the Royal Veterinary College. Grumbling somewhat at the lateness of the hour, he came immediately to our laboratory and examined the dog hairs.

"These hairs," he said finally, "are from an Alsatian—a German shepherd, as he is sometimes called."

"Are you sure?"

"Absolutely positive."

Forthwith, this admirable man started on a piece of research which was to go on for several months. Even after a suspect was found and the hairs of his dog were secured, the question of irrefutable proof remained. Professor Palmgren tried over and over again to establish identity or nonidentity between the hairs on the trench coat and the hair of a suspect's dog. I don't think anyone put in so many man-hours on this case as he did, working patiently while his eyes smarted under the powerful glare of the microscope. Thinking back, he reminds me of Arthur Koehler, who solved the ladder mystery in the Lindbergh kidnapping case. Mr. Koehler was the man, who traced *the* board out of the billions in the Untied States, from which that ladder had been made.

We were making some progress. Now, besides knowing that the girl's body had been in a place with an Alsatian dog and some

vegetable sacks, we also knew from the tire tracks that her body
had been brought to the dump in a car. It was fair supposition,
then, that what we had to look for was a man who owned a car
or truck, probably a light truck, in which he transported vegetables, and who also was the owner of an Alsatian dog.

At this time the population of Stockholm and its environs was
about 700,000 people. But of course they did not all own cars, and
the police were fortunately able to locate a car dealer who, for his
own sales purposes, maintained an alphabetical list of all car owners
in the area. This list was a godsend to us, because in Stockholm
the index of car owners was kept by license-plate number, while
the register of dog owners was kept alphabetically. By using the
car-dealer's index we saved thousands of tedious hours of cross-
checking and were able to compile a list of automobile owners
who also had Alsatians.

Next, we were able to reduce this preliminary list to a small
group of primary suspects, each of whom owned both an Alsatian
dog and not merely a car but specifically a delivery truck. All of
these proved able to clear themselves except one. This man we
will call Carl Johansson.

Johansson was a tall, dark, sneering sort of man with an overbearing manner. He was also something of a sportsman and athlete
and went in for cross-country running, at which he was quite successful. He owned a coffee shop in the suburbs, and on the side
he used a small delivery truck in which to make minor wholesale
deals in vegetables, usually potatoes. We quickly learned that while
he had no previous police record, he did have a bad reputation
with women, was divorced from the only one he had ever married,
and fancied himself as a ladies' man.

The circumstantial evidence against him was so strong that the
Public Prosecutor, Eugen Glas, at that time head of the detective
force in Stockholm, had him arrested. Later, returning to his
duties as District Attorney, Glas was convinced of Johansson's guilt
and prosecuted him. I was equally convinced that we had our man,
but the question was whether he could be convicted on the evi-

dence in hand. This seemed doubtful because of his absence of previous record and the fact that the women with whom he had dealt in the past had apparently succumbed passively, or even enthusiastically. He had no history at all as a rapist. However, there are few surprises in police work. The person to whom the evidence points is the person to concentrate upon until something occurs to direct suspicion elsewhere.

We made a most detailed search of Johansson's house. Our men found the basket where his Alsatian had slept, but the dog was gone. He admitted he had owned a dog, but he said that the animal had become ill and he had put it to sleep. The dog's sickness presumably accounted for the fact that the basket had been sterilized with a blowtorch. Even so, we found enough hairs in the crevices to establish, with Professor Palmgren's help, that the dog had been an Alsatian, and it was no trouble to prove that the dating of the veterinarian's receipt for the dog's killing had been crudely changed. We were able to show, with the help of other evidence, that the dog had not been killed until after the discovery of Gerd Andersson's body.

The interior of Johansson's delivery truck was almost barren of clues. He swore that he had never had a woman of any kind in the back of his truck, and this statement might have gone unchallenged if we hadn't made a curious discovery which threw light on the kind of man Carl Johansson was. When we reexamined the interior of his truck we noticed on one wall the faint mark of a rubber scrape which could have been produced by a rubber boot. Microscopical examination confirmed the finding. After we had confronted the suspect with this evidence, he admitted that he had lied and that indeed he had once had a woman in his truck.

His story was that one day, in the course of making a country delivery of potatoes, he had given a lift to a girl who was on her way to a meeting of a certain religious sect. After some advances on his part, he said, she had agreed to get into the back of the truck with him and that was how the boot mark had got on the wall of the truck.

This did not sound very likely, but the interrogators went to the district where he claimed the event had occurred and, sure enough, they found the woman. She not only corroborated the story in full detail but blamed herself for the whole thing. Her idea was that she had led Johansson on.

Our chain of circumstantial evidence was not strengthened by Professor Palmgren's reluctant report that after much effort he had not been able to work out an airtight method of proving that a particular Alsatian dog hair came from a particular Alsatian. Since there are plenty of Alsatians in Stockholm, the defense could claim that the child might have picked up the dog hairs on her coat from almost any such dog in the city. There were, of course, plenty of vegetable sacks also, and the fibers from them were equally unspecific.

Naturally, our suspect had his own story. He did not deny his interest in the opposite sex; he admitted it freely and with a kind of ostentatious pride. He asserted, over and over again, that he had spent the early evening of the day on which Gerd Andersson was murdered on a barge in Stockholm harbor in the company of a prostitute. He named the woman without hesitation, and after a short search the police found her. She did not deny her profession and declared that she had indeed had a number of assignations with Carl Johansson, but her recollection of dates was cloudy.

In time the case came to trial. It had been a newspaper sensation for weeks, and there were apparently few people in Stockholm who were not convinced of the guilt of Carl Johansson. I myself was certain of it, but a certainty in judgment is not the same as proof, and that element the case lacked, at least in the form in which it had to be presented to the court.

Johansson's life had been of such a kind that any decent person would have felt offended by it. He was a real rogue, but there was one thing which still makes me hesitate to declare him guilty. My entire experience has taught me that sex murderers are single-minded—one-track maniacs with a tendency to repeat their crimes.

The thing about Carl Johansson was that he had never been known to molest children.

There is no death penalty under Swedish law. The three judges who sat on the case were able and accurate men, and they must have found it hard to make a decision. There was no confession from the accused and no finality in the evidence, only the strongest possible presumption. Johansson was convicted of manslaughter and given a sentence under which he spent eight years in penal servitude.

Many years were to pass between the Gerd Andersson case and my final separation from the National Institute of Technical Police, just as many years of training and experience had preceded it. Yet it was a case I never forgot because it illustrated so many of the facets of a policeman's work—the horror and sordidness of crime, the necessity for attention to detail, the strain on any man not armored with the hide of a rhinoceros. The memory of it returned to me vividly, years later, when I was resigning from my post and looking back over the years which had taught me what a policeman's lot really is.

2

LEAVE-TAKING

A case like Gerd Andersson's murder is in itself not a major event in the life of a working policeman. Murder is uglier than many crimes, and the murder of a child is the worst of the whole category, but all crime is vicious and, as my career in criminology went on, year after year, I became increasingly aware of the cumulative weight of all the cases which had come under my responsibility. After fourteen years in my post as Director, I began to feel that, before I grew too old to enjoy it, I ought to sample a life in which the normal was the rule, not the exception, and in which the people among whom I lived and worked belonged to the great majority of normal and decent folk. I wanted a different kind of air in my nostrils. Therefore I chose to resign rather than to reenlist, so to speak, under the Swedish civil service system for another six years.

Eventually the last day of my tenure rolled around. In my familiar office the personal souvenirs had all been packed the day before. I could see the empty place on the wall where the largest of them had hung for fourteen years—the honorary plaque from the New York City Police Department, with its crossed nightsticks, handcuffs, whistles, and cap badge. Not far from that vacancy there was another empty space. The Tyrolean *bergmannstock* which had belonged to a Nazi police captain I once arrested had occupied

14

that gap. And there were still others where several special photographs had hung. The one of M. Locard, in particular; the office seemed empty without that. My desk, too, was bare. It did not look like the same piece of furniture without the old polished-metal baton, which had belonged first to my father and which somehow symbolized his essential qualities—the ruler edge for precision and the heft sufficient to subdue any interviewee foolish enough to make trouble. For the first time I wondered if my father had ever used it. I certainly never had. Well, it would be at home now, waiting in my study. It was time for me to go.

One formality remained. I took the safe keys and my police badge out of my pocket and walked into the outer office through the doorway with its two thick, wooden, soundproof doors. I laid the keys on the cashier's desk; my successor would pick them up. In this outer office, too, everything was as familiar as breathing. I noticed, as I had a thousand times before, that the place had outgrown its allotted space: the rooms were dense with typists and jammed with furniture and bookshelves. That overcrowding would be a problem for the next man. The very familiarity of everything around me made this departure seem suddenly difficult. I found it hard to believe that after today all this would not be a part of my life any more. My mind had been made up for a long time, and I did not doubt that my resignation was the better part of wisdom, but there had been no way of anticipating this final pang.

As I returned to my own office I was aware of it more intensely than ever before. I stood for a moment looking at the big writing desk, the bookshelves, and the oil paintings which officially belonged to the Swedish people—to the state, in other words. Years ago those paintings had been lent to the department by the National Museum of Art; they had been a part of the office ever since, but it was impossible to believe they represented the best the museum had to offer. They bore no connection with the work that had been done inside these four walls. Over the desk was the portrait of an unknown English clergyman of the eighteenth century, pudgy, serious, and hardly a good influence on the questionable characters whom I had interviewed here with small hope of their redemption. On the wall to the left was a still life which seemed even worse to me than others of the genre. There was also a portrait of a lady, not identified, but optical evidence suggested a blameless life devoid of temptation. Next to this was one with which I felt a kind of indirect identification because, like me, the subject had troubles: in her case, lice. She was clearly French, eighteenth century, young, and very refined. Her bright face was lit with an attractive, half-anxious smile as she examined her bosom, which was in evidence (as a policeman learns to express it), preparatory to pinching one of the small trespassers between her fingernails.

Farewell, then, to the clergyman, the lady, the flowers and the fruit, and the girl with the parasites. They had been an almost unconscious part of my life for a long time, and maybe my successor would appreciate them more than I had. The last good-bys had already been said; I had shaken all the friendly hands and heard the familiar voices vouchsafing good wishes for the future. These are the best rewards for a man who has enjoyed the privilege of working with a first-rate staff. Farewell indeed, now—so I went out of my office, into the department's lobby, where the sign said STATENS KRIMINALTEKNISKA ANSTALT—National Institute of Technical Police.

The gigantic old policeman who guarded the entrance hall on the first floor snapped what we both knew to be a last salute. I was a truly private citizen again, free to come and go as my own affairs demanded; free to sleep through every night with no abrupt summons to the scene of any crime, no matter how heinous.

In the street, my car was waiting with one of my farmhands at the wheel. In less than fifteen minutes we had left Stockholm behind and were running south in the direction of the family farm. The past was past.

3

WHERE THE HEART IS

Within fifty minutes I was sitting with my wife and our three children in the library of the farmhouse, drinking coffee, eating home-made cookies, and feeling like an almost-young god. It was a day ordained for feeling fine—the afternoon was golden, the windows to the garden were open, bees were humming, and from the small swimming pool in the garden came the happy cries of children. Far away I could hear the steady mutter of a tractor harrowing a fallow field. The air smelled of summer. All around me were the people and the things I loved best, and a sense of peace flowed over me. This was how the world was intended to be, how life was supposed to be lived.

There was every reason for experiencing such a feeling. A law of physics states that for every action there is an equal and opposite reaction, and our farm represented a good reaction to all I had just left. I had bought the place at the end of the last war, when the urge for a peaceful and orderly pattern could not be resisted; all through the years it was a deep and necessary part of our lives, my life and my family's. Without moving from my chair I could feel the extension of the place all around me, its landscape and its people.

The land first, of course—about a hundred and fifty acres under cultivation and another two hundred in woodland. Near the center of the place there was a small lake, with a mile of beach. In the fall the lake offered good duck shooting, and in the winter there was skating.

Our home itself was an eight-room frame farm house which we had modernized. It stood on top of a hill overlooking a rolling landscape which to me was enormously satisfying with its subtle curves and gently molded hills and swales. Through the library window I could actually see the cluster of other buildings that were far enough away from the manor house to allow a sense of privacy, but constituted integral parts of the farm.

First the red frame guest house, which dated from the middle of the nineteenth century. Then, farther away, the guildhall, built by our own farmhands out of an old granary. It was our social center, a huge place with great beams, an open fireplace that a man could walk into, and heavy benches fixed to the walls. Fifty or sixty persons could be seated and served there. For harvest feasts, we decorated it with sheaves of wheat and barley, beets and flowers, and invited the farmhands and their families and all the surrounding farm families. An accordion and a violin furnished the music, and we ate, drank, and danced till sunrise. Next, the barn where two tractors and the combine were kept, and near it the stables, one for the horses and one for the cows.

Beyond all these stood the three red frame houses in which our farmhands lived. We were especially proud of these dwellings, which had every modern convenience, including central heating. As I thought about each of our three farmhands I felt a sense of gratitude. For a man whose life has been spent in dealing with the dark and ugly aspects of human nature—the violence, fear, desperation, and bitterness which are so much a part of criminality— these men had always been unshakable testimony to the essential worthiness of human life.

Senior of the three was old Pettersson, the foreman, who at seventy was still far from retirement—vigorous, alert, and hale. He had the dignity that comes with responsibility, maturity, and self-possession. Such a man is almost part of the landscape he inhabits, a figure of strength and solidity. He would probably have regarded his life as its own justification, but I have often thought of what he might have accomplished if he had started out with a few more opportunities. He came, though, from a family of twelve without any resources, and he lived most of his life in the neighborhood where he was born.

In the second house was gentle Eriksson, always friendly, always hard-working, living only for his wife and four children. Finally, there was Björnberg, gay and, like the others, hard-working. Thinking about him made me reflect again, as in the past, that disaster and violence often touch even the quietest life. Björnberg's wife had been drowned in the little lake, and his only child, a daughter, had been crippled by polio. Still, Björnberg made a happy life in spite of his troubles. I have thought of him time and again when I was investigating one or another suicide; many of them had far less reason to despair of life than Björnberg had.

This country paradise was certainly mine, yet I was not to be allowed to stay in it even for a full twenty-four hours. The criminologist's world, of which I had been a part for so long, could hardly be shuffled off by the clearing out of a desk and the closing of a door. There were still some loose ends.

The first of them was my association with the International Criminal Police Commission, of which I had been a member for many years. Tomorrow was the date of its annual convention in Oslo, and it behooved me to attend, because I was the organization's Reporter General and a member of its Board. I had to take the night train to Oslo.

Of course it was an occasion I should not have wished to miss. There would be old friends, and much good talk and useful discussion. All the same, it was inevitably another appointment with the world of crime. In a quarter century I had not taught myself to like all the aspects of my profession. In that respect I was like many of my colleagues.

4

NIGHT THOUGHTS

As the train rolled through the night to Oslo, I could not help reviewing the things I had learned about criminology. The sensations of journalism and the entertainments of fiction are all very well for the general reader, but they do not mean much to the man who has spent his life with the raw material from which the eventual stories are derived, distilled, and denatured. I had no illusions about having surrendered a dramatic or privileged way of life.

The policeman's lot is not, indeed, a happy one. I had retired from my job voluntarily, not because of age or incapacity. As the wheels clacked away under my compartment, it seemed to me that the decision to experience the normal human pattern—to live, before it was too late, some years relatively free of professional concentration on the bleak and tragic failures which the human adventure produces—was a wholesome one, intensely practical.

A belief in the romance of crime is possible only for those insulated from it by the comfortable barriers of the printed page. It is a great deal easier to be entertained by accounts of crime than by actual crimes. This thrill, this *frisson* as the French would put it, was not what I had relinquished. At the simplest of all levels, no matter how toughened he may be, even the working policeman repeatedly finds his strong stomach turned by the sheer details of his job. He knows that most major crimes are disgusting. That is why I have never been a reader of detective fiction—with the sole, grand exception of the Sherlock Holmes stories, which I devoured in my early youth.

I hope the reader of these pages will not find an undue emphasis on the sordid aspects of crime, but there is no way of glossing over its most essential and commonplace elements. Murder, for instance, is the favorite subject of certain story-tellers, but in real life—and real death—it is a revolting and nasty business. Even the pathologist who makes the autopsy or the reporter who writes the account has less awareness of what murder is physically like than the unfortunate policeman who has to work on the case. His job demands that he be spared none of the details. He has learned that, from the moment the telephone rings in the homicide squad room until the murderer is behind bars, there is great pressure, both physical and psychological, on the detective in charge. The pressure has many aspects; one is sheer sordidness, from which the policeman cannot retreat. Often he must examine the body of the victim with his own hands, without avoiding any detail. It is those physical details which the author or reporter spares the reader. Frequently these include blood, vomit, the stench of decaying flesh, and even more repulsive matters.

Even worse for any man with heart is the human side of murder. Small children are left alone, or an old mother is bereft of her only son. The victim is always a human being, and there are very few human beings who do not have someone to mourn them when they are murdered. The detective is the man who has to bear the tears, the terror, and the despair of the bereaved. There is no joy in any of this. And, as if that were not enough, many cases necessitate weeks of hard and patient work, under constant pressure of public opinion. Finally, if luck is on the detective's side, the murderer is caught. Then a second tragedy is added to the first, because killers, like their victims, are also human. Even after that the relentless demands of his job require the detective to go over the entire experience again in order to prepare the case for court.

The ability of human beings to create evil is not so diverse as might be supposed. Fiction is apt to be more varied than fact. Therefore a detective's work in time becomes mostly routine, and when he handles a new case he is able to draw upon parallels with earlier cases. "There is nothing new under the sun," said the ancients, and this truism is conspicuously illustrated in detective work. Admittedly, life is very complicated and, like every other biological manifestation, will repeatedly display fresh details. Still, details are only details, and the general patterns do not change. This, too, the thoughtful detective learns, and it does not make his work any the more attractive.

The cheap and often morbid publicity given to the detective may attract some vain spirits to the career. However, though publicity may sell newspapers, it cannot make police work glamorous nor transform a policeman into a genius.

Detective work is mainly teamwork; only very rarely can one man take the credit for solving a case. Certainly there are some heroes, men who put everything at stake—including their lives—to make a daring arrest, but often they are not the ones who developed the leads to make the arrest possible.

This does not mean that police work is best performed by dolts. The requirements are constantly growing stiffer and the prerequisites more complex. Even men who are good at teamwork will not measure up to the job of the future unless they average a higher general education than most members of the forces now have. Many detectives today meet the highest standards of loyalty, courage, diligence, cooperation, and innate intelligence, but serious crimes involve deeply intricate elements of human behavior, and therefore their solution requires not only understanding but also a broad base of theoretical knowledge.

Perhaps in a hundred years people will look back on the average detective of the present in much the same light as today the barbers and bone-setters of the Middle Ages are regarded. Even in my own youth, training was necessary for the aspiring policeman and neophyte criminologist. For that reason I had gone to Lyons. Like an interne under a famous surgeon, I wanted to learn the rudiments of my profession from one of its greatest living practitioners. The world of criminology was not a large one in those days, and the name of Edmond Locard stood at the head of the roster.

5

MAÎTRE LOCARD

My first meeting with M. Locard was fairly brief, but even after more than a quarter century it remains fresh in my mind. The encounter reminded me, both then and now, of the gist of the famous conversation reported by Boswell:

Boswell: Will you, Sir, assume direction of me?
Rousseau: I cannot. I can be responsible only for myself.
Boswell: But I shall come back.
Rousseau: I don't promise to see you. . . .
Boswell: Yes, you will see me.
Rousseau: And a good journey to you.

Locard was decidedly a busy man, and at once he gave me to understand that even if I were to study under him in the Lyons Sûreté, I would have to stand on my own feet. Then he glanced at my testimonials from Sweden and Germany, shrugged his shoulders and remarked, "This is not much." But he made the comment in such a friendly way that my feelings were not hurt. Instead, I was more eager than ever to work under him. I suppose the idea behind his words was to put me on a kind of probation; at least, I soon discovered that he was one of the kindest and most considerate men in the world.

At that time Locard was about fifty years old—a thin, well-groomed man of average height with a small black mustache under an aquiline nose and keen, humorous eyes. He had a very distinct and cultivated voice. The indefinable thing about him was the effect of his presence. It conveyed an impression of personal greatness, and I felt it from the first moment. Locard had a brilliant criminological career and probably could have had several others as well. From early youth, for instance, he had had a strong liking for music and the theater. It is said that even as a schoolboy he could quote Molière, Voltaire, Shakespeare, and Goethe by the hour. However, after receiving his medical degree he became an assistant at Professor Lacassagne's famous Laboratory of Legal Medicine. Police science, due mainly to the contributions of Alphonse Bertillon and Hans Gross, had already become a partially independent profession, and Locard, strongly attracted by it, passed his bar examination in 1907. In 1908 he studied with Bertillon in Paris and then made a criminologist's world tour. That was unusual, for Frenchmen had a reputation for staying at home. He investigated the police methods of Berlin, Rome, Vienna, and even those of New York and Chicago. He returned to France in 1910 to find a heightened interest in modern detective work stimulated by the rising number of murders, many committed by *les apaches*. Locard used to tell us about a benevolent and mild-mannered deputy who introduced in the French Chamber a measure for the abolition of the death penalty, to which old Clemenceau retorted, "Let the murderers begin that."

A police laboratory was set up at Lyons to serve the east and south of France, and young Locard was appointed its first chief. In a few years he had become an authority on all phases of police work and a notable originator. He put the analysis of handwriting on a firmer footing, systematized the analysis of the dust in the clothes of suspects, invented a modified method of analyzing blood stains, and invented poroscopy, whereby the pores in the papillary ridges of fingerprints are used as a means of identification.

Locard was always interested in cryptanalysis, and during World War I he deciphered codes in five languages in his work with the

French General Staff. The year 1918 he spent in the United States as liaison officer with the French Medical Corps. In 1919, back at the laboratory, he began his prodigious writing. Year after year he produced works on various aspects of police science, crowning his achievement with the seven-volume treatise, *Traité de Criminalistique*. Moreover, he was also the music and theater critic of a leading Lyons newspaper. His students used to claim that there were just as many singers and ballet dancers waiting in his anteroom as there were criminals to be interrogated.

Studying under such a man was, of course, a great experience. Locard and I grew to be good friends, and the more I saw of him the more I liked him.

Our last encounter was during World War II. In February of 1942 I had to go to Switzerland for some talks with Colonel Werner Muller, an old friend who was Chief of Intelligence in the Swiss Army. After a week at the headquarters in Interlaken, I decided to visit Lyons, which is only a few hours by rail from Geneva and located in that part of France then presided over by the Vichy Government.

It was a bitter cold day when I set out from Geneva with an enormous package of sandwiches and chocolate as gifts for friends. At the border it was necessary to transfer to a French train which looked as if it belonged in a museum. The two over-crowded passenger cars were so ancient that they were heated with coal stoves and lighted by kerosene lamps. The Germans of course were not allowing trains from a foreign country to enter Vichy France without control, and they had made a station into a little enclave full of SS men in their black uniforms with the skull and bones on the cap. As the train halted, it was boarded, and the papers of the passengers were examined very closely.

As a neutral, I had obtained in Geneva a visa to enter the Pétain-governed section of France, but an elderly woman and a teen-age boy were arrested and dragged from the train in spite of their protests and cries. I asked my neighbors if they had any idea about the reason for the arrests, but they shrugged their shoulders and refused to reply. This reminded me that the law in force was different from the kind in which Locard was proficient.

It was late in the afternoon when we arrived at the dimly-lighted Gare Perrache, the principal railroad station of Lyons. I had telegraphed the police about my arrival, and a companion from my student days, Duffaux, was waiting for me on the platform.

"You have real courage to undertake a journey to this *sacré* country," he said. "Locard will see you tomorrow," he added. "He is tied up this evening. He says you will understand."

Then he escorted me to a hotel, where we made a supper of my Swiss sandwiches. Duffaux went out and came back after a while with a bottle of red wine.

"It is hard to get the stuff nowadays," he said. "The Germans take all new wines and distill them to get alcohol to drive the cars and tanks."

He pictured the miserable life of Vichy France—almost no food, no wine, no liquor, no tobacco, no clothes. Old people and infants were dying from lack of nourishment. The personnel of the laboratory had been out fighting for a while but were now all back on their old jobs. Every facet of life revolved around the question of food, and most arrests were connected with black-market deals. Almost all the famous restaurants of the city were closed, and many of the owners and chefs who had formerly delighted our palates were now behind bars because of infringements of the ration rules. Duffaux was thoroughly depressed.

The following morning I walked through the familiar streets down to the Palais de Justice. The temperature was 20 degrees below zero, centigrade, an extremely low temperature for France. Such weather would have been bitter even in peacetime, but without coal, clothing, or liquor, the cold was savage. On every conceivable wall surface there were big posters with portraits of Marshal Pétain or Admiral Darlan admonishing Frenchmen to behave and assuring them that eventually conditions would improve.

When I reached the laboratory, I was greeted by Locard and all my old friends. Locard was a trifle less worn and more cheerful than I had feared he might be. He said that he was comparatively comfortable because he had owned two race horses at the time of the capitulation. His family had lived on one of them for the last six months, and they had just killed the second horse and pickled a part of it for the future.

"You may not know it, my dear Harry, but pickled horse flesh is no delicacy," he said with a rueful grin.

I wondered if he meant to offer me a sample, but he took me instead to a small restaurant where he succeeded in getting us a chicken and a bottle of red wine.

It was an unexpectedly cheerful luncheon, for Locard can never be wholly down-hearted as long as he can work at his profession. Despite his grief over the humiliation of France, he grew enthusiastic as he recounted how he and the Detective Division found proof that the head of the German Military Mission at Lyons had cheated not only the French but also the German Government. Locard was thoroughly cheerful about that man's downfall.

Next day I invited some of my detective friends for luncheon at a famous eating place, in memory of the feasts we had enjoyed there in the old days. The meat we got that February day was equally memorable, in a different way. We were each served a lump of bad brown bread; the *hors d'oeuvre* consisted of a small pickled sardine for each; the main dish was lentils cooked in salt water. This repast was topped off with a small piece of *ersatz* cheese and a glass of tea brewed from some kind of local leaves. After an argument, the tavernkeeper did produce a bottle of thin red wine.

When I took leave of Locard, his eyes were full of tears. He embraced me, kissed me on both cheeks, and murmured: "We French have been bad boys, and now we have to pay for it."

It cannot have been an easy thing to say, but to accept things as they are and make the most of them has always been a part of Locard's greatness.

6

FRIENDS AND MENTORS

An apprentice detective in the Lyons Sûreté of a quarter century ago was not pampered. Our accommodations put the minimum strain upon the public purse and were designed for the comfort and convenience of the taxpayers rather than the pupils of the greatest criminologist of his day. There was a single room, big and drab, with plastered walls originally a light gray but now darkened by time and not time alone. Between the two high windows stood a vast and temperamental iron stove which emitted billows of coal smoke unless it was tended with meticulous care. Winter after winter had left deposits of soot which were never washed off or painted over.

There was a single old-fashioned writing desk with places for four, two on each side. Its double-sloped surface was composed of four hinged lids, under which we stored our papers and books. Each of us had a chair. The rest of the furniture consisted of two big filing cabinets and the stand for taking anthropometric measurements. Next to the entrance door was another room where we kept a large pile of coal. The windows of this room had been equipped with iron bars, and on the mornings when there were too many prisoners for speedy fingerprinting, photographing, and measuring, we locked the surplus in with the coal.

At the start of each day's work, the desk-table was fully manned by Detectives Duffaux and Poux, who were regular members of the police, Yovan Savitch, a Yugoslav police captain, and myself. On most mornings Duffaux and Poux would disappear for a while to visit the scenes of recent crimes, and Mohammed Zaki, an Egyptian student who is now influential in the Egyptian Criminal Police Department, would slip into the vacancy. We were a truly international assembly.

Detective Duffaux was a blond, slightly stocky man, originally a sturdy peasant from the Jura. He had been assigned to the laboratory because he was the nephew of Armand Chevassus, who had become in effect the assistant chief of the laboratory by virtue of his personality and intelligence. Duffaux himself had plenty of brains and eventually succeeded his uncle. At first he was a little gruff toward me, probably because of an inherent suspicion of foreigners. Eventually we became very close friends, and we still exchange letters. In those early days, Duffaux had scarcely any interests aside from fingerprints and handwriting comparisons. He devoted all his off-duty hours to his family, and every summer for his three weeks' vacation he took them to the mountains to visit his parents on their farm. Years later I had a heart-warming glimpse of this part of his life.

One summer in the middle thirties I happened to be motoring through France and, remembering Duffaux's unvarying schedule, I made a point of looking him up. I was directed to a field, through which ran a stream, and there, amid much splashing and the cries of a dozen children, was a figure something like a big white dog. It was Duffaux, laughing and playing with the children of the village. When he recognized me, he gave a howl of joy, waded out of the water and embraced me with his wet body.

"*Mon dieu*," he cried, "now you must have luncheon in my home. I will tell my mother about this."

Thereupon he put on his clothes, and together we went down to the village. There he introduced me to his old parents and to the rest of the village inhabitants, most of whom seemed to be his cousins or at least second cousins. Mother Duffaux made a fire under the big, black cauldron in the summer kitchen and sent some of her offspring to fetch vegetables and kill chickens. Then with all the men of the village we walked to the village tavern, where we had apéritifs of red or white wine.

There must have been more than twenty of us seated at the huge lunch table, but there was food enough for everybody, and more. Madame Duffaux served the steaming soup directly out of the cauldron. We washed the delicious chickens down with good red wine, and the meal ended with great chunks of the famous *gruyère de Jura*, which to my mind is the best cheese in the world. In this way I learned that, like me, Duffaux had his other world, his private kingdom, which like mine, was far from the city and far from the world of crime and criminals.

Not only was Duffaux the nephew of Chevassus, but the other detective, Poux, was a cousin. Poux was a swarthy young man with the head of a Roman emperor and a mind as quick as lightning. His specialty was examining and photographing scenes, as we called the places where crimes had occurred, and whatever I know about that business I owe largely to him. Every time there was an interesting case, Poux took me with him. We would start out with his heavy, old-fashioned camera and tripod, the fingerprint outfit, and some modeling wax to make casts of the marks of burglars' tools. Seldom were we offered a car from the Detective Division; instead we lugged this heavy paraphernalia all around the city, often on foot but using street cars wherever we could.

At the time, Poux was betrothed to a charming little seamstress, and he rented a very cheap three-room flat. Since the proprietor of the house refused to repair anything, Poux himself put in a bath-room and a new kitchen sink, papered the walls, and painted the floors and woodwork. I attended their wedding, and afterwards they lived like two doves. Within a year they had a little girl, and Poux was so proud I thought he would burst. But their happiness was not destined to last. When I visited Lyons in the terrible days of 1942 I found a haggard and despairing Poux.

"I have lost my little wife," he told me with tears in his eyes.

"She died of consumption a year ago but, thank God, I have succeeded in getting my little girl into a convent where she has food and shelter."

Still, human nature is elastic. I saw Poux a couple of years ago, and he was almost the jolly fellow I had known in my youth, though he had grown fairly fat and had arthritis in one leg. He had married the owner of a prosperous tavern and was quite well off.

My fellow apprentice, Yovan Savitch of Yugoslavia, was older than I and very popular with all of us. He had fought as a Serbian officer in World War I and afterward had held a position in the administration of the new Yugoslav state. He was a gentle and mild-mannered man who seemed ready to embrace the entire world, and he admired in others the quality he himself so conspicuously possessed. His favorite way of expressing his admiration for someone was to say, "You really have the great Slav heart."

Savitch's own Slav heart resulted in his having to witness, along with the rest of us, a tragic episode. A compatriot of his, Dragorad, came to Lyons at Savitch's urging, to study legal medicine under Locard after he had taken an M.D. in Yugoslavia. He was extremely likable—young, brilliant, and with an insatiable appetite for life. But he accomplished before our eyes the difficult feat of drinking himself to death in a single year.

We began to notice that Dragorad was red-eyed in the mornings. Then, though he had at first always been dapper, he began coming in unshaven and wearing rumpled clothes. His hands trembled, and several times each morning he went to the tavern across the street for Pernods, the stuff that is closely related to absinthe. Then he took alcoholic breakfasts with Lacharnier, the police sergeant in charge of our jail. It was alleged that he had at least two bottles of white wine and a few Pernods with his breakfast every morning. The next downward step was his stealing of pure alcohol from the bottles in the laboratory. This was incredible in France, where good liquor could be bought at decent prices.

Soon he was evicted from his rented room and took to sleeping on the benches in the park, making a hasty toilet at the laboratory each morning. The police were embarrassed, but Dragorad met with so much sympathy that he was never arrested for vagrancy. Locard had several talks with him in the hope of persuading him to abstain, without result. Finally, Locard reported the matter to Dragorad's family in Belgrade, and they sent his sister to fetch him. This devoted woman put him in a hotel, had him given a bath, a shave, and a haircut. That afternoon he entered the laboratory and told us meekly that we was going home.

"I will probably never see you any more, but thank you, anyway, for all your patience," he said.

The following month we heard that he was dead. I have seen many drunkards but Dragorad was an outstanding case: a man only thirty years old, apparently quite normal and good-humored, who stubbornly drank himself to death.

Naturally, Duffaux, Poux, and we three apprentice criminologists did not constitute the entire staff of the police laboratory in a city the size of Lyons. By the twenties, the science of crime detection and prosecution had become enormously ramified, and some aspects of it, such as legal medicine, had to be handled by pathologists. Therefore we had two staff experts on legal medicine working under the direct supervision of Locard. Both these young men were able and brilliant, though poles apart in character and personality. Berger was quiet and diffident, willing to display his really deep knowledge only when it was absolutely necessary. He was, in addition, an idealist who suffered anguish over some facets of his work. Taupin was also attractive, but where Berger was shy he was brash. On the surface he was a perennial freshman, always full of laughter and convinced that he was on all occasions absolutely right. This trait was not always easy to live with, but its basis was a sensitivity not very unlike Berger's.

This part of Taupin's nature was displayed to the rest of us in the account he gave of a case on which he had been called. It was not the kind of case that ordinarily appears in polite conversation—

though it did become a *cause célèbre*—but the outcome aroused Taupin's inherent hatred of injustice.

He had been working late at the laboratory when he was summoned to accompany two members of the Detective Division to the outskirts of the city, to a pseudo castle owned by a silk manufacturer, one of the wealthiest men in the region. When Taupin and the two detectives arrived, they found a young man beaten to within an inch of his life on the floor of a corridor, groaning in pain.

The manufacturer's wife had been having an affaire with the victim. When he turned his attentions to her seventeen-year-old daughter and scaled the wall of the castle to climb through the girl's window, the jealous mother had already got wind of the project, locked the girl up in her own bedroom, and put herself in the girl's bed, with the valet and the gardener hidden in an adjoining room armed with sticks. When the young man entered the girl's room he was attacked.

The gardener's wife was aroused by the howls of the victim and telephoned a police station, from which the Detective Division was alerted. When Taupin and the detectives arrived, the valet and the gardener were standing beside their victim like two dumb creatures, apparently astonished at what they had done. The furious mother was leaning over the body, screaming invectives. From a nearby room the detectives and Taupin could hear the sobs and cries of the daughter.

"Never saw a place like it in my life," declared Taupin. "The whole corridor was splashed with blood; there was even blood on the ceiling. I thought that we could arrest that old hag on the spot. But what does she do but go to the telephone and get the District Attorney on the line. He ordered us to take the young man to a hospital and to make a written report, but not to make any arrests until he himself had gone over the affair. And that's supposed to be justice?"

The young man later emerged from the hospital disabled for life. The valet and the gardener stuck stubbornly to their story that they had thought he was a burglar molesting the lady of the house. After they got hold of the story, most of the newspapers ran angry editorials, but nothing official was done and soon the episode was forgotten. I have heard that the silk manufacturer did settle quite a fortune on the young man in order to keep him quiet.

Taupin's story made a deep impression on me. It was the first case in my experience in which, without a doubt, wealth and social standing had hampered the course of justice. I was to see many comparable cases afterwards in different countries.

Taupin became the resident medical man of Réunion, that lonely island south of Madagascar, where the French Republic was then holding important prisoners of state. I think Taupin was induced to take this step by Réunion's Chief of Police, who visited us one day in the in the laboratory. This little sunburnt man told wonderful stories about Abdel Krim, the rebellious Moroccan chieftain who had spent many years on Réunion with his harem, and about several Indo-Chinese princes who were incarcerated there for life, and many other anecdotes of that godforsaken place.

The most stalwart of all Locard's staff was Armand Chevassus—good old Chevassus, as we all thought of him—like his nephew, Duffaux, of peasant stock. He had an intellectual's acumen and the sturdy physical vigor of his breeding. He was a man of a somewhat portly stature, around fifty, with a magnificent forehead and straight-looking, steady gray eyes. He was the right hand of our boss, and chief of the laboratory's personnel. The greater part of his life had been spent in the laboratory, except for the World War I years which he had spent as a noncommissioned officer fighting the Germans in the trenches at Verdun. He sported several ribbons of military medals as a souvenir of those days.

Without Chevassus the laboratory would have been a lesser thing indeed. Peculiarly enough, he was not a detective but a simple plainclothesman and still, officially, also a sergeant in the uniformed branch. When there was rioting or other major trouble, he would, with much grumbling, put on his uniform and go out on duty.

On one occasion, in the line of duty he nearly crowned me with a nightstick. That was at a Communist demonstration accompanied by riots. Every detective on the force was out, mixing with the crowds, and I among them. All at once, an echelon of the uniformed police attacked the part of the mob where I happened to be in circulation. There I was, face to face with old Chevassus, who, not recognizing me, was lifting his nightstick to hit me on the head.

I ducked, crying, "Chevassus!"

He reacted at once and the nightstick took another direction and landed on the ear of one of the demonstrators, who sank senseless to the ground.

"Well, my boy, you had a narrow escape there," hissed Chevassus, as he resumed his steamroller movement through the crowd.

Locard used to give Chevassus part of the fees accrued from the handwriting cases, so I suppose he may have been in comfortable circumstances. Many times he invited me to dine with him and his wife and daughter. He was very fond of the red wines of the region, and there would inevitably be *sauté de lapin*, the famous French rabbit stew at which Madame Chevassus was a specialist. Every time I sat down to the repast, Chevassus would jokingly assure me that the raw material of the stew was not cat's meat. Once Chevassus and I, traveling together on an investigation, had a tasty stew at a country inn in the mountains. After the meal, Chevassus said to the innkeeper, "This was really good cat." Thereupon to my horror the innkeeper nodded and said, "Yes, there are some very good cats around here."

Chevassus' personal plans as to the future were quite definite and characteristically French. He meant to retire in a few years and had already bought a small house near his native village in the Jura Mountains. Here he would plant his cabbage, as the idiom puts it, go fishing in the mountains, and live on his pension and savings. No matter how badly paid French officials are, they always manage to have a savings account. And almost all of them dream of an early retirement to the country. There is probably no other nation where pensions are such a burden on the national budget. When a few years ago the government, in a frantic effort to save money, proposed to raise the retirement age by a few years, a howl of protest arose from thousands of small officials.

Chevassus had the soundest judgment I have known. As long as there are in France plenty of his type among the men in the street, and there are still many, one need not despair about that country. Locard once styled him "an unknown but true scientist, the most remarkable self-taught man I ever met."

Alas, Chevassus was destined never to revel in the delights of retirement. Shortly after he moved into his little house, he developed serious heart trouble and was an invalid for a year before he died. A few months before his death, I visited him. What I saw was only a shadow of the sturdy old Chevassus of the laboratory days.

His voice was barely a whisper: "No more *beaujolais* for me, my friend. I am sorry I did not have more of it when I could. But you, my boy, should drink a bottle."

While we were sitting together before his house, watching the sun slowly sink behind the massive Jura Mountains, I emptied a bottle and we talked about life, about the Great Doctor, about his daughter who had just married, about everything except his illness. When I grasped his hand for the last time, I found that my eyes were wet.

Last, and in many ways least, of the old laboratory crowd was the author of this book. It seems to me that in those days I was strong and healthy with some knowledge of chemistry and physics and their practical applications. Besides my native tongue, I spoke German fluently and had in my journeys picked up a working knowledge of French and English. Earlier I had acquired an odd and in some ways intimate first-hand knowledge of Asia and its inhabitants. I had a theoretical knowledge of criminology, which was to prove very helpful. And then there was my insatiable lust for reading.

At the School of Science at Lyons University I took courses in

Legal Medicine and, of all things, Roman Law, a subject which has always fascinated me although I can now see that I might have used my time better. The School's chemistry professors were Meunier and Grignard, the latter the 1912 winner of the Nobel Prize. It was Grignard who stopped me one fall morning in 1928 on the stairway and honored a mere Swedish student by remarking, "My friend, the last universal genius is dead. There will never again be a man like Svante Arrhenius." Thus I first learned about the death of one of the heroes of my youth, the great Swedish physicist, chemist, astronomer, and author who looked like a cabby but had the soul of a Leonardo da Vinci. I remember still how proud I was in high school, when, because of my good grades in chemistry, I was awarded a copy of Arrhenius' book, *Worlds in the Making*—incidentally the only prize I ever won.

As for my personal circumstances, I rented a cheap but comfortable room from the old widow of an Army captain. She was more than kind to me and invited me every Sunday morning to her breakfast of *café au lait* and delicious hot *croissants*. These latter were especially welcome to a young man nearly always hungry. Because I did not want to ask my mother for more money, I worked out a frugal and sane method of living. Every evening on my way home, I bought a big chunk of crisp French household bread. This I cut in two and had one piece for supper, washing it down with water from a faucet. Early the next morning I ate the other half, and for luncheon I had nothing except water and two pipes of black Caporal tobacco. The luncheon money was thus saved for the afternoon snack. This method was very practical since it freed my lunch hours for reading and laboratory work.

This may sound like hardship, but it did not seem so to me at the time. My police studies and my academic work engrossed me in every waking hour, and there was no time to feel sorry for myself. I enjoyed everything I did, and my travels in Asia had taught me not to regard a full stomach as a prerequisite. Besides, I had other pleasures which were far more important than food. There was the companionship of the men in the laboratory and the rich satisfaction of working under Locard. I must admit that I have always been fond of good food, and lots of it, and no doubt these months in Lyons on short commons whetted my enthusiasm in later years for the excellent meals I have since consumed. But it is possible to exist on bread and water, as both criminals and criminologists can testify.

7

LYONS VIA A MOUNTAIN

The route which had taken me to Lyons to study under Locard was not, perhaps, extraordinary, but it had been full of experiences and events which often stood me in good stead in later years. As a schoolboy, I had been the despair of my teachers, chemistry and physics being the subjects that interested me to the exclusion of the rest.

I finally went through the Chemical School of Malmö in southern Sweden in order to become an industrial paper chemist. Even then I was of a divided mind. Even while still an adolescent I had become interested in criminology. At the start it was a mere hobby, like collecting stamps, and several years elapsed before I saw a chance to turn it into a profession. But I do not think there were at that time many boys in the world who had seriously read so much as I had about crime, criminals, and the different methods of their detection and treatment.

How did such a taste match up with the science and the practical techniques of a pulp and paper chemist? Well, not closely. Without too much enthusiasm I worked for a short time in a pulp mill in northern Sweden, decided that further study was in order if I were to advance in that field, and promptly enrolled in a special school for pulp and paper chemists in Altenburg, Saxony.

Now I was treated to my first look at a really sick society. Postwar Germany, in the grip of inflation, was something quite incredible. Because any kind of sound money would buy anything at all in Germany, many Scandinavian boys of my generation took the opportunity to study in Germany, and the experience scarred them for life. They acquired tastes, vices, and diseases they could not throw off later; the inflated money cast a sort of spell over their minds which could not be resisted. One morning, I remember, I received a hundred-crown note from my mother. That hundred crowns would normally have been worth about thirty-three dollars, but in postwar Germany it was a minor fortune. With it I bought a riding horse (saddle, bridle, and all), several suits of clothes, and a shelf of books. Some of my fellow students traveled in private compartments and ate luxurious meals served to them outside the dining car, to avoid contact with the wretched Germans. Another might buy an entire tavern if he happened to like the wine served there.

The thing that kept me comparatively sane in that nightmare world was my insatiable craving for reading. I soon spoke and read and wrote German fluently, and I began to collect a small library of German titles dealing with criminology. This taste rather puzzled my friends, who would thumb through the books looking for lurid illustrations, without understanding my interest in the nature of crime and its causes. They felt it was somewhat macabre. Perhaps so, but during that exposure to every conceivable form of temptation and evil, books were my refuge, and collecting them was a harmless hobby.

I even graduated from the Altenburg school, though not with any particular distinction. Most of my time had not been devoted to the chemistry of pulp and paper, but I had learned enough to get ahead in the industry if I chose. At the moment it seemed scarcely worthwhile to return to it because soon I should be called to serve my term in the infantry regiment of my province, the Jämtland Rifles. It seemed wiser to use the intervening time as a sort of *Wanderjahr*, as the Germans call a period of traveling.

I spent the next few months in Paris and Rouen, acquiring some knowledge of French. Then one day I received a letter from my mother, my chief source of income, saying that she could no longer support me and that I ought to come home. I decided there was plenty of time in the future for those immense forests of northern Sweden, and I did not want them to swallow me up just yet. Accordingly, I signed on for two months as a fireman on a small Norwegian steamer running between England and continental ports. Young and strong as I was, the first few days of that nearly broke me. At the end of my watch I would stagger up the ladder from the boiler room with the curses of the engineer still ringing in my ears, too tired to eat or even wash, and throw myself on my berth. But after a week my muscles hardened, and I became quite expert at stoking. When my two months were up I went home, and I would not have missed this sea-going episode for anything.

During the six months of my military service I kept myself in funds and at least partly in mental trim by giving private lessons in chemistry and physics to various lazy students at the local college. All the time I was thinking about the future, and one decision emerged more and more clearly. I wanted to see a great deal more of the world, and in particular Asia. Even as a boy the countries of the East had held a fascination for me, and now I determined to see them, come to know their peoples, and study their police systems. Such a trip would be a tremendous adventure, I felt, and indeed I was not wrong in that. But easier said than done. A young pulp-and-paper chemist living in the north of Sweden does not find it easy to get to Carthage and Cathay with limited means. Nevertheless, over the strenuous objections of my patient mother, I set about finding a way.

In a rather complex fashion I finally solved the problem. I met a benevolent gentleman of considerable wealth who was the director of a bicycle manufacturing company. He was sympathetic not only to my dream of travel but to its inherent publicity possibilities. He promised to pay my expenses if I rode one of his bicycles through the Continent down to Constantinople. Furthermore, he agreed to support me in a modest way if I continued my journey through Asia. With this financial backing, it was easy to persuade the editors of a Swedish police magazine, as well as those of a large Swedish weekly, to engage me as correspondent on a free-lance basis.

In preparation I paid a visit to Sven Hedin, the famous explorer, who knew more about the interior of Asia than any other living man. He was very kind, gave me good advice as to the route, and promised to keep up a correspondence with me. This promise he more than lived up to. I still cherish a big packet of hand-written letters from this Marco Polo of modern times. His advice proved especially valuable while I was traveling camelback from Persia to India across the Beluchistan desert.

One chilly day in autumn, 1923, I set forth. Some day the story of that trip may be worth the writing but, so far as the present narrative is concerned, it can only be summarized. I did go to Constantinople by bicycle, and then on to Asia, where I spent eighteen months. I even got as far as China. In the course of my wanderings I employed every conceivable means of transportation besides the bicycle—elephants, canoes, camels, and a dozen others. Almost the entire time I lived with natives of the countries through which I passed. I came home a man who understood himself far better, and I was more deeply interested in criminology than ever before. I had seen policemen in many countries, had studied their methods, their successes, and their failures, and I was determined to become a criminologist myself.

Once again, this was a decision easier to reach than to follow. I knew that a further period of study lay ahead of me, and that might prove difficult. All the higher police jobs in Scandinavian countries were held by lawyers, and it seemed that without admission to the bar I could not hope for any high-echelon niche in police work. Even if I studied law and passed the bar, I should be remote from my real ambition. It did not seem that a career in criminology was possible in my native Sweden.

The place to go, then, was France. The first great modern policeman, Vidoq, had been a Frenchman, a felon turned policeman. His flamboyant career which ended with his death in 1857 had seemed to prove that an understanding of crime and criminals was one key to success. Vidoq had organized the first modern detective squad, and in the fifteen years he supervised its work he developed the techniques of detection to a high degree. Another Frenchman, the great Alphonse Bertillon, had developed the descriptive measurement of criminals and other methods of identification, adding a new dimension to police science. Then, too, France had been rocked time and again by sensational criminal exploits, like the work of the Bonnot gang, the first to use motor cars in the carrying out of organized criminal exploits. The wave of apache murders had also shocked the country, and public pressure had helped to develop the finest police operation of its time. The very French character, with its intellectual curiosity and passion for logic, contributed to this result.

And above all, there was Locard, the one under whom, above all others, I wished to study. It seemed a dream unlikely to be fulfilled on a purse as empty as mine.

The opportunity to realize it came about in a completely unexpected way. Not long after my return from the East I was spending a few days at a small mountain resort in northern Sweden. There I fell in with a distinguished judge and sportsman. We found ourselves with a number of tastes in common and decided to make a trip together to the top of a mountain not far away. This was not a feat of mountaineering but only a long stiff tramp of about eight hours. At the summit there was a small lodge which, in the summer season, provided bunks for climbers and facilities for simple meals. The trip seemed to promise exactly the sort of recreation for which the judge and I were looking.

Early one morning we met in the judge's room to pack our rucksacks. While we were discussing the relative merits of our heavy hiking boots there was a knock on the door, and the maid entered. She had come to ask us if a certain M. Moleyre, a French diplomat who had just arrived at the resort, could join us on the trip. She said that he was waiting downstairs. We assured the maid that we would be happy to make the acquaintance of this gentleman. A few minutes later, she knocked again at the door and asked if an elderly person, also waiting downstairs, could join us. We gave her the same assurance.

In the lobby we were greeted by M. Moleyre with many gestures and a torrent of French. He was about thirty-five with black hair, a protruding nose, and intelligent eyes. He was impeccably dressed *pour le sport* and had on his back an enormous rucksack. Already he was panting under the weight of it. The second recruit to our party, a parson, was waiting shyly behind M. Moleyre. He must have been at least sixty years of age, but he carried his years well. He had mild blue eyes and a sloping white mustache.

Soon we were engulfed in the jungle of tall, thin birches which covered the mountainside. In the midst of this forest, we came upon a small farm, the last human dwelling on our way. Since two cows were grazing in the meadow, the judge led us to the farm house to try to buy some milk for our lunch. In the kitchen we found a tall strong woman, plainly dressed and with dirty bare feet. She was ministering to a baby in the immemorial way but, when she saw us, she removed the source of supply and in a far from ladylike tone asked us what we wanted. When we explained our errand, she proceeded to pour milk from a big pitcher into some empty bottles which we had with us. While doing so she stared at us with obvious curiosity.

Then, pointing at the parson, she said, "You must be a parson, aren't you?"

The parson, slightly blushing at the thought that, dressed as he was in sports clothes, he was still recognizable as a man of God, admitted his vocation. She asked him if he would baptize the child, since the farm was far away from the church and she could not leave it on account of the cows. The parson agreed, though somewhat reluctantly, and asked her to produce a prayer book. It was the woman's turn to blush; she said that there was no prayer book in the house. To our astonishment the judge produced one from his rucksack.

The woman escorted the four of us to the parlor and excused herself. It was furnished with dark-painted wooden furniture which was not very comfortable, starched white curtains, a wide cloth spread over the table in the center, several hideous porcelain figures and colored enlargements of photographs of farm people, probably the woman's parents. Later we learned that her parents were dead and that she herself was running the farm without the aid of any man. About this time we heard some fuss in the kitchen which seemed to indicate that there were other children than the baby, but we did not pay any special attention.

In a short while the woman came back. In one arm she carried the baby, nicely pinafored, and, in the other, a porcelain washbowl with some water in it. The parson had removed his rucksack and put on a black tie which partially offset the levity of his light-colored sports shirt and augmented the solemnity of the occasion. He inquired the mother's name and other necessary data, but when he asked for the father's name, she blushed and said that she did not know it—he had been a chance acquaintance. The parson had to accept this, of course, but he was remarkably red in the face when he took the child in one arm, blessed it, read the usual prayers from the book which he held in the other hand, and finally baptized the little creature.

When the ceremony was over, the woman asked if he would care to baptize another child for her and, before the parson had time to answer, she went into the kitchen and returned with a little girl about five years old, with a very runny nose. Again she had to confess that she did not know the name of the father and, even redder in the face, the parson repeated the ceremony. But when the woman went to the kitchen a third time and returned with an urchin of about ten, it was obvious that the parson was very near preaching a sermon on morals instead of the baptismal service.

In the meantime the Frenchman, who understood some Swedish,

was becoming more and more amazed with every child she produced. When he saw the last little scamp he burst into a fit of uncontrollable laughter. Our parson abandoned all thought of a homily and performed the ceremony as quickly as in common decency he could do. He bade the woman a hurried farewell, and we went out.

However, the judge, whose curiosity had been aroused, went back in and had a short private talk with the woman. He came back chuckling. Apparently the fathers of these wood's colts had been sundry snow-shovellers temporarily employed by the state-owned railroad during bad snowstorms. Since the rail line did not become snowbound every year, the conception of these children was more of a meteorological phenomenon than anything else.

The path became steeper and steeper. We stopped to have a belated lunch before continuing the more strenuous part of the climb. Largely thanks to our farm-house interlude, we had grown to feel acquainted with one another. Our numerous jokes on the menage below us heightened our friendliness, except for the strain they placed on the parson's decorum.

When we recommenced our journey, I noticed that our French friend was breathing heavily and did not look at all well. We had left the forest and there were only cliffs and rocks along the way, with an occasional green patch. The Frenchman was last in line and, after a while, when I turned around, I could not see him. Suspecting that something was wrong, I took off my rucksack and ran back down the path. Behind a cliff I found him lying on the ground almost unconscious. I took off his heavy rucksack and poured water from my flask into his mouth. After a while he staggered to his feet.

"I was a fool to pack the rucksack that way," he said, looking helplessly at it. Then he blushed a little and continued, "You see, I thought it would be good if I brought a few bottles of red wine with me, not knowing how I would suffer under the weight of those damned bottles."

I was as strong as a young ox and, despite his protests, I slung his rucksack on my shoulders and took to the path again, the French-man following meekly. Afterwards I learned that he had a weak heart (to which he succumbed twenty-five years later).

The party was complete once more and we continued the climb, I with two rucksacks. In the late afternoon we arrived at the hut on the summit and had a magnificent view of the surrounding mountains in the twilight which at this time of the year would continue all through the night. We lit a fire, had supper, and then went unsuspectingly to sleep.

We awakened in the morning to a blizzard. There was no ques-tion of leaving the hut until it was over, although we were sched-uled to be back at the resort the next evening. We had to nurse the fire and cook our food. There was no danger of starvation, since the Tourist's Association kept a stock of canned goods in the hut. And now M. Moleyre's claret came in very handy.

What could we talk about, four men who had never before met but who were brought together by fate in such a lonely spot? We spent three days and three long evenings in that hut, and at the end of them we knew one another as well as if we had been friends for many years. Each of us talked mostly of the thing that was most precious to him, and that was his own life. The judge turned out to be a dreamer and a poet, with a strong religious touch in him. The parson, with his mild eyes and manner, was in reality a very practical man who, after having served for many years as a missionary in China, had succeeded in getting a com-fortable parish in Sweden. The Frenchman, who had studied law and economics, was a close friend of the great European statesman, Aristide Briand, and the famous General Foch. He had just been appointed Commercial Attaché to the French Legation in Stock-holm. I have often wondered since why a man of his abilities had accepted such a humble post, and why he stuck to it all the rest of his life, retiring only during World War II when Pétain assumed leadership of his country. His home in Stockholm, which I was to visit many times, was filled with antique furniture, paint-ings, and rare books, and he was a most cultivated gentleman.

Compared with theirs, my own life story seemed very simple, not to say dull. There was only one highlight, my journey through Asia.

My companions listened to me with great courtesy. Perhaps they were too experienced to expect much of youth, or too charitable. At any rate, they listened attentively while I finished my recital with a reference to my dream of going to France and studying to be a criminologist.

M. Moleyre looked at me thoughtfully and said, "Perhaps I can help you out. By chance, I am acquainted with a great criminologist in France."

My pulse began to quicken. "May I ask who it is?"

"No doubt you have heard of him," M. Moleyre replied. "He lives in Lyons; he is the head of the police laboratory there. His name is Edmond Locard."

"Yes!" I exclaimed. "Certainly I have heard of him. He is the greatest living police scientist. It is under him that I want to study."

M. Moleyre nodded. "I'll write Locard about you and ask him to take you into his laboratory."

Of course I thanked him warmly. The coincidence of finding a friend of Locard's in a mountain hut in northern Sweden struck me as a good omen, but the whole thing was really no more than a kindly promise. Very probably Locard would not think it worthwhile to receive a young man like me, whose knowledge of criminology was self-taught except for the small amount of first-hand contact with police work which I had enjoyed on my Asian trip. M. Moleyre continued to talk about Locard's wonderful investigative methods but, when the path down the mountain was finally clear enough to permit our descent, I was far from convinced that anything would come of it. Indeed, when we shook hands back at the resort, I did not even feel certain I should ever see the amiable Frenchman again.

Nevertheless, in the two weeks that followed I could not help thinking wishfully about M. Moleyre's promise and hoping earn-

estly that he had acted upon it. I had under consideration at the
time a most challenging offer from Karen Jeppe, whom I had met
on my Asian travels and who wanted me to go to Armenia to serve
as a combination schoolteacher and local chief. I had learned to
admire her inordinately, and the work was certainly both fascinating and important. The only trouble was that it did not lie in the
direction of my main interest. I put off answering her from day to
day. It was well that I did.

One morning the envelope came: small and yellow, made of inferior paper, and furnished with an inferior gum. Printed across
its face in bold letters were the words REPUBLIQUE FRAN-
ÇAISE: *Liberté, Egalité, Fraternité.* The postmark was Lyons.
Well, I told myself, M. Moleyre has been as good as his word.
The enclosed letter contained only a few lines, but they told me all
I wanted to know. On the basis of strong recommendation from
the French Legation in Stockholm I had been accepted as a
stagiare of the Police Laboratory of Lyons.

The dictionary informed me that a *stagiare* was a student pro-
bationer, or assistant of the lowest degree. My appointment would
carry no pay, but I knew it was priceless. I told my mother of this
stroke of the greatest good fortune. Once again she urged me to
remain at home and warned me that I could expect very little
family support in the future. She knew, I am sure, that she could
not dissuade me.

With a small amount of money in my pocket and a vast amount
of excitement in my heart, I set out for Lyons.

8

THE FIRST FEE

Money was a recurring problem in those early Lyons days. The small amount I had would not last long, even with the utmost frugality. I began to cast about for ways to earn more, and it did not take long to discover that, as far as police work was concerned, the most lucrative aspect was the analysis of documents. Even the great Edmond Locard made most of his living in this fashion, his salary as head of the laboratory being nominal. However, he was allowed to set his own price for his work on questioned documents, whether for lawyers, for the state, or for private individuals. Detectives under him occasionally did this kind of work also.

Before coming to Lyons I had never thought much about the importance of handwriting analysis. Although I knew that Locard was famous for his work on questioned documents, the extent of his practice was a surprise to me. Under his tutelage, I gradually became fascinated with the entire science of document analysis. Still, it was apparent that even with my background in the field of pulp-and-paper chemistry and Locard's encyclopedic knowledge, it would be a good while before I could hope to earn fees as an expert.

Nearly a year passed before I had my initial chance. When I first arrived in Lyons, I put up at a hotel called the Regina. Modest though it was, it was well beyond my means, and soon I located lodgings with the widow I have mentioned. While I was still at the hotel, however, I made the acquaintance of an elderly lawyer named Maître Robert, whose habit it was to sit in the parlor and play cards each evening. Usually his companions were the proprietor, the wife of the proprietor—who was, in effect, the actual proprietor—and a retired French colonel. Maître Robert himself was about seventy, portly, white-haired, and the possessor of a magnificent blue wine-nose. He was always dressed in a black suit and wore a high, starched collar.

To this day I am not sure what it was that drew Maître Robert and me together. There cannot have been much in common between a staid, elderly Frenchman and a young Swedish student criminologist. All the same, his pale blue eyes used to light up when I came in. Gradually, I came to know that his past was darkened by a good many tragedies. He had lost not only his wife but all his children except one, a girl, who had entered a convent. Outside his work, he had little except a few cronies and, like most lonely men, he loved to talk. In the course of many pleasant evenings I learned a good deal about French judicial procedure.

After I had moved to my furnished room I continued to drop in at the parlor of the Regina to see him, and on one occasion I found Maître Robert in a somber mood. He said briefly and glumly that he was working on a case and felt certain that he would lose it.

"How so?" I asked.

He drew a worn paper out of his wallet, unfolded it and gave it to me to read. On the paper was written in a neat hand:

In addition to the clauses of the contract of the sale to me of M. Joseph Grasset's farm, I herewith consent that M. Grasset may use the small barn at the side of the stable in which to store machines for a period of two years. Dur-

ing this period M. Grasset also has my permission to take
from the farm up to 5000 cubic metres of top soil.

(*signed*) André Olivier

Lyons.

Feb. 3, 1926

"I don't know what to make of this," said Maître Robert, sighing. "I am M. Olivier's lawyer. He signed the document all right, but he maintains that that final sentence about taking away soil has been added since he signed his name. Obviously, this fellow Grasset intends to take away soil and sell it to gardeners and house owners in the suburbs. This will ruin the farm for all time, and it wasn't worth much anyhow. The trouble is that Grasset wrote out this deed for Olivier to sign, and when Olivier wrote his name on it he left a little space between the last sentence and the signature. The disputed sentence seems to be in Grasset's hand and, so far as I can see, was done with the same ink and the same pen. There were no witnesses. Though it is inconceivable that my client would ever have consented to ruin his farm in this way, I don't know how to prove it. It would be a long, costly process, and I could not be sure of winning."

I eyed the document curiously. The signature of M. Olivier, who was obviously a good calligrapher, was a real orgy of penmanship. It is said that a paraph—that flourish with which signatures often end—is added to prevent forgery, but in France and other Latin countries there are often signatures which are completely illegible and which actually consist of only one elaborate paraph. One of those bold strokes of M. Olivier's pen curved upwards and crossed the disputed sentence in two places. Here was the crux of the matter. If the disputed sentence had been affixed to the document after it had been signed by M. Olivier, then the track of the pen would be above the strokes of the signature; if M. Grasset was right, it would be underneath it.

My excitement was very great. This was my first chance to do something on my own. I wanted to ask Maître Robert to give me a crack at that document even if I had to pay him for the opportunity. I would almost have mortgaged my future for it.

"Lend me this paper for a day, Maître."

He looked doubtful. "I cannot spare it for long, my young friend."

"I promise to return it to you, here, at this same hour tomorrow evening."

His expression remained unhappy, but finally he nodded. "Very well. The case is as good as lost anyhow."

I put the document into my own wallet, trying to conceal my excitement. It would not do to let conservative old Maître Robert know how anxious I was to test myself. He had taken something of a risk in entrusting the paper to me, since it belonged to the opposing side of the case and had been put at his disposal by M. Grasset's lawyer. I stayed only to kibitz a final round of cards, and then trudged out of the lobby. I maintained this pace only until I was sure of being out of sight and then broke into a run toward the laboratory.

It was eleven at night, but late hours were no rarity in our work, and the sleepy-eyed detective on duty barely glanced at me when I burst through the door. I went up the five winding flights of stone steps like a squirrel and arrived breathless at our attic emporium of criminology. There on the bookshelf behind the desk was the powerful German microscope which was Chevassus' special pride. It had taken him about four years of bureaucratic jockeying and maneuvering to have it assigned out of German reparations to the Lyons laboratory, and even to touch it in an unauthorized way was sacrilege. No one was allowed to use it without express permission, but I cannot recall feeling the least hesitation.

In a matter of seconds I had the instrument out of its polished wooden case. I plugged in the electrical connection and had the beam of the lamp focussed on the mirror under the examination surface. With unsteady fingers I put Maître Robert's paper on the small metal "table" and wiggled it round till I could see, in the illumined area, the first place where the strokes of the signature crossed the last line of the text.

It took only a few moments to examine the two points where the lines intersected. After studying them as carefully as I knew how, I conducted several experiments on the crossing of inked lines under various conditions. These proved that if the ink of the stroke first made was not entirely dry beforehand, the ink from the second stroke would spread over the first at the crossing in such an obvious manner that there could be no doubt about the second stroke's have been made above the first one. At both the crossings on Maître Robert's document, the strokes of the final sentence flowed out into M. Olivier's paraph. There could be no doubt that the disputed sentence had been added after M. Olivier had put his signature to the paper.

I was burning with eagerness to show the proof to Maître Robert at once, but when I hastened back to the Regina, all was dark. I would have to wait until morning. At that point it occurred to me that I had never been to the old gentleman's office and did not even know where it was. The sensible thing would be to wait until tomorrow evening, and get some sleep in the meantime. Instead, I found myself back in the laboratory. I had to know everything there was to know about handwriting, and somehow the remaining hours of the night vanished in alternate concentrated reading in every book I could find and fresh inspection of my precious questioned document. About dawn, fatigue and hunger drove me out of the laboratory, and I welcomed the day drinking a bowl of onion soup at a bistro in the market place.

That evening I finally came off duty and took the document back to Maître Robert. In a voice which must have trembled with pride, I told him my findings. Some of the gloom lifted from his face.

"Well," he observed, "it will be interesting to hear what our good M. Grasset has to say to this!"

Apparently, there was not much that he could say. Maître Robert reported to me that Grasset immediately withdrew his claims.

Indeed, he even offered to pay M. Olivier a handsome sum not to prosecute. Prompted by honest Maître Robert's wise counsel, M. Olivier declined the bribe and settled for Grasset's merely paying the lawyer's fee.

"This," said Maître Robert with one of his rare smiles, "I have already collected. And a portion of what I collected was on your behalf." Once again he drew out his worn old wallet and extracted from it no less than two hundred francs. "This is yours," he said, "and with my thanks."

I had earned my first fee.

9

THE MOVING FINGER WRITES

The story of Maître Robert and the deed of sale has anticipated the story of my early months in Lyons. I could not have brought the matter to its successful conclusion without a long grounding in the science of questioned documents. Training under Locard was intensive. He was undoubtedly one of the two world authorities on the subject, the other being the late Albert S. Osborne of New York City. Locard's fame was international, and the laboratory was continually flooded with documents from all over the world. Their variety never ceased to astonish me. There were business agreements written in Chinese characters on long slips of paper and signed with thumbprints in India ink. There were drafts from Moroccan Jews, incunabula from the Renaissance, yellowed wills in the trembling handwriting of old people, and anonymous letters of all descriptions.

Handling this flood of work was not rendered easier by several of the circumstances. Although the science of document-analysis is extremely exacting and intricate, almost everyone seems to consider himself capable of rendering an opinion. French law fostered any number of these self-appointed experts. In penal cases the law compelled the *juge d'instruction*, the examining magistrate who constitutes the link between the Sûreté and the prosecuting attorney, to appoint only one expert to examine any documents which might be in question. On the other hand, in civil suits the law prescribed three experts and permitted the use of even more.

Assume that a reputable, professional document-analyst has been assigned to a civil case. He is perfectly capable of rendering a valid opinion singehanded, but the law stipulates he must have at least two corroborating experts to sign the declaration and swear to it in court. This means that the fee for the opinion has to be divided three ways. Frenchmen are as reluctant as other people to part with money unnecessarily, and the way around this impasse was to keep a string of humble friends, such as retired schoolteachers, former customs officials, or anyone with a reasonable reputation to confirm his findings for the least possible percentage of the total fee. These worthies would go to court for a small number of francs, sign the declaration, and swear to its accuracy.

The trouble with this ingenuous system was that the humble friends seldom remained humble. Having participated in a few cases and noticed the lucrative fees involved, they began to envy the professionals. Before long, they invariably went into business for themselves, thereby augmenting the large number of dubious handwriting "experts." There was never, at any time, a shortage of handwriting experts, and I have seen civil cases in which there were ten for each side.

Perhaps the system is not quite so bad as it sounds. My own experience suggests that an expert—a trained professional—can feel positive about his opinion in only about twenty-five percent of his cases. Even so, there is also the possibility of personal error to be considered. A good half of all the cases must be judged on varying degrees of probability, and the remaining quarter are those in which no opinion can be rendered. The comic court dramas in which numerous dissenting experts are ranged on each side of the case are generally staged when the decision falls in the fifty percent middle category, the area of possibility but no certainty.

The employment of private experts is open to serious objection, for they are only human, and it is natural for a man to sympathize

with the side of a case from which his fee comes. Unless he keeps
an open mind and conducts himself according to the highest professional standards, the private expert will inevitably become biased.
Such delicate work as the analysis of handwriting should be carried out in a government laboratory where the expert has no personal interest in the outcome of the case.

In criminal cases, the comparison of handwriting requires caution. Personally, I should hesitate to hang a man on the basis of
handwriting analysis, however expert. Of course, the physical and
chemical tests with regard to inks, typewriting, and erasures are
just as reliable as any other scientific procedure and constitute
genuine evidence. But the techniques of comparison are not so
precise. I have carried out or supervised thousands of such comparisons, and I remain a little afraid of them. To my mind, their most
important function is to point the best probable route for further
investigation; at the start of a case they may prove invaluable.
Many times an accurate comparison solves an otherwise impossible
problem and, at the very least, it may save time and effort. When
it was my task to organize police laboratories, I always assigned
handwriting experts to work with the detectives, and that system
has proved wise.

The caution with which the whole subject has to be approached
is underlined by numerous fearful blunders that have studded the
history of handwriting analysis from the days of the Emperor Jus-
tinian down to the present. The most dramatic error of all was
made by Alphonse Bertillon, one of the founders of police science
and the greatest criminologist of his day. It happened in the
famous—and infamous—Dreyfus case. Alfred Dreyfus, a French
artillery captain of Jewish descent, was court-martialled, convicted
of being a German spy, and sent to Devil's Island for life. The
central piece of evidence against him was a *bordereau*—a memorandum—which revealed French military secrets and which was
found in the wastebasket of the German military attaché at the
Paris embassy. Bertillon testified that the memorandum was in
Dreyfus' handwriting.

After a lapse of fifty years it is interesting to scrutinize Bertillon's testimony. Obviously, he did not rate very highly the intelligence of the officers of the court. He framed his testimony in a fashion sufficiently childish for their comprehension, using a primer-simple military metaphor. The handwriting, he said, was a kind of fortress in which Dreyfus was trying to hide from justice: here he was defending himself from *M*, hiding in the trench of *Q*, searching for cover at the bastion *B*, or holing up in the dungeon *K*. Apparently Bertillon's estimate of the intelligence of the court was accurate, for the officers swallowed this fantasy whole and brought in a verdict of guilty. In Bertillon's defense it could be said that he rarely made handwriting comparisons, that he was probably oversure of himself, and that he was actuated by patriotic zeal. These considerations may palliate his mistake, but they are cold comfort in the face of a vicious miscarriage of justice.

When Emile Zola, the brothers Reinach, and others devoted to justice succeeded in getting the case reopened, it developed that Dreyfus was innocent and that the memorandum had been written by a Hungarian in the French army, a Major Esterhazy. Bertillon's testimony was completely discredited, and the Dreyfus affair resulted in an almost mortal blow to handwriting comparisons. It required many years of effort by Locard, Osborne, and others to restore it to good standing.

As I worked under Locard, I soon discovered that most of the work of handwriting comparison is tiresome and even exasperating. It strains both the eyes and the patience. But every now and then we had a case that revealed the human drama behind the tedium.

One rainy morning in November Chevassus returned to our workroom after his regularly scheduled morning conference with Locard. He tossed some papers on the desk, the uppermost of which was a photostat of a handwritten letter. Under it were typewritten pages on the letterhead of a prominent Belgian lawyer and six or seven assorted bits of paper with handwritten texts of different lengths. The envelope in which all this had reached us instantly proclaimed the country of origin, for it was a big yellow envelope characteristic of Belgian business correspondence.

With a gesture toward the dossier, Chevassus said, "Read it all. And then roll up your sleeves, my boy. Two sets of experts have said the stuff is genuine, and now we're supposed to prove it isn't." He paused and added, almost regretfully, "*Le Patron* has a feeling about it."

Well, if Locard had a hunch, there must have been some basis for questioning the documents. As I waded through the file, a curious story emerged. It concerned a wealthy manufacturer in Brussels, about seventy years old and a bachelor. One day a young insurance man called on him, declaring that he was the manufacturer's illegitimate son and claiming that his mother had been an actress whom the manufacturer had enjoyed some thirty years before. The businessman examined his conscience and denied the connection. When the alleged son refused to accept the denial and continued an argument, the manufacturer had him thrown out of the office.

Subsequently letters arrived from the insurance man, filial, polite, and humble letters. The manufacturer answered them, trying to prove to the young man that he was totally mistaken and that there was no possibility of their relationship. Presently the correspondence died out. However, before long the manufacturer was sued by the insurance man for recognition as son and heir. The basis of the suit was a letter in which the manufacturer recognized the younger man as his son and wrote regretfully of his heartlessness toward his former mistress. This letter and the envelope in which it was alleged to have been mailed were on deposit with the court.

The handwriting of the letter and the address on the envelope appeared identical. The older man admitted to having addressed the envelope, but he said that he had done so in the course of correspondence with the plaintiff months earlier, and he claimed he had never written the letter. This denial was not convincing because the young insurance man had collected some compromising and apparently corroborative evidence to support the letter. It seemed very likely that the manufacturer was going to get a son whether he wanted one or not.

The more I looked at the samples of the old man's handwriting and compared them with the questioned letter, the more puzzled I became. I could not imagine why Locard had "a feeling" about the case. Finally I looked up at Chevassus, who had been watching me go through the dossier.

"What on earth is there to do about this?" I asked him. "These handwriting samples, including the letter, are obviously all from the same hand. Why do we bother with this case?"

Chevassus shook his double chins, and focussed his determined, steady eyes on me.

"My young friend," he said, "you are too sure too quickly. The Boss has a feeling, I told you . . . and I've hardly ever found his feelings wrong. So now let's get to work."

He put aside all the papers except the photostat, laid that on the desk, and ran his finger along the lines.

"Look," he said. "The connecting strokes between the individual letters of some words are rather hesitant, uncertain. It's only the shadow of hesitation, though. Whoever forged this, if it is forged, never stopped when he came to certain words. He drew in the letters at intervals and then went back to connect them, the way some bunglers do. You can barely see that the connecting strokes in *some words* do not have the same swing, the same shadowings that the letters themselves have."

Light began to dawn, and my comfortable feeling of certainty disappeared. These Sûreté men knew more than I had got out of all my reading and study of theory. The wisest thing I had ever done was to come to Lyons; my greatest piece of luck was in being here.

"You are right," I humbly admitted to Chevassus. "It is almost as if someone had pasted letters in a row, then connected them, and then had it all photographed. Well, it's solved. All we need to do now is to write a report."

Once again Chevassus shook his head.

"Not so fast, my boy. Just our opinion, even le Patron's opinion, is not enough. We'll have to prove it. Take the stuff down to the photographer and get some enlargements—let's say, ten times original."

About noon the enlargements were delivered to us: the letter which had formed the basis of the paternity claim and half a dozen pieces of the rich old man's acknowledged letters, notes, and pages from a business diary. The large print of the paternity letter was still wet when we laid it out on the desk. Both Chevassus and I leaned over it eagerly. We read it through again and again, and with our fingers we followed the strokes of the handwriting. We still saw what we had seen on the original; we were more than ever convinced that there was something wrong. But our hypothesis that the individual characters had been cut out, pasted up, and then photographed into a letter did not seem to hold up. There were no visible telltale shadows of overlapping paper-edges, no hairlines that usually appear when paper is pasted edge to edge. But another peculiarity about the paternity letter fairly leaped to view on the enlargements: there was a complete change in the character of the rhythm of the handwriting in certain words.

We then embarked on a speculation which today might be called "psychosemantic." We weighed each word that displayed this negative characteristic, each phrase in which the word was contained, each thought that the word might have evoked in the writer's mind. Our purpose was to test whether the intellectual and psychic motivation of the writing might not have automatically impelled the writer to disguise himself. In such a case, the inner blocks of his mind might, we conjectured, cause him to hesitate so much that each letter would seem like the start of a new word. We determined that in the authentic samples the businessman did start words in the fashion of the individual letters in the disputed document.

Our speculations continued for hours. We did not merely rely upon our own judgment, but at lunch in our favorite café we tested

·it by posing fictional situations to our colleagues, the proprietor, our fellow guests, and even the waiters.

Just before closing time Locard came into our office to ask whether we had prepared a report. We explained our hypothesis that the alleged son had in some way used words and particularly individual letters from epistles written by the older man, but we were still unable to explain how he had done it. Locard smiled; it would not be difficult to prove it, he assured us.

Locard's confidence that further research would substantiate our theory proved well founded. When the original of the paternity letter was subjected to painstaking analysis, the technique by which it had been forged became apparent. The letter was a peculiarly ingenious form of tracing. The young insurance man had concocted a plan which had produced a document devoid of the usual stigmata of tracings. For he evidently realized that no cutting and piecing together of pieces of paper and no ordinary forgery could stand up under the scrutiny to which such a letter would be subjected in a case certain to involve a great amount of notoriety. His method was new—at least to me—and the amount of pains he had taken with it was certainly worthy of a more commendable end. He could have sold a lot of insurance in the time he spent perpetrating this fraud.

First of all he must have cut from the correspondence he had wheedled from the old manufacturer most of the words he needed for his paternity letter. Of course, the subject matter of the actual correspondence was a great help in this respect. And then he composed his own letter and, using the words purloined from the genuine epistles, pasted up almost the whole of the text on a sheet of cardboard. Unfortunately, he had made one small mistake: in composing his false letter he used certain words which had occurred nowhere in the genuine texts. In fabricating these new words he had had to build them up out of individual characters abstracted one at a time from the correspondence. He had connected these characters by strokes of the pen, and thus succeeded in producing a document with a very high degree of verisimilitude.

Next he had photographed the synthetic letter to actual scale and had used this photograph as a model, tracing it over and over again until his pen followed the letters almost automatically. In this way he managed to write the paternity letter so surely and easily that it might almost have been the old man's fingers that guided the pen.

Almost, but not quite. What tripped the rascal was a small but fatal matter. The manufacturer's handwriting had many peculiarities, as the handwriting of old people especially is likely to have. One of these was a marked tendency to start off individual words with fairly high letters; the succeeding ones tended to dwindle down until the final ones in each word were much smaller than the initial letter. From the enlargements of the words in the incriminating letter, we noticed that several of the characters had zigzag profiles instead of a regular downward slope. In the genuine samples of the old man's calligraphy there was no such irregularity —only a steady sort of diminuendo from the start of a word to its end.

As soon as we hit upon this discrepancy, we telegraphed the Brussels police. A search of the insurance man's home brought to light a camera, an enlarger, and even the very cardboard model of the forged letter. Incredible as it still seems, the young man had even preserved several test tracings which the police promptly impounded.

For persons with a predisposition to forgery, paternity seems to offer a series of irresistible temptations. Perhaps only a fraction of the cases reach the police. For many that came to our attention, however, Locard was far too patient and inspired an opponent for even the cleverest of the fakers in this pseudoromantic field. Still, his fame was apparently no deterrent to the crime. Paternity cases frequently attract newspaper publicity, and a good many of the forgeries which Locard spotted made headlines. One more account will serve to illustrate the hope that springs in a forger's breast regardless of the existence of a Locard.

A certain Herr Stauffer, a Swiss who lived in Lausanne, died leaving several million francs to his sister, an elderly married lady. Shortly after she had inherited the fortune she received a call from a Pauline Veuve, who claimed that Herr Stauffer had had relations with her twenty-odd years previously. In the course of what must have been a fairly awkward interview, Madame Veuve informed Stauffer's sister that she had borne a child by him and that, on the occasion of the birth of the child, Stauffer had willed a fourth of his fortune to her. In proof of her contention, she produced a letter from Stauffer to her. The first and second pages consisted of the usual matters of such correspondence, but on the third page, after the close of the main body of the letter, appeared a codicil:

> The undersigned gives to Mme P. Veuve on the occasion of the child for which I am responsible, one fourth of my fortune, to be paid to her at my death.
>
> *Made and signed*, Gottlieb Stauffer
> Chaux de Fonds, 2 Dec. 1910

The heiress refused to give away a fourth of her inheritance, and Madame Veuve, on her part, refused to take no for an answer. The result was a lawsuit which resounded all over the Continent.

Locard was called as an expert witness on the authenticity of the letter, and I began to understand why there is little new in the unravelling of crimes, and why Locard sometimes had a "feeling" to guide him. Locard was able to prove that Pauline Veuve had added the final paragraph to Herr Stauffer's letter.

The District Attorney stepped in, and Madame Veuve was prosecuted for forgery and fraud. When the case came up for trial, the courtroom was packed with the curious, and they were destined to get their money's worth. There was a vein of never-say-die in Madame Veuve, perhaps because at this point she had little, if anything, to lose. In court when the indictments against her were read aloud, she jumped up from her defendant's seat and cried, "God has inspired me!"

Before anyone could quite grasp what was happening, she tore out of the lining of her old handbag another letter which she handed to the judge. Then she collapsed in hysterics and had to be carried out. The court adjourned.

This second letter, unlike the bequest in the Stauffer letter, was not a forgery. Madame Veuve had learned her lesson in that regard; the new epistle was one written by herself and addressed to her mother. The document was stained with what looked like age, and the ink was pale with what looked like time. Its text was full of grief and despair. In it the author described how she had been raped by Herr Stauffer and how she had fears that she was pregnant as a result. Upon later interrogation, Madame Veuve declared that the handbag had belonged to her mother, that the letter, by some coincidence, must have been resting between the lining and the leather of the bag for all the intervening years, that at the critical moment some divine inspiration had caused her to become aware of its presence.

The jury was composed of petty bourgeois from Lausanne, and all devout Catholics. To a man they disapproved of rape, and to a man they were prejudiced in favor of divine inspiration. She stood excellent chances of acquittal, and even had some hope of getting a share in the Stauffer estate.

Locard, of course, was not present at this dramatic moment, but the skeptical Swiss authorities sent the letter to the Lyons laboratory for analysis. Alas for the ingenuity of Pauline Veuve; Locard quickly established that the stains were not those of years, or even of tears, but of a more prosaic liquid, urine, and the ink had not faded with time but had merely been diluted with water.

Madame Veuve got several years at hard labor.

10

THE NICETIES OF COUNTERFEITING

Most forgers and their cousins in crime, the counterfeiters and false-document artists, are eventually brought to book. But as long as there is the possibility of rich reward for success in fakery, there will always be patient and extremely resourceful felons to try it. For every precaution that ingenuity can devise there is some method by which it can be circumvented. The perfect protection against this kind of crime has yet to be invented, though many useful devices and techniques have been developed in the last few decades.

In recent years, for example, the use of the so-called security inks has become widespread. These inks are used both for printing and writing, and theoretically any tampering with the original text will be self-revealing because the use of an eradicator produces a white spot or colored stain where the mischief is done. Checks, passports, and all sorts of important business and legal documents are printed and filled out in these security inks. Special papers for use with these inks have also been developed, and on the whole they offer a high degree of protection. Therefore more talent is now required to forge or alter such documents. But the talent exists.

We finally got on the track of such a forger in Lyons itself. The time, patience, and skill he devoted to his work was remarkable. After eradicating the section of the check he wished to raise or

68

the document he was going to alter, he set to work with a strong magnifying glass. First he prepared the surface of the security paper where he had altered it, restoring its natural glossiness. Then with minute brushes and water colors he imitated flawlessly even the most intricate background pattern, so that the alterations were invisible to the naked eye. The skill and steadiness of hand this process required are hard to conceive.

As for printed matter, if enough time and resources are brought to bear on the operation there is probably nothing in the world which cannot be counterfeited. Hitler's infamous henchman, Heinrich Himmler, relied on this fact when he organized his secret concentration camp for specialists in printing and engraving. These captive experts were used for the preparation of all sorts of counterfeits, even Swedish passports and Bank of England ten-pound notes. These assignments were formidable, for Swedish passports employ practically all the most effective security measures known, and Bank of England notes are generally regarded as impossible to counterfeit. Himmler's results, however, were spectacular. His imitation Swedish passports were so good that even the state printer could scarcely distinguish them from the authentic ones. To protect ourselves we changed our passports immediately, thankful to have discovered the counterfeiting when only a few spurious specimens were in circulation.

Himmler had an even more notable success with his Bank of England notes. Only the Bank's own experts could tell the imitations from the genuine. The German capitulation occurred before all the fake notes were in circulation; in fact, almost the whole printing found its way into the black market only after the war. Hotels on the Continent had to refuse to take ten-pound notes from their guests, and in London itself, anyone who wanted to change such a note, even at a bank, had to identify himself. The Bank of England had to withdraw all ten-pound notes and issue a new series.

Even before Himmler's example, I had personally run up against a similar problem. In 1936 I was invited to go to Ireland and give some advice on a planned reorganization of the police of the Free State. While I was there I met General W. R. E. Murphy, the head of the famous Irish Hospitals' Sweepstakes. This organization raises funds to maintain hospitals in Ireland. It is closely connected with the Garda Siochána—the Free State police—at the supervisory level. Its executives were confronted with a tough problem: a good proportion of their total funds came from the sale of tickets in the United States, where this kind of gambling is against the law, and the result of this legalism was the forging of great numbers of counterfeit tickets. Americans had no way to protect themselves, so thousands of people were mulcted.

The Sweepstakes executives wanted to know whether there was any way of making the genuine tickets counterfeit-proof. For several days I pondered the problem. First of all, it was evident that no matter how intricately the tickets were designed and printed, and no matter how effectively security inks and papers were used, imitation was still possible. Next, it occurred to me that perhaps a paper could be used which would enable even a housewife to test a proffered ticket for authenticity. For instance, if a drop of some common household liquid, such as vinegar or ammonia, were placed on such a paper, a spot of color would appear. There could be a different color for each year that the Grand National was run—red one time, green the next, then blue, and so on. Chemically this was entirely feasible. Nevertheless, experience with forgers had already taught me that the scheme would not work. Within two weeks after a set of tickets with their new secret color came on the market, the counterfeiters could catch up with the situation and arrange the fakes to respond to the test as successfully as the authentic tickets.

I never earned that fee. The core of the problem was not in the tickets themselves but in the fact that under United States law the purchaser had no way of having his ticket validated. So far as I am aware, the problem remains unsolved to this day.

Many people believe that the most profitable form of forgery is in counterfeiting banknotes. Apparently this belief rests on the assumption that the easiest way to make money must be to make it. The cost accountancy of experience does not support this view. Counterfeiters seem never to be affluent in spite of all their "money." They ought to be well rewarded considering all the time and skill they expend on the felony but, by the very nature of the crime, the forger of banknotes has to strew around a whole series of clues which are themselves his stock in trade. Sooner or later he is always tracked down. Once caught, he is almost certain to be convicted.

In the past, the sentences for counterfeiting were very severe. Several countries issued banknotes bearing the warning that any counterfeiter would be hanged. In France, only a few hundred years ago, anyone who counterfeited coinage was boiled alive in oil. Nowadays, the penalties are still formidable. And, if the counterfeiter has been indiscreet enough to scatter his imitation money in several different countries, he may inadvertently become an expert in comparative prison systems. While he serves sentence in the country where he was apprehended, other countries wait to take him in turn, handing him along from penitentiary to penitentiary. It is possible to spend the rest of a lifetime in this dreary fashion.

Such a fate has an element of waste about it. Really skilful forgers could make a handsome living in the engraving industry in which many of them began. Only the obsession to get rich quickly prevents them from living comfortable and secure lives. Their inventiveness and ingenuity at the technical level sometimes amounts to genius, and, as a rule, their paraphernalia is unbelievably simple for the results they get. I remember one of them whose product was a work of art, yet all he had to work with was an old-fashioned camera, a small hand mangle which he used as a printing press, and some pots of dyes. Even the police could not believe he had produced such competent work with such primitive equipment. He obligingly ran off a few notes before their eyes to demonstrate.

Counterfeiting is by no means confined to money and passports. Almost any piece of paper which seems to have value can be the basis of a fraud. Even the gentle madness of stamp collecting has produced a surprising number of felons. Valuable stamps are counterfeited or forged so frequently that quite a few experts earn a nice living in the field of authentication. Like other forms of forgery, these fakes often require enormous patience and skill. Locard had a great reputation with stamp collectors.

One morning in Lyons two gentlemen appeared, obviously at odds with each other, and one, a well-known stamp collector, demanded to see the boss. His companion, I gathered, was a dealer, whose entire bearing expressed outrage at the idea that his potential customer should wish to consult Locard at all. In the Chief's office they poured out the story.

Apparently in the middle of the nineteenth century some sheets of French stamps had been accidentally printed with one row face up and the next row inverted. Two vertically adjoining stamps from this issue that exhibited this defect were considered of great value. The dealer possessed such a pair and had shown them to the collector, naming a stiff price. Just as the deal was about to be consummated, the collector became suspicious. The stamps happened to be in his hand at the moment and, pocketing them firmly, he marched off to consult Locard, followed angrily by the dealer.

Locard listened quietly until the tumult subsided and then examined the stamps under a magnifying glass. After a couple of minutes he went over to the windowsill on which stood a small glass bowl. This he filled with water and set the stamps afloat on the surface. All four of us watched the little squares, and for a time nothing happened. In about two minutes, a large rectangular portion of one stamp detached itself from the rest and floated separately on the surface. Locard turned to the collector.

"Do you want to have this man arrested?" he inquired.

Even before the collector could reply, the dealer was running out the door. Apparently the collector did not want the trouble and notoriety of a lawsuit, for he made no move to follow the dealer.

Locard explained that the rascal had secured a relatively valueless pair of stamps from the same issue as the one containing the valuable printing error, both adjoining stamps originally face up, of course. With astonishing skill and patience, he had then cut away the engraved part of one of the stamps from its edges, even slicing the paper obliquely, to create an empty frame. Next, he had inverted the design and put it in place, fastening it to the frame by means of gum. This operation had been so deftly carried out that it could not have been detected with the naked eye.

11

APPRENTICE POLICEMAN

The course of study in police science which Locard laid out for his probationers was not confined to theory and laboratory technique. We were expected to do a great deal of apprentice work with actual crimes and criminals, but this presented a problem. As students (some of us not even French nationals) we had no legal status and only an amorphous power to conduct investigations unless we were accompanied by a regular detective. We did not have the power to make arrests, for instance, and outside the walls of the laboratory only the sponsorship of the powerful Dr. Locard distinguished us from any other foreigners. Inside the laboratory we enjoyed complete freedom as long as we took our responsibilities seriously.

This lack of a clearly defined status was not so hampering as it may sound. I discovered that the attitude of the members of the local Detective Division and the uniformed police was benevolent. I made some close friends, especially among the personnel of the laboratory and the skillful investigators from the Detective Division. This was fortunate, because the student criminologist had to be friendly in order to learn anything. I was interested as much in the cases and the actors in those dramas as in the laboratory findings.

I usually succeeded in keeping on good terms with officials, but one exception was the man in charge of the Alien Section. Every alien living in France had to obtain a *carte d'identité*. The Alien Section, to which it was necessary to report in order to obtain this precious card, was located in the Palais de Justice between the Detective Division and the jail, but it had its own entrance from the street. It was a big, drab room, and the detective in charge sat at a table on a dais at one end. The room had a few old benches which were always packed, mostly with poor Polish or Italian laborers and their families. They were unhappy people; mostly they were not very clean, and always they were shabbily dressed. The odors they brought with them, the reek of the big coal stove in winter and the airless heat of summer, produced a combination of stenches which added up on all occasions to a full-bodied stink. Since then I have never smelled garlic without being reminded of that room.

Soon after I arrived at Lyons, I had to go to this miserable place to get my papers in order. On entering the room, I was repelled by its unattractive atmosphere and, as I was really in a hurry to go out on an investigation, I went straight up to the detective in charge, smiling genially, and told him who I was and what I wanted. He was a little fat man with bloodshot eyes and a red face. While I addressed him, he was busy writing, and never lifted his head or paid any attention to me. When I spoke to him a second time, he snarled, "Sit down and wait your turn. You have no right to come up before the others."

Humiliated and with my smile gone, I went back and took my place in that endless queue of aliens. When I had been standing for an hour, I calculated I would probably not be through for another three or four hours. Thereupon I left and went to see M. Sarbach, the head of the Detective Division. He listened to me sympathetically, took a slip of paper, and wrote across it in bold strokes, "Do the necessary. Sarbach." Back down I went triumphantly and showed this passport to the little detective. He grew still redder in the face, but I got my *carte d'identité* immediately.

Most visitors to France find Lyons a drab, uninteresting industrial and commercial town, in spite of its Roman ruins and a history of resistance at the time of the French Revolution that led to death and disaster. (When the guillotine finished the chore of cutting off the heads of all the loyalist burghers of Lyons, the Commune even changed the name of the city to be "for all eternity" *la ville affranchie*, the liberated city.) Yet this sanguinary past could not make Lyons anything but what it is, the third largest city in France, a silk-manufacturing center, and a metropolis devoted to commerce.

Prosaic though it might seem to the tourist eye, the Lyons of those days was the most interesting place in the world for a young man bent on becoming a criminologist. Aside from the fact that it was the seat of the laboratory over which the great Edmond Locard presided, the very modernity of the city, the commercial and manufacturing traffic which passed through its arteries, its identification with the contemporary world, all made it exciting to me.

My exhilaration was compounded of several elements. Locard was an exciting man to work for. There was also the freemasonry and sense of brotherhood that came from working with the young French policemen, and stimulation in the discipline of my university studies. It is not pleasant to be poor, and I was extremely poor in my first months at Lyons, but it was a city where that fact was less bleak than it might have been elsewhere.

For me and my fellow students, one of these pleasures was the feeling that to an unprecedented degree we were an actual part of the life of the city. When I was launched into the practical, on-the-spot aspects of my apprenticeship, I discovered the excitement of knowing, or supposing I knew (and the difference is not great, perhaps), everything that went on in the town. I was full of secrets, which I kept discreetly and proudly. I knew why the keeper of the little police prison had become a drunkard. I knew why the Bulgarian who owned a big silk store at the market place was covering up for a man who had stolen thousands of silk stockings from him. I knew why Madame Bertrand could never get a license to open a tobacco shop, although she applied for it every second day. These items of inside information were the kind of "intelligence" which is the bread-and-butter of any alert police department anywhere. All well-run police operations accumulate masses of this kind of material, but this was the first time I had had contact with what amounted to a new, and intensely practical, way of looking at a society in operation.

The police knew a near infinity about a huge number of persons and actions. The knowledge was necessary, but a great percentage of it never came into active use. Either there was not enough tangible evidence to support action, or. . . . That "or" is hard to define. Perhaps it implies the words "Better not." Anyhow, there is an indefinable entity which invariably participates in the work of the police, an almost metaphysical presence which seems to hover over their activities. The function of this entity is to suggest that since you cannot do everything, certain things are better left lying just as they are.

12

THE DAY WITH THE ENDLESS EVENING

In those golden Lyons years our daily schedule followed a pattern, but within the routine performance of duty there was always some incident or aspect of our work which was unexpected, like the appearance of the joker in a deck of cards. No two days were ever duplicates, and it was never possible to predict at dawn what would happen by sunset. This perpetual variety was a stimulus to me and my fellow apprentices. I enjoyed it all, or almost all. But on one occasion I could cheerfully have foregone the joker in the deck. This was when I was fated to undergo the most embarrassing evening of my life.

The day began ordinarily enough. I rose at six o'clock in order to be at the laboratory by seven, the hour at which French police work commences. My landlady was away from the house; to supplement her pension she served as a nurse for old and wealthy people, and her cases sometimes lasted two or three months. During such periods I had the place to myself, an ideal situation for anyone whose hours were as irregular as mine.

I sallied forth for breakfast, and that, too, was as pleasantly conventional as usual. Since I had begun to earn extra money, I could afford a more agreeable breakfast than bread and cold water. I had acquired the habit of eating on the quay of the Saône River with

78

other early-morning workers. I ordered a big dish of cheese soup *fondu,* a slice of crusty bread, and a generous glass of white wine.

Thus fortified, I set off for the Palais de Justice. This edifice was—and still is—a huge monument of a place, with columns and an enormous flight of steps running down toward the river. Those grandeurs were not for the police. The entrance to the Detective Division was situated in the rear and was the reverse of imposing. The door opened off a narrow side street and into a passageway. Here was stationed a venerable telephone switchboard, presided over by one or another elderly detective with some disability, such as gout, which kept him from active duty. His title was *le planton*— the orderly—and beyond him was a narrow corridor leading to the jail.

Opening off this corridor was a large, indescribably dusty chamber stuffed with ancient filing cabinets. Here was the great working tool of the French police system, a kind of giant memory. French police files were supposed to be the most thorough in the world. Certainly ours were encyclopedic and must have weighed countless tons. Anyone who had ever come to the attention of the police had a dossier, and each dossier contained all the information available about its subject. These records were kept up to date by annotations supplied by detectives on matters that might turn out to be useful at some future date. I cannot vouch for its truth, but there is a legend that every prominent Frenchmen has his official record, and that in Paris when a new Chief of Police is installed it is the custom of the Chief of Records to present him with his dossier for burning. Whether this courtesy is extended or not, it is a certainty that even the Police Chief is on file.

The laboratory was three stories above the file room, reached by a winding staircase. On this morning I got there a few minutes before seven and was on duty by the time the noise of many people climbing the stairs became audible. Just as always, the door swung open and in came the turnkey, whistling the latest tune, his peaked uniform cap tilted over one ear and his keys swinging merrily around one finger. This jollity and air of well-being resulted from his habit of polishing off a bottle of white wine for breakfast. Behind him came the motley collection of prisoners that it was our function to process. I had by now learned that the popular supposition of the romantic scoundrel or dashing criminal was nothing but a myth; if a bird of such plumage had ever appeared in the net he would have received special police treatment out of pride in his rarity. Our usual customers were a drab lot, most of them vagrants and petty thieves, not infrequently of Arab or Chinese origin. The bulk of the women were young prostitutes who had been picked up for failure to register. Beginners in this profession seemed to avoid registration and medical control as long as possible, and therefore among them was a high percentage of venereal disease.

Since Lyons was a city of about a million inhabitants, the night's criminal haul was always twenty or thirty, and on this particular day the number was larger than usual. In those days for registering and classifying criminals the French police were still using the old-fashioned anthropometrical system invented in the 1880's by Alphonse Bertillon. The core of this system was a set of eleven measurements of various parts of the body which were considered to remain unchanged in the course of a lifetime. Each measurement was further divided into three categories, small, medium, and large, and there were other technical subdivisions. As a result there were about 80,000 possible final classifications. One of us would do the actual measuring of each prisoner, and another would note down the figures as they were called out.

After completing the measurements, our job was to make what was called a *portrait parlé*, or spoken picture, of the subject. This was necessary because the Bertillon classification did not constitute a complete identification. This "speaking likeness" began with a painstaking description of every detail of the head, with special attention to the ears. Second, we noted down such details as the color of the eyes, hair, and skin. The last stage was a very detailed description of any indelible marks, such as scars and tattoos. The

Bertillon system was already in the process of being supplanted, even in France, by simpler means of identification, so we also fingerprinted and photographed each prisoner.

All this took a lot of time, even though fewer measurements were made in the case of the women. An obsolete law required us to go through the entire Bertillon catalog, even though in our actual work we relied almost wholly on fingerprints and photographs.

On this day the process seemed more tedious than usual, and I was beginning to wonder if the line would ever end. I was conducting the interrogations and recording the measurements, and the pile of papers in front of me was mounting. I looked up to question the next man and received something of a surprise. Unlike his predecessors, he was a well-to-do middle-class businessman with an air of solidity that contrasted markedly with the others. He answered my questions about his name and age and address willingly and politely.

"For what crime are you here?" I asked him.

The man's tone remained perfectly calm. "I killed my wife last evening."

It was not my business to ask, but I was so startled that the word slipped out. "Why?"

Even more calmly he answered, "I have been thinking for twenty years of doing it."

I finished filling out his record in silence. His calm, emotionless words had given me a glimpse of a chasm into which my life has often since compelled me to look.

Finally the line came to an end, and I was thinking hopefully of a brief recess, but just as the room had been vacated, there was a fresh commotion at the door, and in came a second delegation. One look and we all groaned inwardly. In the van was a big, bearded man, a perfect patriarch and obviously a Gypsy. After him shuffled his numerous womenfolk and a multitude of children who at first seemed countless but later turned out to be only seventeen. The group amounted to a tribe.

"Look at that!" Savitch muttered to me. "One Gypsy family is more work than a murder."

French law required that every Gypsy, old or young, male or female, have a special sort of identity book. We had to photograph and fingerprint the entire lot and also go through the complete *Bertillonage* with each of them. Three of us took them on, one doing the photographing and fingerprinting, a second making out the identity books, and the third hauling the Gypsies over to the window, one at a time, and shouting the details of the measurement and *portraits parlés*. By dint of cutting all the amenities very short, we disposed of the lot by noon.

Even though the police day started early and ended late, the noon hour was always a two-hour break. The married detectives went home to their wives and children. After I emerged from my bread-and-water regime I used to go with some of the bachelors to a small and ancient street near the Palais de Justice named the Rue des Trois Maries. In a fourteenth-century house was a small restaurant run by an old man named M. Volpière, and Madame Volpière presided over the kitchen.

The front of the place was merely an ordinary bar for anyone who wanted a glass of good Beaujolais, a Pernod, or one of those liqueurs which are the special glory of France. Beyond the bar there was a room with a long table accommodating sixteen. Here the good M. Volpière received his "boarders." They certainly could not be called customers, for they were all carefully chosen for their congeniality and capacity to appreciate what was set before them. Membership in this gastronomic club was regarded as an honor.

Still without any forewarning of what was to happen later, we sauntered down the Rue des Trois Maries and into M. Volpière's haven. The regulars were all there, M. Volpière was wearing his cheap cloth cap, his blue apron, and his habitual slippers. The two commercial travelers had already arrived, and I was especially pleased to see one of them, who remains in my memory as scholarly and well-informed on the history of literature. There were also two

police inspectors, companionably chatting with a couple of gentlemen who were proud of their indiscriminate interest in women.
There was, too, a lady who was making her living at the time
by playing the piano in a motion-picture house but who had
spent her youth in quite a different kind of house in Barcelona.
This foreign professional background gave her a standing of considerable eminence in the circles where she was now moving.

Each noon the first arrivals were expected to go down to the
cellar with M. Volpière and fill the bottles out of the casks he had
stored there, and now the big bottles of red wine were already on
the table. The food was what the French call *impeccable*—fault-
less even to our critical palates. What Madame could produce from
her damp, dirty, little kitchen was past believing. It was, as always,
a carefree and magnificent meal.

The afternoon stint at the laboratory was a full five hours, from
two to seven. On this particular day we were occupied with examinations of questioned documents, an inspection of two scenes-of-
crime, work on fingerprints, ballistics, and footprints. When half
past six rolled around we were beginning to think gratefully of
going home in a few minutes.

But the old-fashioned telephone on the desk shrilled, and Duffaux took the call. He listened, nodded, and hung up.

"An order from the Chief," he said loudly to all of us. "All prefecture phones are turned off as of now. No employee will be
allowed to leave the building for any reason. The public will be
permitted to use only one entrance. We're all to get sandwiches
and wine later." He sat down again and commenced working.

The married men looked disgruntled, but I think most of us
felt at least a small stir of excitement. We knew well enough what
the order meant. Some sort of raid was scheduled for the evening,
and Sarbach had decided to take no chance on a leak. Police experience has proved that no security is possible for projected raids.
No matter how good the force, how carefully disguised the plans,
if the police themselves know ahead of time that a raid is planned,
the news gets out. "To keep a raid secret, begin by arresting the

police," the axiom used to run. Without such drastic precautions as Sarbach was taking, a major criminal would never be caught in a raid.

Evidently this was to be a big affair. Every squad of the Detective Division was on hand to participate, and only a corporal's guard was left behind to man the offices. To my delight I was assigned to the Chief's own squad. We still had no information about the object of the raid, and the old hands did not seem to expect any. They spent the time of waiting as men in such situations always do—reading, sleeping, or playing cards. When the signal to come along was finally sounded each man made a final check of his gun—generally a .32 automatic pistol—and we all went down to the street. By then it was about ten o'clock.

A nondescript cavalcade was waiting for us in the dark and narrow back street. Because the Lyons Police Department had no regular fleet of automobiles, whenever a raid was scheduled it had to be made with an assortment of vehicles gathered from whatever sources were available. This night the convoy consisted of a few old-fashioned limousines and two elderly trucks normally used to transport prisoners. These last had wooden seats built into them and furnished their passengers with a pretty rough ride. But, being assigned to Sarbach's squad, I got to ride in the best of the limousines.

As we rolled through the almost empty streets, Sarbach said, "We are going after Georges Reme."

One of the men beside me gave a small grunt. The reason for so much secrecy was immediately apparent: Reme was the Houdini of French criminals. We had almost caught him a few days earlier, but to our shame and to the delight of his admirers he had managed to escape, as he had invariably done when arrested in other cities. Here in Lyons he had been posing as a Navy captain, living in high style and paving his path with worthless checks. He was a small dapper man, good-looking in a genteel way, and mild-mannered. We knew from his record that he never resorted to violence but lived only by his wits, and his well-publicized exploits had

ABOVE Looking across the Saône River toward the *Palais de Justice*. The Sûreté's Lyons office was in the upper rear of the columned building.

BELOW Members of the Police Laboratory staff at Lyons, 1928. In the first row, second from the left, is Savitch; third from the left, Locard; and right, Chevassus. Center, Locard's secretary, Maggie Guiral; to her left the author and Poux; Duffaux on her right. The others are visiting students or staff members not mentioned in these pages.

The studio portrait given to me by Edmond Locard when I left Lyons to return home to Sweden.

My father, the redoubtable Pehr Söderman, wearing his official sheriff's uniform on the occasion of Emperor Chulalonkong's visit to Sweden.

earned him something of a popular following, so naturally his escape was regarded as a good joke on us.

It is true that Reme thoroughly outfoxed the two detectives assigned to take him before the examining magistrate. They were familiar with his reputation for clever escapes, but for some reason they neglected to handcuff him to either of themselves, though his hands were cuffed together in front of him. When the trio reached the door of the magistrate's office, the judge was occupied and could not admit them immediately. They stood around, waiting their turn, and suddenly Reme made his break.

Dropping the greatcoat slung around his shoulders, he bent low and began to run toward the dead end of the corridor, the detectives after him. Halfway down, he made as if to tackle, swerved, retraced his steps, and raced to the main staircase. Down the bannister he slid, and out onto the sidewalk. Across the street there was a grammar school, and at the moment the children were all out in the yard for morning recess. Somehow little Reme managed to dive into that schoolyard, get himself down on his hands and knees, and start making comic faces and funny noises. In a few seconds he was surrounded by scores of children.

"We simply could not see where he had gone," one of the detectives explained later.

That was all there was to the escape. No doubt some benevolent locksmith or mechanic removed the handcuffs, and Reme was free as air again. The hunt for him had continued for several days without result, but now there was reason to suppose he might be hiding out in a red-light district in a part of the city known as La Guillotière.

It did not take us long to get there, and we found the district already shut off from the outer world by a cordon of uniformed police. We began to go through one house after another, systematically searching them from cellars to attics and asking every denizen to show his identity papers. Building after building was covered methodically, and still there was no sign of Reme. Finally we came to a small bistro that had a large window opening on a back yard.

The bar was packed with sinister-looking characters from the underworld, and we rushed in with pistols drawn.

"This is the police!" Sarbach shouted. "Be quiet and remain seated."

All but one of them obeyed. A man sitting near the big window dived through it into the darkness outside and disappeared. Several detectives plunged after him, but they never caught him. All we ever knew for sure was that he was not Reme.

The raid turned out to be a disappointment. True, we rounded up almost two hundred questionable persons, but Reme was not among them. Our haul was taken back to headquarters in the Division's trucks, to be fingerprinted and questioned. Since they were unregistered prostitutes, foreigners without identity cards, and the miscellaneous riff-raff to be found in any large city, we decided to postpone the examinations until the next day.

It was well on toward dawn.

A sense of disappointment pervaded our force, and this was most evident in Sarbach, for whom any of us would have gone through fire and water. It was not his way to ask any such sacrifices however; he was considerate and kind in everything he did, a man of great personal bravery, with a gift for making rapid decisions. As the prisoners were led away, he sighed and turned to us with the suggestion that we take the taste of the evening's fiasco out of our mouths with a round of drinks.

About ten of us trooped down to a café near the Saône River. As we sat over our beers one of the detectives began to describe an illegal gambling joint he had spotted in the middle of town. According to him, the entrance was unusual in that it was through a bakery where two men worked all night preparing the long crusty loaves which are the staple of the French diet. Apparently the technique for admission was a knock on the bakery door. One of the men inside would then inspect the caller through a small window and, if he looked satisfactory, would admit him, conduct him through the bakery, and send him up a small spiral staircase to the second floor. Up there, the detective said, there was reputed to be a large, elegant room in which gambling took place every evening.

The same idea must have formed in all our minds as we listened. Sarbach was leaning forward, his mild blue eyes beginning to light up. Even the droop of his blond mustache seemed less despondent.

"Let's have something to show for this miserable night's work," somebody exclaimed.

"Not so fast," Sarbach said reflectively. "This requires thought." He stroked his mustache and took another pull at his beer. "First, there is the problem of getting in."

"We can manage that," I said. "Look at my friend Savitch here, all dressed for a society evening he never got to attend. He's just about the best-dressed man in Lyons—black coat, those elegant white gloves, and even white spats. He looks absolutely loaded with money."

Savitch gave me a grin. "Loaded is right, Harry, but not with money. Why don't you and I impersonate a couple of drunks? They're pretty sure to let us in. They can tell we're foreigners and won't be thinking of police in connection with us."

"There is merit in that," Sarbach agreed. "However, you both know that the law requires that cards and money be on the table at the moment of arrest, and neither of you can legally make an arrest. It takes only a couple of seconds to sweep up the cards and the bets, and if that happens we won't be able to make our case hold up in court."

"Harry and I will take care of that," Savitch said with a twinkle.

"Also," Sarbach went on, "the gambling paraphernalia has to be officially seized. No detective is empowered to make such a seizure. A commissaire of police is required for that."

"You, Sarbach," said one of the others.

We were all beginning to take fire at the idea of the raid.

"True," said Sarbach with a smile, "true. I am a commissaire. Well, we shall try it on for size. Here's how we'll work it."

He outlined the main elements of strategy while we downed our beers, and then we set off in a warm glow of anticipation.

At the bakery Sarbach and the rest of our friends hid around the corner while Savitch and I, reeling convincingly, went up and knocked. The man who looked us over must have been satisfied with our act because he admitted us immediately. We found ourselves in an ordinary bakery, with a pile of flour sacks on the floor and two bakers busy at the big oven. The spiral staircase was visible at the rear of the room, and I headed immediately for it, while Savitch loitered behind to make sure the door was open for the main body of the attack, which was to follow in two minutes.

Up the stairs I went with a rush, dropping my hand onto the butt of my automatic as I climbed. At the head of the stairs was another door. I opened it with one quick jerk and found myself in a large room with many indications of ancient splendor. The house had been built in the eighteenth century, and this room had evidently been the salon of some nobleman or wealthy burgher. Its ceiling was molded plaster; there was an enormous fireplace with porcelain tiles around it; the walls were lined with mirrors. Under present circumstances, however, I had no time for these glories; my attention was instantly focused on a big green table in the middle of the room, around which about thirty persons of both sexes were sitting. They were all holding cards in their hands, and there was a pile of money in front of each.

My entry produced a momentary silence. I drew my gun and shouted, *"Haut les mains!"* In plain English this means "Hands up!"

Every hand went up instantly. There are few arguments more convincing than the muzzle of a gun.

Time passed. Nothing happened. The room was still; none of the gamblers wanted to say anything at all. Several minutes went by, and there was still no sound of feet on the stairs to indicate that Sarbach and his cohorts were arriving. I began to perspire gently.

Finally, a husky Levantine at one side of the table lowered his hands, still holding his cards. Perhaps his arms had begun to tire. I leveled the automatic at him and said, trying to sound wholly calm, "Hands up, or I'll shoot." His hands went up again. It was plain that he was the black sheep of some royal or moneyed family from some Mediterranean country. All the reigning houses used to have one or more of these lively skeletons in the family closet, to the despair of hotel managers, jewelers, businessmen, and, last but not least, the police.

More minutes dragged on. Still there was no sound of rescue from the stairs, and I could see that my customers were beginning to tire. It is physically difficult to keep one's hands in the air for any length of time, and by a natural process of fatigue all their hands were beginning to sink, especially those of the older people. After about ten minutes a Chinese quickly lowered one hand and snatched his money off the table and pocketed it. The gun and I looked him hard in the eye, so reluctantly he pulled the money out again and put it back on the table. The hands returned to the air.

By now, every minute seemed to me to be an eternity. The situation was desperate. The thirty people I was holding at bay would clearly enjoy rending me limb from limb. I, on the other hand, would hardly dare to shoot. Killing a man just because he had been gambling was unthinkable. My throat was dry as dust, and I could not have spoken if I had wanted to. And still there was no noise from below. Thirty pairs of eyes were watching me, and there was murder in every one of them. The conviction grew in my mind that some of the gamblers were about to make a rush. The sweat stood out all over me.

At what I was convinced was the very last possible second of this ordeal, the tension was broken by a thunderous crash which shook the whole house; then another and another. This new development made the gamblers forget their aching arms, and they stopped staring at me to listen. The crashes stopped, and five seconds later Sarbach was in the room. He gave one lightning-fast glance around the room, smiled, and said, "You can all put your hands down on the table now. I've seen enough."

As for me, I was weak with relief.

Downstairs I found my unfortunate friend Savitch. His elegance was completely gone. He was covered with flour from head to foot, and was as white as a snowman. Also he was breathing hard. It seemed that when the man who opened the door to us saw me hurry up the spiral staircase he became suspicious and tried to haul Savitch away from the door. Savitch hung on like grim death, but the man wrestled him away and threw him into the middle of the room, where he landed on a heap of flour sacks. The guard bolted the door and leaned against it. Savitch made a rush at him, trying to open the door to admit Sarbach and the squad. A heroic struggle ensued, in which the bakers took an enthusiastic part.

Meanwhile the detectives had made their scheduled rush to the door, only to find it bolted. They realized at once that they would have to force an entrance, but it took quite a while to find a suitable battering ram. Fortunately there was in the vicinity a house under construction with several rafter beams not yet installed. The squad rushed one of these to the bakery, and heaving together, they broke down the door. Sarbach estimated the whole affair took twenty minutes. Twenty years, it seemed to me.

13

APACHE AND GUILLOTINE

Often around seven o'clock in the evening, when we had finished our work in the laboratory, Chevassus, Duffaux, Poux, and I used to stroll over the big bridge in front of the Palais de Justice to stop at a café located in a small street on the other side of the Rhone. This place was named *Au Mal Assiz*, which means that one sat badly there. The name was not inappropriate because instead of chairs the seats were small wine barrels. Even the tables were bigger wine barrels. At *Au Mal Assiz* almost nothing but the red Beaujolais wine of the region was served, but what a wine! As served there, it was what the French call "open wine," meaning that it is on draft. In the cellar of the tavern the delicious Beaujolais rested in huge barrels from which were filled the thick green service bottles so characteristic of this kind of French café.

Over the counter hung an assortment of bulky, odd-shaped sausages from the Jura. These with white bread and the wine constituted the sole bill of fare, but it was more than good enough. The place was full of customers from early morning to eight in the evening. Promptly at that hour M. Dubut, the proprietor and a man of principle, closed the place firmly and tightly.

What attracted me to the establishment was not so much the Beaujolais, the wine-keg seats, the atmosphere, nor even the waitress—a fine, fresh country lass—as an interesting habit of

M. Dubut's. This same habit also attracted the attention of Poux, Duffaux, and some of the other leading detectives of Lyons. We spent many a convivial hour at *Au Mal Assiz* trying to get to the bottom of the matter, and the length of time it took us to figure it out is a measure of the fallibility of the deductive process.

On the face of it, there should have been almost no problem in fathoming what happened in plain sight. M. Dubut, as proprietor, did not usually wait directly on the customers. This was the job of his excellent waitress, who was tipped by the patrons in the ordinary way. But sometimes she was absent, or overworked, and on these occasions M. Dubut would serve the wine himself. Strangers to the place would sometimes, in ignorance of M. Dubut's proprietary status, tip him. These philistines were referred to by M. Dubut (if at all) as "suckers." The tip generally consisted of a couple of heavy copper sous, and our host would receive the offering without thanks or comment. Then he would march behind the counter and ostentatiously wrap the coins in a twist of paper, so that the package looked like a tadpole. By this time the innocent tipper would be looking at the proprietor as though he were insane.

The next step would do nothing to reassure him. With a flick of his wrist, the good M. Dubut would send his little parcel of coins spinning through the air and up to the ceiling. There it landed with a thud—and stuck. The miraculous part of it, even for us, was that the trick was done right before our eyes. As the months progressed the ceiling became ever more densly plastered with these paper squills, until, on New Year's Eve, M. Dubut would grasp a broom, brush them all down and collect them, count the coins, and invite all the customers present to consume Beaujolais up to the value of the total.

How the lot of us racked our brains over this peculiar violation of the law of gravity! Why did the little packages stay on the ceiling? Many afternoons we conducted surreptitious experiments at the laboratory, but they were always failures. Once we settled for the theory that the sly M. Dubut had put some glue in the paint of his ceiling. But, on the other hand, we could see that the ceiling looked dry. Finally, after countless close observations of every movement of M. Dubut's hands, we discovered his secret. Quick as a magician, he used to put a thumb tack on top of the coins before he wrapped them up. The point of the thumb tack, hidden under the paper when it went spinning up in the air, would emerge and enter the ceiling when it had been tapped from beneath by the heavy coins.

An innocent bit of sleight of hand like M. Dubut's was only an interlude in a business which for all of us was nothing if not serious. Perhaps our very enjoyment of food and story-telling was a reaction to the emotionally disturbing matters which made up the bulk of our daily work.

In fact, violence was so natural a part of our lives that once in a long time we made mistakes in taking it for granted. Such a case involved one of the best detectives on the force, my old friend Durand. He was about forty, a portly, stately man with a fine, sloping black mustache and a wisp of beard to reinforce it. He had sharp eyes which scrutinized the world in front of his aquiline nose. Durand was D'Artagnan in the body of Porthos and would have made an excellent, resourceful musketeer if he had been born in the right era. His own century made of him no more than a humble French detective, compelled to make ends meet on a low salary. His personal budget was slightly eased by the fact that he was a bachelor, something that could readily be observed by a glance at his trousers: they were incredibly baggy on all occasions, and wholly free of any caress from the iron of a devoted woman. His appearance was decidedly Bohemian, and some of his tastes matched it. What he did not know about food and wines was not worth knowing, and in me he found an enthusiastic pupil. His direct thinking, his matter-of-fact approach to problems, his love of human beings, his ready laughter, all made him a magnificent companion.

It was Durand's custom, if he was not out trailing some suspect, to sneak back in the afternoons to the laboratory to smoke a cigarette and have a chat. He generally managed to arrive at the moment of our *casse-croûte*—"break crust," or snack. When we felt in the mood—and that was nearly every day—we would donate a few centimes apiece, and Poux, the youngest on the squad, would go to an *épicerie* across the street to buy a few bottles of Beaujolais, some ham or a piece of Jura sausage, and one of those crisp loaves of French bread.

On one such afternoon Durand seemed distracted.

"What's the matter with you, old chap?" Chevassus asked as he handed him a glass of wine.

Durand gulped it down, lit a cigarette, and leaned back. "Thanks, *mon vieux.*"

Chevassus nodded. "What's the case this time?"

Durand looked almost sheepish. "It concerns a woman that some of you know. She eats in that little restaurant in the Rue des Trois Maries—Mademoiselle Olivier. She plays the piano in a movie house on the Place de la République. You probably know that in her youth she worked in a brothel in Barcelona. What she doesn't know about Spaniards isn't worth knowing."

"Yes," I said, "but that was long ago. Why, she must be well over fifty."

He gave me a reflective look. "She's fifty-five," he said. "But when you reach fifty-five yourself it may not seem so old. Anyhow, when she retired officially she came here with her savings. She has musical talent and makes a good income from her playing. She still takes a lover on occasion, and there's a brutal little Spanish pimp who has been her regular visitor for months."

This could hardly be called a surprise.

"A couple of hours ago," Durand continued, "we got a call from the concierge of that old apartment house at 23 Bis, Rue des Trois Maries. One of the tenants had just been found in her own bathroom, savagely cut up and unconscious. It turned out that the victim was Mademoiselle Olivier."

He paused and drew strongly on his cigarette.

"Well," he resumed, turning to Chevassus, "I had been more or less expecting trouble in that quarter. 'The Spaniard has done it,' I said to myself. I sent young Claude and that chap Heguette out to pick the fellow up and bring him in. I myself went directly to the apartment.

"The woman was lying naked on the floor of her bathroom. She was face down, and her behind was cut practically to ribbons. I never saw anything nastier; there were quarts of blood all over the floor and, even though she was still breathing, she looked to me to be on her way out of this world. The place was a wreck; even the porcelain washstand was smashed. Every indication of the worst kind of sex murder was present, and I was thinking that the guillotine was too good for that Spaniard.

"While I waited for the doctor I sat down on the lid of the w.c.—there wasn't any blood there, at least—and began to reconstruct the crime in my mind. The terrible wounds were hideous, all right, but they didn't look as deep as I should have expected. Lying right beside her was a curved piece of the shattered washbasin with blood all along one edge. I picked it up and looked at it and then at her. Finally I leaned over and tried the piece against one of the wounds. It fitted."

Chevassus began to grin. "Aha!" he said. "I see what you are getting at."

Durand nodded. "Yes. There had been no crime. The poor woman was obviously washing herself at her own basin, sat down on it, and it smashed under her. She is no featherweight at best. When the doctor arrived he confirmed my judgment. They carted her off to the hospital, and they had to take so many stitches the surgeon didn't bother to count them. Mademoiselle Olivier will have to play the piano standing up for a while."

Durand's expression darkened. "When I got back to the Sûreté I found that Claude and Heguette had arrested the Spaniard. That odious little creature was flaming mad and shouting out his innocence in two languages. I'll bet it was the first time he had told the truth in years."

The apache is a common type in the rogues' gallery of French criminals. The polite dictionary definition of the term is "ruffian" or "hooligan," but this seems to me a mild way of defining a felon whose means of livelihood ranges from pimping to burglary. He occupies a position in French crime somewhat parallel to the American gangster, but there are several differences. For one, he is apt to be less well-dressed than his American counterpart, although he no longer wears the picturesque costume still perpetuated in drama and ballet.

This kind of a criminal is more ruthless than any American counterpart in his attitude toward his women. No "gun moll" in the United States would put up with the treatment the apache accords his loved one. This holds especially true for the subspecies *maquereau*, or pimp. When a maquereau gets his hooks into a prostitute there is almost no way she can escape from him except by death. Even so, I once came upon a case of a pimp who had cut the throat of his woman, and her last words were, "I love you." Their women seem to like the revolting treatment they receive at the hands of these men. The relationship between the maquereau and his captive has been analyzed by many experts, who agree that it is a masochistic trait, a taking of pleasure out of the pain inflicted upon them. They seem almost to illustrate the old Russian peasant maxim that if a man does not thrash his woman often enough she will take it as a sign that he no longer loves her. At any rate, a maquereau will beat and torture his victim if she fails to earn as much money as he expects. Often he will beat her for fun, without any overt reason.

The apache of Paris or Lyons, like his counterpart, the *nervi* of Marseilles, frequents small restaurants and cafés. Here his capacity for innocent enjoyment is much the same as any other man's. He enjoys the good food and takes pleasure in the wine—this latter almost always in moderation because the apache gets his stimulation in other ways and is apt to content himself with a couple of bottles a day. Drugs seldom tempt him. The social part of his evening is generally spent playing cards and telling jokes. At such times it is difficult for the inexperienced observer to suspect his inherent viciousness.

The curious nature of French law made it almost impossible, in those days, to do anything much about pimping. Not all the pimps were apaches, by any means. There were so many and so many different types of them that they constituted a sort of cancer in the social body. There were even university students who maintained themselves in this fashion, and maquereaux were to be found in the most unlikely strata of society. Under the criminal code they were nearly untouchable because pimping was legally defined as "special vagabondage." To be convicted of this special vagabondage a man had to be shown to be without work, income, and legal residence. The maquereau was almost always able to prove he had one of the three and so evade the law. The owner of his favorite restaurant would swear that he resided there or that he worked a couple of hours a day as a waiter. Under such circumstances the police were powerless.

The frustration, intensified by the loathing we felt for these men and the way they lived, produced a reaction in the police that was not altogether healthy. Since the law restrained the police, the police would sometimes decide, when the evil became intolerable, to take matters into their own hands. A group of the worst pimps would then be rounded up, generally on a quiet Saturday afternoon, and thoroughly thrashed. Perhaps the practice did some good, but I suspected it of doing an equal amount of harm, since it is likely that the victims gave their beatings back with interest to their women during the ensuing evening.

Of course not all apaches were averse to shooting it out if the occasion arose. The worst case in my memory was that of André Dupont, the only man I ever saw pay the death penalty. He was a brutal little rat of a man, about twenty-two, with no doubt a very low I.Q.

One Sunday afternoon André was taking a stroll in a remote corner of a park in Lyons. He came upon an old man sitting on a bench examining the contents of his wallet. The temptation was too much for André. He stepped over to the old man and demanded the wallet. The old man handed it over, even though Dupont did not draw his .32-caliber pistol. Just as the wallet was changing hands, there was a faint noise on the path behind, and André whirled, drawing his gun.

Two policemen mounted on bicycles were coming up the path. Every French city has its bicycle squad of uniformed police and, old-fashioned though they may look, they are more effective for work as park patrols than motorcycle cops, because they move silently. These two were upon André before he knew it; he fired at once. In two seconds both policemen were dead and André was in full flight, not bothering even to pick up the wallet. The old man staggered to the nearest police station and reported what had happened.

The murder enraged the entire police force. The two victims had been well liked. More tragic still, each was the father of a large family. An intensive manhunt commenced, aided by the old man's excellent description of the murderer. His picture of the assailant was so accurate that the police virtually identified André at once, and in a few days he was found, hiding out with a new girl he had got hold of.

In a case of this sort, French justice works speedily. In no more than a month's time Dupont had been tried, convicted, and sentenced to death. I was invited—perhaps under the circumstances the word "instructed" would be more accurate—to be one of the witnesses at the execution, in compliance with the regulation that executions must be conducted in a public place. The scaffold was erected on the sidewalk in front of the prison, and at the moment of the execution a cordon of mounted police surrounded the spot to keep uninvited spectators away.

Early in the morning the witnesses were summoned. There were about ten of us, and we forgathered at a small café opposite the prison. We fortified ourselves for what was ahead with black coffee and stiff brandies. I confess I had a feeling of nausea and a longing to be somewhere else. We were a silent group as we started across the dark street, lighted by a single arc light. The scaffold stood out with the raw yellow of new wood. It had been built during the night, and I wondered whether André Dupont had spent the dark hours listening to the carpenters' hammering.

To the people of other countries the guillotine sometimes seems a barbarous way of taking a man's life. It is, however, just as quick, if not quicker, than hanging, electrocution, or the gas chamber. No other method of execution has been employed in France since the time of the Revolution, but the practice of beheading is centuries old. The guillotine was introduced at the time of the Revolution to make mass executions swift and efficient.

For a hundred years before the Revolution, executions in Paris and in much of the rest of France were the monopoly of a family named Sanson, which enjoyed a royal charter. The legend is that the first Sanson was a seventeenth-century Gascon nobleman, an officer of a regiment stationed in the town of Honfleur. One night, while he was in his cups, he made the acquaintance of a beautiful girl and followed her home. In the morning he discovered to his horror that he was in the home of the local executioner. In those superstitious times the executioner was considered to be a social leper condemned for life to associate only with his own family and fellow craftsmen. When the father of the girl complained to the regiment's commanding officer, Sanson was cashiered and compelled to marry the girl. There was nothing he could do but become the assistant to his father-in-law. In due course he was advanced to the post of Executioner of Paris.

This first Sanson is reputed to have been uncannily skilled with the sword. Once a young nobleman was sentenced to die by the sword and, not trusting the skill of the local axman, the authorities sent to Paris for Sanson to carry out the sentence. A platform was erected in the market place, and on the fateful morning it was surrounded by the entire population. The condemned nobleman threw Sanson a purse of gold and said, "Dog, do your work!"

Sanson replied humbly, "It is already done, Your Grace. Just shake your head."

The son of this virtuoso was only eight when his father died, but his mother managed to retain the royal charter on his behalf. The actual tortures and executions were performed by his father's oldest assistant, but the boy's presence made the matter legal. Less than three hundred years ago, unhappy as it may be to recall the fact, the official executioner was kept extremely busy, and the Sansons became a wealthy family. Their work was varied, and beheadings were the least of it. There were highwaymen to be quartered alive, counterfeiters to be boiled in oil, felons to be crippled by the crushing of their legs, and all sorts of tortures to be inflicted. The fees for this kind of work ran high. Furthermore, because the work was intermittent, executioners were entitled to an excise tax on goods brought to the local market place.

Out of so much torture one humanitarian virtue gradually evolved: the executioners learned a good deal about human anatomy and entered into the practice of medicine at which they often earned a high reputation.

By the time the twentieth century came round, executions were rare enough so that only one man was required for the entire country. He was known as *l'exécuteur des hautes oeuvres*—the performer of capital operations—and in my day his name was M. Deibler. His official title, Executioner of Paris, ranked him among connoisseurs as the most distinguished among his European colleagues. M. Deibler had already come from Paris, bringing with him the blade of the guillotine, and what is called the *bois de justice*, the wood of justice, as the French call the grooved upright and the crossbar from which the blade is dropped.

Reluctantly we crossed the road and went into the prison. In the sentry room we were welcomed by the warden and introduced to M. Deibler, who proved to be a stately man in his late fifties, funereally dressed in a top hat and black coat. He had brought two aides, who were obviously employees of some butcher shop.

With the warden at our head, we marched through the main prison building and into the death cell. Almost every French prisoner under death sentence appeals as a last resort to the President of the Republic for pardon, and in many cases it is accorded. If the request is denied, this fact is not communicated to the prisoner until the morning of his execution. André Dupont, then, could not be certain that he was to die this morning. As we entered the cell, he was peacefully snoring on his bed, with a prison guard at his side since, after sentence of death has been passed, a prisoner is never left alone. The warden went over to the bed and shook André by the shoulder. He woke up startled and began rubbing his eyes.

The warden then uttered the classic words, "Be courageous, my friend. The President of the Republic has refused your pardon."

André was then proffered the assistance of the prison chaplain, but he brushed aside the consolations of religion. A prison guard carrying a tray with a bottle of rum, a glass, some lumps of sugar and some cigarettes now stepped forward and offered André these refreshments. He gulped down a couple of glasses of rum, got to his feet, and followed us.

We all returned to the sentry house. Deibler's assistants put André in a chair and cut off the thick hair from his neck and the collar from his shirt. M. Deibler gave the warden a receipt for André. There is nothing more final than to be receipted for in writing by the official executioner.

André had now to stand up and clasp his hands behind his back. A pair of light handcuffs were put on him and, with one of the assistants at either side, he was led to the prison entrance. The sun was rising and, blinking his eyes, André could see the guillotine and the gendarmes. His body was fastened to the plank, which went down with a thump, and his neck was under the knife, fastened by a wooden device. M. Deibler stood immobile at the side of the guillotine, in his black-gloved hand holding the cord to release the knife. The knife came down with a thud, and André's head rolled into a basket. His body was loaded into a bigger basket, and the two were placed in the morgue's delivery truck. Sawdust was spread over the blood, and the carpenters began to pull down the guillotine.

The end of André Dupont confirmed me in a decision never to witness an official taking-of-life again.

14

THE ORDEAL OF SUZANNE DUBOIS

Every execution implies a kind of criticism of society. It means that society is compelled to resort to violence in order to punish or prevent violence. Our work in Lyons brought this home to us time and again.

Locard believed passionately in the usefulness of every technical analysis which could be brought to bear upon the problems of crime. To him, a police laboratory was an essential part of crime prevention as well as crime detection. I think in his most optimistic moments he wanted to believe that a scientific approach would make crime too difficult to perpetrate. The certainty of detection and punishment is undoubtedly a deterrent to many delinquents, especially those who have time for premeditation.

One conspicuous illustration is the crime of murder by poison. Advances in chemistry and medicine were even in those days making poisoning unpopular, and today, although poison cases are still to be found, almost every potential murderer knows how refined police detection methods have become and hesitates to resort to a method which by its very nature will leave physical evidence. Faint traces of poison can now be detected even long after death, and all calculating criminals wish to believe that they are destined to belong to the supposedly high percentage of unapprehended felons. Indeed, if criminals were certain they would be caught, a

103

preponderance of crimes would be those committed on the spur of the moment.

It was not always so. The premeditated murders of the Borgias were almost unprovable except by inference, because no techniques existed for identification of poisoning. In seventeenth-century France there was a popular prescription called heritage pills; they were used on elderly wealthy relatives who seemed to the impatient heirs to be living beyond their allotted span. But by the opening of the nineteenth century the popularity of poisoning declined with the improvement in scientific detection techniques.

Not all poisoners were well enough informed to be deterred by the new police techniques, and I can remember one instance in which the perpetrator nearly got away with the murder in spite of them. The case was a village crime and one committed with unusual ingenuity. It baffled us all for a time, and even now the final solution is not actually established, though the presumption is overwhelming. . . .

"There's enough arsenic here to kill a cow!" my friend Taupin exclaimed one day as he emerged from the small lab in which we conducted chemical analyses. "Look," he said, holding out a test tube and pointing to the characteristic arsenic film of the Marsh reaction.

Inside the test tube were samples of the alimentary canal of the late Madame Geneviève Dubois. A few days before a large glass jar had come to us containing quite a little of the lady's insides, and since she had been resting peacefully in the cemetery for more than two years the job of analysis had not been a welcome one. But police work is seldom a bed of roses, even olfactorily.

The evidence was so indisputable that a task force was sent to the village of St. Fontain, where the good Madame Dubois had lived most of her life and where she died. Next day at noon three of us set out for the place—Duffaux, a detective from the Division, and I. The train took us to a town not far away, and there we found the gendarme of the village, who had been notified to meet us. He had bicycled to the station and was dressed according to regulations in his picturesque uniform, with its *képi,* or peaked cap, black jacket, blue trousers, and black leather leggings. His pistol was holstered at one side of his broad belt, and on the other side was his small leather pouch. I smiled to myself when I saw it. Inside the pouch I knew there would be his supply of the small blank forms on which gendarmes report every disturbance of the peace from traffic violations to tavern brawls and poaching. We had read endless numbers of them and invented hundreds of jokes, good and bad, about them. The printed text began:

"I, the Gendarme.............., dressed in his uniform and obeying the orders of his Chief, report...................."

Gendarmes are the rural police of France, and they are stationed all over the country in squads of five and ten. With their wives and families they live in a group. They work under the direction of the Minister of the Interior, but they are all noncommissioned officers and the force as a whole is supervised by the Minister of War. Theoretically, a gendarme may investigate anything that happens in his district, but all difficult cases, especially those involving major crimes, are taken over by the detectives of the Sûreté. That is what had happened in the matter of Madame Dubois.

St. Fontain proved to be one of those fortified villages characteristic of many regions of the Continent. Built on a hill, it consisted of a castle, a church, and a cluster of small buildings surrounded by a large wall. A few hundred years earlier feudal barons or counts lived in such a village, and the inhabitants were their subjects and serfs. For my taste, the fortified villages of Italy are too austere in their architecture, too sun-baked, and too poverty-stricken. But in France a fortified village is often like an illustration for a fairy tale, bowered in trees, the walls mantled in vines, the people busily cultivating the fields at the foot of the hill or carrying on their trades and crafts. St. Fontain was just such a charming place.

As we went toward the town along a narrow road which wound through green fields bordered with fruit trees, the gendarme related the facts of the case as he had ascertained them on preliminary investigation.

"Naturally, messieurs, in a place like St. Fontain, where everyone lives close to everyone else, there are not likely to be many secrets among the inhabitants," he observed.

The exhumation for which he had obtained the order was the result of a series of vague rumors of foul play which had seeped through the village. He seemed himself somewhat surprised that they had proved to have foundation in fact. Madame Dubois was not the kind of person who is ordinarily the victim of murder. She had been a widow for a long time and had no children. Her only heir was her niece, who had lived with her and taken care of her. She had apparently not required much care, for even at seventy she was hale and hearty, and her death had been something of a surprise.

But one afternoon, shortly after a meal, she became ill, vomited, and complained of pain in the stomach. There was no doctor in the village, and, shrinking from the expense of summoning one from a neighboring town, Madame DuBois decided to let things go until the following day. By then she was better, and her illness was attributed to food poisoning. A week later she was ill again with the same symptoms. Once again she recovered, and this cycle was repeated several times until, one night, she died in great agony. No autopsy was made; the old doctor from the next town simply concluded that she had died of some undiagnosed internal illness. So Madame Dubois was buried, and all the villagers mourned. Mademoiselle Suzanne Dubois, her niece, continued to live in the small house on the market place.

That would have been the end of the story if a certain M. Fontvieille, a solicitor in a neighboring town, had not been in the habit of drinking wine every evening with a couple of merchant friends. Fontvieille had been in charge of Madame Dubois' affairs and was the administrator of her estate. One evening about six months after the old lady's burial, M. Fontvieille may have had a few glasses too many. At any rate, he forgot the professional secrecy proper to his occupation and informed his companions that Mademoiselle Dubois had recently asked him to convert a large part of the mortgages and bonds of her newly acquired fortune into ready cash.

"There is something wrong with her," said M. Fontvieille. "She seems to be under great pressure; I have a feeling she is giving the money away to somebody. How terrible that such a snug little fortune should be dissipated in this way."

By the next day, the story was being whispered from ear to ear, and if anything can arouse a sense of outrage in the breast of a Frenchman it is the thought that one of their number may be throwing money away and dipping into capital to boot. Mademoiselle Dubois *was* one of them; she was supposed to live comfortably in their midst until her soul departed, leaving the fortune unimpaired. They were outraged.

Mademoiselle Dubois, the gendarme said, was a pleasant-looking woman in her middle thirties. She had a kind, mild nature, and everyone liked her, although she was rather retiring and did not talk much. No one knew her intimately enough to tell her about the solicitor's revelations, and the gossip about her continued to spread. Under ordinary circumstances there is not much to talk about in a fortified village, and anything the least out of the usual is therefore canvassed from every angle.

"And when one talks and talks in this fashion, messieurs," said our gendarme friend, "things begin to take on special meanings. Now that one has perceived that the affair is out of the ordinary, even apparently ordinary matters are to be considered in a new light."

"Precisely," said Duffaux. "What sort of matters?"

"Well," the gendarme replied, "shortly before her aunt had the first abdominal seizure, Mademoiselle Dubois spent a couple of months in Paris. We are not so provincial here that a visit to Paris is remarkable, but. . . . Then, too, why didn't the niece call the doctor when her aunt became violently ill the first time? Perhaps Mademoiselle Dubois had secured some poison in Paris and come home to—"

Duffaux grunted noncommittally. "Poison is not so easy to get even in Paris," he observed. "We can look into that later. Meanwhile, how did all this talk come to your attention?"

The gendarme shook his head. "One of the inhabitants came to me, saying that things were going too far. Apparently this M. Fontvieille, having once blabbed about Mademoiselle Dubois' affairs, considered he might as well go on doing so. He said he had been ordered to sell the house in St. Fontain and that Mademoiselle had made up her mind to go to Paris to live."

"What did you do then?" Duffaux asked, watching the man's expression.

"As monsieur knows from the report," the gendarme replied, "I went to Mademoiselle Dubois and interrogated her. She denied any knowledge of how her aunt had died. She affirmed to me that the reason no doctor had been called was her aunt's anxiety to save the money. She would tell me nothing of why she had gone to Paris or what she had done there. As for selling the house, she replied flatly that this was no one's business but her own." He returned Duffaux's glance. "We then reported the whole matter to the Sûreté, and Mademoiselle was interrogated again with equally negative results, or so I understand."

"That is correct," said Duffaux. "That is why we authorized the exhumation of the body, and it was found to contain more than enough arsenic to kill her."

We had only to collect evidence on how the niece had obtained the arsenic. Had she found a way to buy it in Paris, as the villagers seemed to believe?

It was a warm day. The long walk from the station had given us a good appetite and climbing the hill a nice thirst. When we entered the village, Duffaux declared that we would have luncheon before we started work. He asked the gendarme to show us the local inn, but the officer merely glanced at his wristwatch, remarked that it was already ten minutes past two, and informed us calmly that there would probably be no lunch at all because of the lateness of the hour.

"Come, now!" Duffaux said. "Every restaurant in France serves luncheon between twelve and two, and ten minutes will not make so much difference."

The gendarme answered, "Then you don't know this innkeeper. He serves excellent food, so good in fact that on Sundays the village street is crowded with the limousines of wealthy merchants from St. Etienne and even Lyons. But he is personally so gruff, unpleasant, and egotistical that he would not serve a king if he arrived after two o'clock."

"Nevertheless," Duffaux declared, "respect for my stomach compels me to make the attempt."

We went to the inn. The tavernkeeper was sitting on a stone at the side of the entrance, smoking his pipe. He was dressed in wooden clogs, a blue apron, and a sports cap, and looked most untidy. When we politely asked him for luncheon he looked us up and down and told us in slightly roundabout fashion to go to hell. He was having his rest now and was not going to cook any more food until that evening at seven o'clock. At this painful piece of information, Duffaux spread a look of misery across his face and began to describe how hungry he was. The innkeeper must have had a soft spot somewhere in his heart, because he finally agreed to prepare a meal for us. He even promised to have it ready in half an hour. Thereupon he whistled to a dirty little boy who was playing in the yard and told him to fish a few trout out of the narrow stream which ran past one corner of the inn. Then he disappeared into the kitchen.

We three investigators settled ourselves at a rough wooden table in the inn and ordered a bottle of the good Beaujolais. Before the half hour had passed, the tavernkeeper spread a white cloth on the table and served several small trout fried in butter and caught only a quarter of an hour before. Then followed broiled filet of pork and, after that, cheese and fruit.

After we had finished eating and while we were still sipping our coffee, our host sat down at our table. Looking to left and right to be sure no one could hear him, he whispered, "I suppose you are here for the Dubois affair." When we nodded, he continued, "Might be that the old woman was poisoned, but I could swear that her niece is not to blame. I have known this girl almost since she was born. She really loved her old aunt. It is impossible to imagine that she could have killed her aunt, even though all the scandalmongers around here are insisting that she has done it. There is some mystery about her journey to Paris, but after the talk around here I don't think there is any mystery about why she wants to liquidate her holdings and get out of this thrice accursed place."

The little man grew more and more excited as he talked. Now he was looking at us with imploring eyes.

"Don't hurt that girl. She is innocent!"

Duffaux returned his look and said, "If she's not guilty, we won't try to prove she is."

The woman who answered our knock at the door of the little house on the market square was not quite what I had expected. She looked older than I had supposed, her face was drawn and haggard, and I could see that she had been crying a good deal of late.

Duffaux told her we were from the Sûreté, and after she had admitted us to her living room, he said directly, "Mademoiselle, I have to tell you at once that enough arsenic has been found in the body of your aunt to account for her death."

Mademoiselle Dubois stared at him but said nothing.

"Have you any statement to make, Mademoiselle?"

The look of surprise on the woman's face seemed absolutely genuine to me. "It can't be true! It can't be true!" she exclaimed. "Why, my aunt had only friends—no enemies at all! Who would have killed her in such a horrible way?"

The gendarme stepped forward. "I am sorry, Mademoiselle, but I am afraid I shall have to place you under arrest. You will be charged with the poisoning of Madame Dubois."

Duffaux looked sadly at her. "Pack your suitcase with toilet articles and nightclothes, Mademoiselle," he said in a quiet voice. "Meanwhile we shall have to search this house."

While the gendarme went off to summon a taxi, we proceeded to ransack the house, keeping a sharp eye on the lady as we did so. After a time the gendarme returned and the taxi also arrived. Off he went to take his prisoner to the county jail. We continued our work with impersonal thoroughness, and it took a long time.

Knowing how to search a house is an important part of a detective's skill. The search must be made extremely methodically, and there must not be a single possibility of anything's remaining hidden at the end of the job. People are very ingenious about hiding things, and the cleverest way is, I think, to put whatever is to be hidden in a conspicuous place. We were, of course, looking for arsenic, prescriptions, medicine bottle, and the like, and we searched that little house from top to bottom. All in vain.

But we did find, not exactly hidden but at least partly concealed among the pages of an old religious book in Mademoiselle Dubois' bedroom, a photograph of a good-looking young man in his thirties. "From Armand to his beloved Suzanne," was written across one corner. I pocketed the picture, determined to find out who the man was.

After we had finished the search we had to wait for about three hours for the next train. We decided to have dinner at the inn. The reception accorded us was not very graceful.

"You arrested her anyway, you rascals!" exclaimed the innkeeper with tears in his eyes.

He refused to serve us, and it was only because of Duffaux's great gift of persuasion that he finally agreed to give us a bottle of wine and some sandwiches. As we were the only guests at the moment, I took the proprietor aside and showed him the young man's photograph, asking if he knew who the subject was.

"Why," he said in surprise, "that's Armand Forgeot, the nephew of our herbalist, old M. Forgeot who sells herbs to the village. Young Armand is a surveyor by profession. In the past he used to spend his vacations at our village, but he hasn't been here for the last year or two." Then he added curiously, "Where did you get that photograph?"

I told him that we had found it in Mademoiselle Dubois' room, and I pointed out that the first name of Mademoiselle was Suzanne.

He looked at the photograph as if he could not believe his eyes.

"This is hard to believe," he said. "Suzanne Dubois is at least five years older than the boy Forgeot, and no one has ever suspected anything between them."

So, then, there was something in the life of Suzanne which she had managed to hide from the watchful eyes of the villagers. We decided to investigate this matter further because a case of such a serious nature required the exposure of every detail of Suzanne's life. But there was nothing more to do at the moment here in St. Fontain. We took our leave of the fortified village and caught a return train to Lyons.

Next morning the photograph was given to the head of the Mobile Detective Unit of the region, M. Villefranche. He too saw the necessity of investigating Suzanne's life in the most painstaking way. Therefore an experienced detective of the unit, Claude Ferrail, was given the photograph and sent to the prison where Suzanne was in custody. I have the rest of the story from Ferrail.

"When I first showed her the photograph," Ferrail told me, "she became instantly upset. Finally she told me that she had not seen Armand Forgeot since he had last spent a vacation at St. Fontain, two years before. She denied ever having had intimate relations with him. Instead, according to her story, they had been good friends, and the photograph was nothing but a kind of affectionate joke between them."

She would not go beyond this statement, but Ferrail formed the definite impression that there was more to the matter. His next move was to get in touch with Armand Forgeot himself, so he too went to St. Fontain. The small shop of the herbalist turned out to be situated only a few doors from Suzanne's place. It was dark, stuffy, and full of the odors of the innumerable spices and herbs which the French use to flavor their food or to prepare medicinal teas. The herbalist was a thin, elderly man with a bald head, large tufted white eyebrows, and an extraordinary mustache. Its thin strands of hair protruded at least five inches on either side. When Ferrail explained his errand, M. Forgeot wanted to know what his nephew had to do with the matter. He seemed satisfied when Ferrail explained that his inquiry was just a routine matter, and he willingly told Ferrail that his nephew was employed in a surveyor's office in Algiers. Having secured this important information, Ferrail left the shop, but on the way out he noticed an incongruity. On the counter were spread the latest quotations from the Bourse (the Paris Stock Exchange). It seemed to him odd that the proprietor of such a small and musty shop should be interested in the stock market.

It was now lunch time, so Ferrail went to the village inn. We had told him about the wonderful quality of the food and the surly character of the innkeeper. The two men were soon deep in conversation, and the talk, steered by Ferrail, soon came round to the subject of the herbalist.

"In the last few months," the innkeeper said, "something has happened to him. He came here (I think from some Paris suburb) about thirty years ago and bought that small shop from the widow of the late owner. In all these years he has never made any friends except Madame Dubois, who used to spend part of every evening in his shop." The tavernkeeper chuckled. "There were rumors that she used to go there to drink liqueurs because she could not possibly come here to the inn, and her strait-laced piety prevented her from drinking at home where her niece was. Anyway, this chap, Forgeot, always had difficulty making ends meet, until recently. He has been getting plenty of mail, mostly from Paris. Now they say he is going to install a telephone. Well, I haven't got one. I think he is crazy. Imagine a telephone in that miserable little shop." And he spat disgustedly.

Ferrail listened attentively. When he returned to headquarters, he immediately telegraphed the Sûreté in Algiers, asking them to question the surveyor, Armand Forgeot, on his relations with Suzanne Dubois. The answer on the following day reported that Forgeot admitted having had intimate relations with Suzanne Dubois. "But she was not a virgin," he asserted, adding, "there may have been half a dozen other chaps who had the same experience as I."

Ferrail now had a fresh interview with Suzanne Dubois in her prison cell. This time he used the age-old police trick of putting her into a rage against her former lover by informing her of what Armand had told the police about her morals.

"What a beast!" she exclaimed. "He knows very well that he was the only man in my life."

She began to weep and confided her story to Ferrail.

"I was so lonely. The years passed by and nothing happened. Armand was kind and sweet; we used to meet in his room at the back of his uncle's shop after my aunt had gone to sleep in the evening. I used to walk out of our back door, step over a little fence which separated the two yards, and knock at his window. No one ever saw us except his uncle, who once happened to see me when I was stepping out of Armand's window early in the morning. A short while after that Armand left the village to return to his job, and I discovered I was pregnant. I wrote Armand several times, but he didn't answer. I was terrified. Finally I confessed to old M. Forgeot in the faint hope that he could persuade Armand to marry me. But the old man told me coolly that Armand was already betrothed and marriage to me was out of the question."

"What did you do then?" asked Ferrail.

She blushed, hesitated and finally cried, "I can't stand this any more! I have to get out of this awful jail! I will tell you the rest. Old M. Forgeot instructed me to get rid of the child, and gave me an address in Paris. I had a little money of my own, and I told my aunt that I would like to go to Paris for a sewing course. She opposed it strongly, but I went anyway. It was awful, and I became very sick and had to spend several weeks in one of the wards of the hospital before I could go home. My aunt was always suspicious about this journey, but I never told her the truth."

"What happened then?" Ferrail was almost whispering. With the instinct of the experienced detective he now thought he was on the right track.

Suzanne Dubois disappointed him. "Shortly afterward my aunt became ill. But, believe me," she said, "I had nothing to do with her death."

Seeing that he would probably get nothing more out of her at the moment, Ferrail asked what she had done with her money. He had to do a great deal of talking before she haltingly replied that she had given it to old M. Forgeot, who said he had some very good tips on how to invest it at a much higher rate of interest than she could obtain here.

Well, thought Ferrail, that explained the list from the stock exchange and the telephone. "Are those investments made in your name?" he asked.

"No, M. Forgeot is acting for me," she replied.

"You must believe he is honest; otherwise how could you put all your fortune into his hands?" was Ferrail's next question.

"Well, to tell the truth, I was forced to do it because he threatened to tell the story of my Paris experience here in the village. And that would have been the end of me."

Ferrail saw at once that here was a clear-cut extortion case but one that it would be exceedingly difficult to prove. And the mystery of the murder remained.

"Have you yourself any idea how your aunt was killed?" Ferrail now asked.

She shook her head. "I knew that my aunt was apt to drink, and it was no secret to me that she went almost every evening after supper to Forgeot's shop. He used to sell her liqueur which she drank in the small room at the back of the shop. After such a visit she would walk the few steps home and then go immediately to bed. Often in the morning she had headaches. When she became ill, I thought it was on account of the drinking. It might happen so when a person has drunk too much, mightn't it?" Mademoiselle asked innocently.

A light began to dawn on Ferrail. Here was another suspect, a man who had profited by the death of Madame Dubois and, furthermore, a man likely to be in the possession of arsenic. He got a staff car at once, took a couple of his colleagues with him, and returned to the village. Old M. Forgeot was already in bed and sleeping when they arrived. He lighted a candle, put on his slippers and came to open the door.

"An incredible sight," Ferrail told me. "The fellow looked as if he were cut out of a drawing of a hundred years ago, with his nightcap, his long striped nightshirt, his long mustache, and the old candlestick in his hand. 'Sorry to disturb you at this time of night,' I said politely, 'but we have to ask you some more questions about this Dubois business.'

" 'With pleasure, sir,' the old chap answered, 'but allow me to put on some clothes.'

"After having lighted another candle, which he put on the counter, he disappeared in the interior of the house. I didn't like the idea of leaving him alone," Ferrail admitted, "but at the moment I had only an unsupported suspicion that he might know something about the poisoning. As for the extortion, that would be damned difficult to prove legally. And so the three of us waited for him up front in the shop. Finally, when more than a quarter of an hour had passed, I took my flashlight and went to his bedroom. There he was, lying outstretched on the bed with his nightcap still on, his eyes open and protruding, and his tongue sticking out of his mouth. The old man had managed to hang himself by his suspenders, which he had fastened to one of the bedposts." He added with professional interest, "That was the first time I ever saw a person hang himself in a horizontal position."

When the detectives searched the house, they made a discovery. Decades ago, before M. Forgeot's time, when the village had been more prosperous, the shop had been a pharmacy. As the years passed it had degenerated into a mere herb shop, but there were a

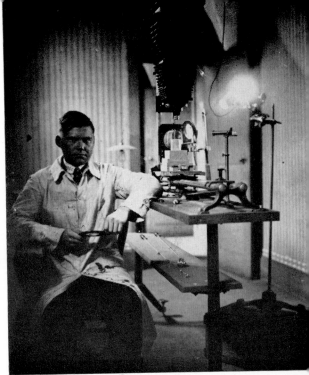

RIGHT The author in the Police Laboratory at Lyons.

ABOVE The elusive Georges Rème, wearing the uniform in which he was impersonating a naval officer.

The explanation of one of our most puzzling cases.

ABOVE Sir Basil Thomson and two of the Siamese police officials in Lyons.

BELOW The Glozel artifacts which Dr. Morlet sent over to me in New York in 1954. They display the runic markings and running reindeer which seemed to me so impressive.

few relics of its former estate. One of them was a whole jar of arsenic, which Ferrail and his companions found cached away in a cupboard.

No one will ever know for certain how Madame Dubois died. Suzanne continued to deny any knowledge of the subject and was in a short while released from the prison. Armand Forgeot was questioned closely by the police in Algiers, but his innocence could not be doubted because he had been far away when Madame Dubois died. Old M. Forgeot was now dead, and there was no evidence to contradict the assumption that he had poisoned Madame Dubois so that her money would fall into the hands of her niece, whom he could blackmail at his leisure.

Personally, I am convinced of this solution, particularly in the incriminating light of the old man's suicide.

There is not much more to add to this story. After many legal difficulties, Suzanne Dubois managed to recover a part of her money from the estate of old Forgeot. I don't think anybody in St. Fontain blamed her when she carried out her plan to sell everything and move away.

15

A PRINCE AND PRINTS

It often seems to me that each step in a career is as complex as the most puzzling of crimes. Certainly there was nothing simple about the fashion in which I came to earn the largest fee of my young life, an amount greater than my entire earnings up to that moment, including Maître Robert's 200 francs. At one stride I passed from the counting of centimes to the banking of francs, and I must confess it was a pleasant transition. I owed it to the generosity and support of my great teacher, Edmond Locard, but the manner of its coming about was so strange that no fiction writer would dare to foist such material upon his readers.

One morning during my third year at Lyons I found Locard closeted with a stranger, a man of about sixty-five, medium in height, with a mustache which stamped him as a Briton. He was dressed with Savile Row elegance, and everything about him suggested affluence and authority.

"Harry," Locard said, "this is my old friend Sir Basil Thomson."

Everybody in the world of criminology knew the great Sir Basil. He had had a long and distinguished career, first as a member of the Executive Council that governed the Fiji Islands and later as a penologist. He had been appointed Secretary to the Prisons Committee of Great Britain and then Governor of Dartmoor Prison. This had led to his appointment as Assistant Commissioner of

the Metropolitan Police of London, a post which he held until
1921. But his most dramatic service was during World War I,
when he was Chief of the Central Intelligence Division of Scotland Yard, a key position in the internal security structure of his
country. After his retirement as Assistant Commissioner in 1921 he
had settled in Paris, and I wondered what business had brought
him to Lyons.

Neither Sir Basil nor Locard came immediately to the point.
We chatted for a while in what appeared to me a rather aimless
fashion, Sir Basil asking me a number of questions about my
travels in the East, about which Locard must have informed him.
Gradually it developed that Sir Basil had a special interest in the
Kingdom of Siam. This had begun when Chulalonkong, Siam's
most progressive monarch in a century, sent his two oldest sons to
be educated in England. When they arrived, they stayed for a
time at the Bishopthorpe Palace of the Archbishop of York, who
was Sir Basil's father. So it came about that Sir Basil spent some
of his youth in the company of the two Siamese boys, who in due
course became successively the rulers of Siam.

This had resulted in Sir Basil's appointment as the secret and
unofficial representative of the Royal Siamese Government in
Europe. He was now, it finally appeared, under assignment to arrange for the training of a Siamese prince and certain Siamese
police officers in modern methods of investigation. For various
reasons, some of them personal, he had come to consult his old
friend Locard.

"I have recommended you, Harry, to supervise the instruction,"
Locard said with a smile. "You are our expert on Far Eastern
peoples."

This was flattering, and I was naturally delighted, but when Sir
Basil mentioned the fee involved, I was even more pleased. My
days of bread and water were definitely at an end. I promised to
do my best, and the interview ended in the utmost cordiality.

As I left Locard's office I began to reflect upon the coincidence
of my new assignment. Except for my *Wanderjahr* in the Far

East, which had certainly not involved any members of the Siamese royal family, I was ignorant of the country and its rulers. But out of the memories of my childhood there began to emerge the realization that I was the second Söderman in a row to deal with that country in terms of its royalty. In fact, Sir Basil Thomson and I each had a connection with that enlightened monarch, Emperor Chulalonkong. His connection was direct, mine through my father, who had sometimes told the tale to his family. On my desk there is to this day one piece of evidence: a photograph of my father in official uniform as Swedish Crown Sheriff. My mother and every friend of his I have ever met confirm the statement that Pehr Söderman could not abide the wearing of formal uniforms, and though he had never worn his dress regalia before and never wore it afterward, he was on one occasion compelled to put it on in honor of Emperor Chulalonkong.

During the 1890's, well before I was born, the Siamese monarch decided to tour Europe in the company of all his wives. To this end the royal yacht was fitted out and provisioned. After many weeks of voyaging and visiting in several countries, he decided to continue his trip clear up into the Baltic. In due course, he arrived at the port of Sundsvall, a town on the Gulf of Bothnia, north of Stockholm. Here he determined to take a look at the interior of northern Sweden and, leaving his wives on the yacht, boarded a private railroad car supplied him by the Swedish government.

The trip took him into my father's county of east Jämtland, where Stockholm authorities ordered he be tendered a state dinner. They telegraphed my father to this effect, leaving it up to him where the function was to be held. After much deliberation, my father selected a resort hotel in the small village of Bispgarden. He so advised the central authorities in Stockholm and plunged into supervising the feverish preparations. In that pre-aviation era there was no time to transport a sufficiently distinguished *chef de cuisine* from Stockholm to Bispgarden. The next best thing was to have the Royal Chef in the capital telegraph instructions for the menu and the preparation of the various dishes. This was arranged.

At the outset, all went well. The slight, elegant, almond-eyed monarch expressed his satisfaction with the reception which preceded the formal dinner. Then, at the side of my father in his full-dress uniform complete with sword, the king entered the banquet hall. There army officers, officials, and leading families of the county were gathered. It was not a vast assembly—only about thirty in all—partly because the district was thinly settled and partly because that was all the room could accommodate. My father conducted the king first to the side table, on which was spread a truly lavish Swedish smörgasbord—fifty varieties of smoked fish, caviar, meats, salads, and appurtenances. Chulalonkong was as entranced by this opulence as any lesser man might have been. The procession came to a protracted halt while he sampled most of the dishes and washed them down with three varieties of Swedish aquavit.

After that they proceeded to the main table for the meal itself.

"The king looked very happy," my father used to say in fond recollection. "I thought his face looked even rounder than before."

Then came a reindeer consommé, with the appropriate sherry. Everything was going along nicely, dignified as a royal banquet should be, but still easy and comfortable. Next came the salmon-trout native to the region, accompanied by the correct Rhine wine, well cooled and fragrant. The king quaffed it with every sign of satisfaction.

The main course was also a regional specialty, reindeer steak, cooked to perfection and accompanied by a noble Burgundy. The king lifted his glass, held it against the light for a moment to admire its deep and glowing color, and took a preliminary swallow. A second later, with true Oriental forthrightness, he spat it out.

There was a moment of consternation. My father held his breath, not knowing quite what to do.

"Always wait a second, my son," he used to say whenever he used this anecdote to illustrate the virtue of patience. "Always wait a second. Things can go any way at all after the first impact."

Without a word, the king replaced his glass on the table, picked up his knife and fork, and began eating the reindeer steak with gusto. The rest of the dinner passed off uneventfully, and Chula-longkong was so pleased that he offered to reward my father either with the highest decoration of the Siamese state—the Order of the Elephant—or a large diamond stickpin. My father, a man of great clarity of mind, chose the stickpin.

Only after the Very Important Personage was safely back on his yacht did my father reflect on the incident of the wine. He found the explanation on rereading one of the telegrams of instruction to the local cook from the Royal Chef: WINES BE SURE TO SERVE ALL TABLE WINES THOROUGHLY CHILLED EXCEPT THE VINTAGES AT ROOM TEMPERATURE. The local man had mistaken the Burgundy for something else and had chilled it practically into vinegar. Father always refused to say whether the champagne had been served warm. Whenever I asked him about this detail he brushed me off by saying, "You know I never drink that effeminate stuff."

During the two weeks while I was awaiting the arrival of my charges, I made what preparations I could to pave the way for their indoctrination in police science. I drew up a schedule of morning work that commenced with a two-hour lecture on the general theories of criminology and its techniques. This was to be followed by some practical, firsthand experience at the scenes of crimes. That would take care of the morning. Fortunately, as it turned out, my plans for the afternoons were less definite.

It did not surprise me that the new Siamese department of criminal investigation was to be headed by a prince. In that country the royal family is usually large because of the monarch's numerous wives and relatives. There was always a glut of princes in the country, and most of the important offices in the land were reserved for them. In this case, Prince Vongsa Nirajara was an uncle of the reigning monarch. I was instructed to address him not as "Your Royal Highness" but as "Your Serene Highness"—this delicate distinction having something to do with clarifying the complex family relationships.

Except for some doubts about my own competence to cover the ground in as short a time as the two scheduled months of the Prince's visit, I looked forward with pleasure to the assignment. When I had been in that part of the world, I had ridden on horseback through the jungle from Burma to northern Siam. Those carefree weeks among the charming and innocent natives and their lovely girls were among my pleasantest memories. I had not had any traffic with royalty, but I felt certain the Prince would be a delightful companion.

Indeed he was. Slightly to my surprise he turned out to be forty years old, a magnificent figure of a man whose bearing puzzled me at first until I discovered that before World War I he had been educated in the famous Prussian cadet school. This experience had given him a military carriage and a somewhat Prussian manner which contrasted amusingly with the gaiety and lightheartedness of his Siamese breeding. His three subordinates also proved to be agreeable.

The Siamese are not a niggardly people, and his government had given Vongsa Nirajara the tidy sum of two hundred dollars a day for expense money. This allowance made it possible for His Serene Highness to gratify one of his most serious hobbies, eating. He was a real gastronome, and it was part of my duty to select a restaurant and order lunch for him each day. Soon I became accustomed to what the French call the *haute cuisine*. Lyons was full of good—and expensive—restaurants and had a reputation throughout France for the quality of its cookery. The opportunity was not one to be missed, and I rapidly became familiar with eating places which a young student would never ordinarily have entered. A typical lunch for the five of us would consist of *apéritifs* followed by a generous variety of *hors d'oeuvres*, a serving of forcemeat balls—*quenelles*—which were one of the specialties of Lyons, followed by broiled chicken, and topped off by a super soufflé of Chinese ginger. This would all be washed down by the appropriate red and white wines of the best vintages. After the meal we would have our black coffee and several brandies.

A lunch of this sort put an end to the serious work of the day. I have never quite understood why the French like to have their heaviest meal in the middle of the day, but my Siamese friends took to the idea with enthusiasm. I learned not to schedule for the afternoon hours anything which required close attention or delicate work. Still, something had to be done with the time, and the idea occurred to me that a visit to the morgue might be instructive.

To this end I got in touch with my friend M. Rollet, the amiable Keeper of the Morgue, and asked him to notify me when he had a corpse to identify. This happened frequently because Lyons is situated at the confluence of the Saône and Rhone rivers, and frequently bodies floated down on one or the other of the streams. Partly for this reason, when I first came to Lyons, the morgue was a barge moored to the bank of the Saône. It was a dirty and noisome craft, but it was M. Rollet's kingdom and he was proud of it. He had grown so accustomed to his work that he handled his corpses as casually as a bricklayer his brick or a porter his baggage. Before the visit of my Siamese friends, however, the city had built a modern morgue, complete with refrigeration, as an adjunct to the medical school of the university. Above the morgue was a tidy apartment where M. Rollet lived happily with his wife and children. His detractors used to say that the entrance to his flat was through the storage room, but this was a canard. Not that it would have bothered the good man in the slightest if it had been true.

In the beginning I felt as most people do about morgues—that there is a grisly horror about them—and it took me many visits in the course of my work to see beyond the surface unpleasantness. Gradually I came to understand that a morgue is in good measure an institution which fills both a moral and a practical purpose. At the very core of our Western sense of the sanctity of the individual is the notion that each life, and hence each death as well, is important to all of society. In Siam, bodies might float down the Menam Chao Phaya clear to the sea—or the crocodiles—without anyone's bothering about them, but in the West we hold to the idea of Christian burial and we know that every death matters to some living person.

On the practical side, establishing the identity of a body simplifies all kinds of bookkeeping. Sometimes an estate may be affected; sometimes a police file can be closed, a search for a missing person discontinued, or a criminal case terminated. If there is any suspicion of foul play, the identity of the victim is the first step in clearing up the crime and tracking down the murderer. All kinds of records are kept, and they are a necessary part of any society as intricate as our Western one.

I decided, however, to base our visit to the morgue on the practical point of identification and, when M. Rollet let me know that an unknown corpse had been picked out of the river, I made an appointment for the afternoon. There had been nothing on the body to establish who the man was, and my Siamese charges would be able to observe just how the police went about the problem of identifying him. After one of our prodigious lunches, we got into a taxi (another evidence of the princely way in which we lived during those two months) and headed for the medical school and the morgue.

"You must be prepared," I told the Prince on the way, "for a certain amount of unpleasantness. In hot summer weather like this a body can be a disgusting sight. Since there is no indication of who the man was, we shall have to fingerprint him as well as make the routine physical description. This fingerprinting can be a messy business if the body has been in the water too long. Sometimes we have to do a crude piece of taxidermy and bring the skin of the fingers back to the laboratory."

I looked sharply at my companions, but they did not quail. The Prince's face wore its habitual Prussian passivity, but the others seemed positively to be anticipating the experience.

"What is the procedure at the laboratory in such cases?" the Prince inquired.

"First," I told him, "we try inking the skin and rolling it against a piece of paper. If that does not work because the papillary ridges have already disappeared, we turn the skin over and photograph it. Generally the pattern is still visible on the under side."

"Very interesting," the Prince observed. "And then?"

"Then we check against our police files. A body can be identified in that way if in life the person was a vagrant, a prostitute, or a criminal, for then his prints are on file. I shouldn't wonder if that would prove to be the case today."

When we got to the morgue M. Rollet welcomed us cordially. He was obviously pleased to be receiving royalty. He led us into the workroom, opened one of the numerous cabinet shutter drawers of the refrigeration unit, and rolled out a zinc stretcher. The Siamese managed to maintain their Oriental impassivity, but I must confess that I was more than a little startled.

The corpse was one of the most spectacular I have ever seen. It was that of an elderly man with a big gray beard. The gray of his beard was the only original color left to the poor fellow; the rest of him would have strained the resources of a modern painter's palette. Almost every conceivable shading of color was represented. The grotesque effect was rendered even more striking by the fact that one eye was opened and seemed to be looking at us.

"There he is!" M. Rollet exclaimed with childlike pride.

The first step was to photograph the body. To my chagrin I discovered that I had left my flash gun back at the Laboratory, so we could not follow the usual procedure, which was to take the necessary two pictures—full face and profile—directly on the stretcher. Cursing myself, I put on one of M. Rollet's smocks and a pair of rubber gloves. M. Rollet never bothered with gloves, the use of which he considered an example of snobbery. Together we carried the body out into the sunny courtyard and seated it in a chair. The four Siamese trooped after us, their faces expressionless.

I put up the heavy, old-fashioned camera tripod and took the required pictures as quickly as possible. It was hot and airless in that small yard, and I have never been able to accustom myself to the stench of putrefaction. After completing the physical description as best I could, I proceeded to the worst part of the job, which was the removal of the skin on the man's fingers. It was impossible to take prints directly; he had been in the water too long. My Oriental friends watched intently, without turning a hair.

At this inappropriate moment M. Rollet was smitten with an idea. It seemed to him that he ought to signalize the presence of royalty in his establishment in some manner or other. He pattered off inside the building and emerged a few seconds later with a bottle of red wine in one unsanitary hand and a couple of murky glasses in the other. Drawing himself up to full height, and in carefully selected words, he made a short, official speech of welcome to the Prince and his companions. Then he filled a glass with wine, handed it to the Prince, filled the other, and thrust it at me.

A flicker of the Prince's eyes informed me that he understood the quandary. On the one hand, it seemed physically impossible to down the wine under the circumstances. On the other, if we failed to do so, we should deeply injure the feelings of our host. Very slowly we raised our glasses, looked at each other with death in our eyes, and took a gulp. Nothing saved us but the fact that M. Rollet turned at once to fetch glasses for the other three Siamese. The Prince and I retreated just in time to get rid of that first gulp and most of our lunch behind a bush.

The three Siamese police officers were beginning to lose their color. They said nothing but stared at the Prince and me in distraction. When M. Rollet returned, one of them—he is now most deservedly the head of the Thailand Central Intelligence Department—turned to me and asked me to explain to M. Rollet that he felt most deeply honored, but that he and his companions were strict Buddhists and hence were not allowed to touch wine. This was pure fabrication, since Buddhists are just as eligible to drink wine as Christians, but it saved the situation. M. Rollet knew that Mohammedans are not allowed to drink, and he innocently assumed that the same thing was true of Buddhists. We put the body back in its refrigerator compartment, and with many protestations of good will on all sides escaped into the street.

"You and I," the Prince said to me, "should have been born Moslems."

My prediction on the way to the Morgue turned out to be true, as we learned when we examined the corpse's fingerprints at the laboratory. The dead man had been a pitiful old vagrant who many years before had got involved in some minor felony and been fingerprinted. He had apparently drowned himself in the river, whether accidentally or intentionally we never discovered.

To be able to make an identification with such relative ease is a recent development in the history of criminology. In the first attempts in this direction, the object was to make anyone convicted of a crime forever afterward recognizable as a criminal. In ancient Egypt, I understand, thieves were punished by having a few front teeth knocked out. Those who had the means tried to conceal the shameful gap by having their mouths fitted with bits of bone or ivory. (This may have been the remote origin of modern dentistry.)

In Medieval Europe, a man with his ears or nose cut off was not an uncommon sight. The mutilation signified that he was a thief who had paid lightly instead of with the usual death penalty. Of course in the event of a second offense death was automatic. Another often-used device of identification was the branding iron, which was used freely on the Continent up to the time of the French Revolution. Every Dumas reader will remember that Milady de Winter of *The Three Musketeers* bore on one of her lovely shoulders the fleur-de-lis brand of the Bourbons.

Branding was abolished during the Revolution but reinstated in Napoleon's time. Criminals not sentenced to the gallows were marked TF for *travaux forcés*, hard labor. Sometimes a V was used to identify a *voleur*, or thief, and after a second conviction, another V would be added. Even as late as the 1860's the lifers who were sent to work in the salt mines of Siberia were branded on the face in big letters, one on the forehead and one on each cheek. Penal codes made drastic punishment mandatory for second offenses, but without something approaching mutilation the difficulty of establishing that a felon was a second offender would often have been overwhelming. Of course, people with some outstanding physical characteristic, such as a harelip or a clubfoot were somewhat easier to identify with assurance. But until the last hundred years no means of identifying people as *individuals* was known.

In the absence of any reliable proof that a person was what he was accused of being, many a criminal caught in a large city like London or Paris could plead "Not Guilty" or "First Offense." The police countered this problem by putting all the suspects through an identification parade that was a forerunner of the present line-up. They would be scrutinized by seasoned policemen and prison guards reputed to have good memories. One old prison guard in England in the first half of the last century boasted he had made a thousand such sight identifications, with only five mistakes. This remarkable record must have been cold comfort to the victims of those five mistakes, however.

The first great step toward accurate personal identification came about the middle of the nineteenth century with the development of photography. The advantages of the process were quickly apparent to the police, but in those early days the operation was tedious. The photographing could be done only when there was bright sunshine, usually on the roof of a building, and the plates had to be exposed slowly. It often took twenty minutes for a single exposure, and to make sure that the image was sharp, the subject was fastened into a solid chair for that length of time. Anyone subjected to this treatment must have been willing to admit that crime does not pay.

As photography became more rapid and less expensive, its police use was increased. Gustave Macé, chief of the Paris Detective Division, was the first to photograph every criminal. Partly because of his belief in this new method, Macé strongly opposed the theories of the great Alphonse Bertillon, who was then only a young clerk in the Paris Police Department. But Macé failed to reckon with the enormous size of the files, and his photographs became prog-

ressively less useful as their number increased. There was no method
of classifying his pictures except by the name of the criminal, and
since every scoundrel changes his name as often as he likes, the
bulging files became useless.

Then Alphonse Bertillon ushered in a new era of identification.
Though a doctor's son, he had no higher education and had to
begin work as a humble clerk in the Paris Police Department. He
was energetic, fanatical, gruff, narrow-minded, and burdened with
what would today be called an inferiority complex, but in many
ways he was gifted. He invented anthropometry, a method of measuring different and unalterable parts of the human body and classifying them. By dogged persistence he succeeded in getting his
method accepted, first in Paris in 1882 and thereafter in the whole
civilized world. Yet in the public mind today his name is connected with the invention of fingerprinting. Bertillon bitterly resented fingerprinting and fought it all his life because fingerprinting threatened to overshadow his own system.

Although to this day the anthropometric system which Bertillon
developed is still in official use by the Sûreté and the Bureau
d'Identité Judiciaère, it appears possible that a new development
may supplant the *portrait parlé*. A Sûreté commissioner named
Chabot has twice used with sensational results the system of
asking witnesses to a crime to look through thousands of photographs of criminals and pick out those which most nearly resemble
the wrongdoer. After a selection of these photographs has been
made in terms of various features such as the eyes, the forehead,
the nose, the mouth, the chin, a composite photograph is prepared.

This composite face is then subjected to the same checking and
recomposing. In the two instances in which the system has been
employed a face emerged which has been nearly identical with the
actual visage of the criminal. In the most recent of these cases a
British schoolteacher named Janet Marshall was murdered in the
summer of 1955 while she was on a bicycle trip through Picardy.
There were of course a good many suspects. Chabot put witnesses
to the crime through the photographic routine described above.

Little by little a portrait emerged and when he was satisfied that it was as close as possible to the visage of the murderer, Chabot asked a number of French newspapers to publish the picture with a story about it.

Identification followed almost immediately. The Director of a prison at Meaux spotted the face as that of a former convict named Avril. Avril was apprehended and confessed.

The difficulties of this method are of course obvious, and it is not applicable in various kinds of cases. But the actual photograph of Avril was nearly identical with the composite face developed by Chabot's system, and it appears that a valuable weapon has been added to the arsenal of criminal identification.

Credit for the first practical use of fingerprinting as a means of identification must be given to an Englishman, William J. Herschel, later knighted, an administrator in the province of Bengal, India, almost a hundred years ago. One of Herschel's duties was to pay pensions to old, retired native soldiers. He found that his pensioners had a span of life able to ruin any insurance company. On pay days he contemplated the phalanx of white-beared men dressed in the uniforms of bygone days and, as they collected the precious small pensions, Herschel felt more and more uneasy.

He soon perceived the trick. When an old soldier died, another old man from the same village would put on the uniform, go down to the town, and collect the dead man's pension, blessing the Great Queen the while. Herschel put a plan into effect by which every pensioner placed his thumbmark beside his name in the register, and every time a stipend was paid, the recipient had to make another thumbmark on a slip of paper, which Herschel then compared with the original. The average life span of the pensioners dwindled considerably after the introduction of this method.

At about the same time Dr. Henry Faulds, a Scot who was a medical missionary and amateur archeologist in Japan, came upon another use for fingerprints. He suspected his servant of having stolen liquor from a bottle. The servant denied ever having touched the bottle, but Faulds proceeded to make the first identification in history of a fingerprint at the scene of a crime. His archeological studies had caused him to observe numerous markings of thumbs and fingers in prehistoric pottery. These markings had been made before the clay was baked; they showed all the details of the ridge pattern. He now carefully examined the incriminating bottle and on it found a faint thumbmark which he discovered was identical with that of his servant.

Asia, where both William Herschel and Dr. Faulds worked, is the classic continent for fingerprints. Since time immemorial the poor and illiterate native workman has put his inked thumbmark on receipts and other documents requiring a signature. In China fingerprints were used for fortune-telling, and for this purpose the Chinese divided the patterns into loops and whorls in about the same way Western classifiers do today. Certain combinations of patterns were supposed to point to certain fates, and it is said that Chinese mothers anxiously examined the fingers of a newborn child to ascertain what life had in store for it. Some say that three whorls and two loops on the left hand destined the infant to a life as a pawnbroker.

The introduction of fingerprinting was a deadly thrust against anthropometry. Fingerprinting was simple and infallible and, in spite of Bertillon's opposition, it won out. The technique was first put to general use in London and from there it penetrated to every country in the world. It has three main advantages: the uniqueness of every fingerprint, the unchangeability of a fingerprint during a lifetime, and the facility with which fingerprint patterns can be classified.

Of course the uniqueness of an individual fingerprint is not without parallels in nature, who seems never to duplicate herself. Two absolutely identical leaves from the same kind of tree cannot be found. Snowflakes are of endless variations.

At first the admission of fingerprinting as evidence was assailed by defense attorneys, who maintained that somewhere else in the world there might be a person with the same set of fingerprints, but that claim is never advanced today. Millions of people have been fingerprinted. In the FBI collection in Washington alone (by far the largest in the world), there are the fingerprints of about 72,000,000 persons. No two have ever been found to be alike. A mathematical calculation as to the chance of finding two similar fingerprints shows there is one chance in 17,179,869,184.

The population of the globe stands today at an estimated 2,500,-000,000. This means there are about 25,000,000,000 fingerprint patterns from all living fingers, and this figure is less than fifty percent larger than the computed possible variations under fingerprint classification. Still, such statistics suggest a minute chance that a parallelism might be found, some time, somewhere. On the other hand, this computation is based on only seventeen main points of classification, whereas in an ordinary well-rolled fingerprint there are over one hundred such points. Moreover, in any fingerprint case the investigator is not dealing with the entire population of the globe. It is rare that he has to reckon even with the whole citizenry of a single country. Very often only the inhabitants of a single district have to be considered. So great are the odds against duplication that in the identification of chance impressions it can be assumed that similarity of pattern and agreement of twelve main points constitute incontrovertible evidence.

Now and again a news story mentions that fingerprints are inherited. In one sense there is truth in such a claim. Certain patterns are inherited, but only patterns. Scores of details are wholly different even when the patterns are similar. The closest approach is in the case of identical twins where both have the same number of papillary ridges. Similarities of pattern due to inheritance are not considered close enough even to establish paternity, for instance.

Regarding the second advantage, unchangeability of fingerprints, even before birth the patterns of the papillary ridges and pores are formed in the womb, and the fingerprints (incidentally the toe-prints and palm and footprints as well) of the newest-born infants are those which they will carry all through life. At many modern hospitals footprints are made shortly after the birth of a child to prevent accidental change of babies in the nursery ward. The patterns do not change; a hundred years later they are the same as they were the day of birth. Even half-dissolved bodies, as my Siamese friends saw demonstrated, retain the pattern as long as there is any finger skin left for examination. Because of this, many identifications of unrecognizable bodies have been made.

Sometimes criminals try to get rid of their fingerprints. I have watched some of them, in their cells the night before the fingerprinting is to be done, methodically and painfully rubbing the tips of their fingers against the brick or stone surface of the cell wall, hoping that by morning the tips would be smooth and without the telltale papillary ridges. The police do not worry much about this device of desperation. If there is any difficulty with the identification, the suspect can be put in a straitjacket for a few days until the ridges grow out again.

Certain well-endowed criminals, generally American, occasionally try a more extreme expedient. They have a surgeon remove the skin from the tips of their fingers and replace it with skin grafted from elsewhere on their bodies. This does of course destroy the papillary pattern, but only at a great price. The sensitive feeling of the fingertips is lost forever. If the man is a burglar, pickpocket, or practitioner in any area of crime where touch is important, he is handicapped from that time onward. Even worse, the police never release such a person until they completely establish his identity, and if the suspect is guilty, his attempt to hide his identity boomerangs.

As soon as the infallibility of fingerprint evidence was accepted, the criminal mind turned to forgery. There is an apocryphal story of a clever Paris burglar who always left the thumbmark of the Chief of Police at the scene of a robbery. Technically, this is quite possible. In the early twenties criminals in the United States and scientists in Rumania demonstrated independently that it is possible to make a rubber fingertip with a fingerprint on it. However, it is impossible to produce such a stamp with pores in the ridges, and therefore no experienced fingerprint expert would be deceived by such a gadget.

The individuality of fingerprints, added to the fact that they cannot be changed, could not have produced such a revolution in police science except for the third aspect: they can be classified. They are biological phenomena, each separate print falling into a broad pattern. Besides, every print conforms to one of five basic patterns: arches, tented arches, radial loops, ulnar loops, and whorls. These principal patterns are in turn divided on the basis of two main distinctions, the ridge count and the ridge tracing. A fingerprint expert, having in his possession no more than a set of prints, can classify it against a coded file and draw from a library of millions of prints the identification of the exact individual under investigation.

Every fingerprint expert in the world seems to have dreams of building up an improved classification system, but the two systems in use are the English one, called the Galton-Henry system, and the Argentinian, called the Vucetich system. Both work well, and proposed new methods always prove to be mere variants on one or the other. Considering their reliability and universal applicability, it scarcely seems necessary to change this one of the few totally reliable police tools.

There is a popular impression that the classification of fingerprints is a profession both highly skilled and esoteric. This is an exaggeration. It is no more than a good and honest craft. It requires not special skill, but plenty of precision and patience. Skill enters in when it is necessary to identify partial and chance impressions left at the scene of a crime, for then experience and a trained eye are necessary. Where the layman might see only a blur, the expert often detects dozens of valuable details.

From my friends in the laboratory at Lyons I gathered that there had been a brief period, after the introduction of classified fingerprinting, when the police had an easy task at the scene of a crime. Prints that were left were easy to develop and invariably useful; felons were caught and convicted with ease. But the word spread, and today any schoolboy can discourse on the danger of such evidence. The experienced modern criminal rarely leaves any prints at all. Either he works with meticulous care to prevent prints, or else he wears gloves. This latter precaution is not always successful. There are a number of cases on record in which criminals have been identified by the prints of dirty gloves.

It is harder to avoid leaving fingerprint evidence at the scene of a crime than many felons suppose. One day in Lyons we investigated a burglary which showed how easy it is to make a slip. The inhabitants of a villa were away for the night and a burglar grasped the opportunity to make a haul. He gained entry by picking the lock to one of the doors and filled a sack with valuable loot. But when he was ready to leave, he found that the lock had jammed. He had to depart by way of a window.

When we examined the scene we were able to reconstruct what had happened. The fellow had worn no gloves; but he had left no prints around the house, so far as we could at first discover. The window by which he had made his exit had been lifted from its hinges, and there were no prints on that either, since he had taken the precaution of spraying the treacherous pane with nature's most available liquid, which made any hope of fingerprints out of the question. However, either in the course of this operation or in lifting the window out of its frame, he had felt the need of candle-light and had used a stub which he had probably brought with him. The candle had melted; some wax had dripped down onto his thumb, and eventually to the floor. On one of the blobs there was a perfect thumbprint. It was the only evidence the burglar left at the scene, but it proved quite enough to identify and convict him.

Even with the precise fingerprint technique there are always borderline cases, and these can produce a troubled police conscience. When the identifying details of the prints are common as to pattern and blurred as to detail, and when the crime is a capital crime, any decision is the occasion for soul-searching. One such case stands out in my memory, largely because the detectives and experts under whom I was studying were bitterly divided. It concerned a twenty-year-old Italian mason named Antonio Fratelli, with whom the police had had no previous contact.

Anatole France once observed that "the law, in its majestic equality, forbids the rich as well as the poor to sleep under bridges." Perhaps so, but in the case of the poor it is not a strictly enforced law, and the victim in this case not only slept under a bridge, in filth and dirt, but operated from there as a prostitute. She made only a miserable living because she was over seventy and could entice only drunken ruffians without the price of a flophouse bed. One morning another beldame of the same profession, who shared the shelter of the bridge, found her dead of strangulation. There was also evidence of assult with an empty wine bottle. This bottle proved to be the only clue, and on it we could find only two faint, blurred fingerprints. We had no idea who the criminal was nor where to look for him.

We started our investigation with the feeling that the cards were stacked against us. Apprehending the murderer of a prostitute is almost always difficult for the police; in every large city the list of such unsolved crimes is long. The livelihood of the prostitute is by its nature a clandestine matter. Seldom does anyone actually witness such a murder, and the guilty one generally doesn't leave a visiting card. Even if he does leave fingerprints, the chances are that he is not criminally known to the police and his prints are not on file. The murder might have been the result of a sudden flare-up of sex antagonism on the part of a man who otherwise has no criminal tendencies at all.

In this case we did the only thing we could do; that was to study the blurred prints on the wine bottle. After we had tentatively classified them we began to compare them with the prints of all recently arrested felons. Of course, every detective on the force was alerted. It happened that the day after the murder an Italian brick-layer, who gave his name as Antonio Fratelli, was one of a group of men arrested in a street brawl. This was only a minor offense, but it required fingerprinting all the same. The detective who was doing the job thought that Fratelli had something under his nails that looked like blood. Immediately he compared the prints he had just taken with those from the bottle found at the scene of the murder. At first glance no identity between the two was evident, but there was enough similarity to justify a thorough examination. Fratelli had his nails thoroughly cleaned by the police; the scrapings were examined microscopically and found to contain some blood and minute pieces of skin. When he was interrogated about the murder, Fratelli denied having had anything to do with it. He was put back into jail and closely watched.

Meantime, a schism was developing among the detectives working in the police laboratory. The fingerprints on the bottle, which had been brought out with a white powder, were re-examined under the magnifying glass. They were certainly blurred. From their position on the bottle it might be assumed that one print came from the thumb of the right hand, and the other from the right index finger. On the print of the thumb an expert could distinguish seven identifying points. On the index fingerprint there were five. The patterns matched Fratelli's. Now, in France it was an unwritten law of evidence that not only must the patterns match, but that at least twelve points of identification must be established. Here there were a scant twelve—and from blurred prints at that. If even one of those points should remain unclear to a judge or a jury in the course of a trial, the police case would fail. This was an important matter because several of the detectives were also fingerprint experts. They were individualists to a man, and no one of them was willing to retreat from his position, pro or con. The dispute over those blurred, faint prints became an obsession in the laboratory.

Old Chevassus was impatient with the doubters.

"Damn it all," he said angrily, "if this were an ordinary burglary, every one of you would swear to the identity and the man would be off to a couple of years in prison. But now, when it's a question of cutting off the fellow's head, you hesitate. Be serious, my chil-

dren, and face up to the responsibility, no matter what the consequences."

"But, Chevassus," said Grangeversannes, the police photographer
and also a ranking expert on fingerprints, "the details are so blurred
you will never be able to convince the judge." His voice sounded
meek, but it was evident he had no intention of retreating. "Do
you think they will cut off a man's head merely because you express your personal belief that these prints are identical?"

"Fool!" exclaimed Chevassus. "Are you implying that you are
going to testify there is only probability of identity? You are betraying the whole science of fingerprinting. Never heard such a
silly thing. Fingerprints are either identical, or they are not identical, or they are too blurred to express any opinion."

"In this special case, I would reckon with probability," replied
Grangeversannes. "And there is the blood under the nails, too. I
think we'll leave the rest to the court."

"You coward!" said Chevassus, who by this time was almost
blue in the face. "Here for the last twenty-five years you have been
giving evidence in court on fingerprint identification. Now you
back out because this little scoundrel might be executed. *I* am
going to testify that the rogue touched the bottle."

The discussions grew so hot that the written testimony was held
up for several days. Eventually Locard settled for the probability
theory and Chevassus grudgingly gave up. This certainly contributed to saving the head of Fratelli, who got hard labor for life in
French Guiana, the place French criminals used to call the dry
guillotine.

This dissension at the laboratory might never have taken place
if a method for photographing very faint fingerprints, introduced
by Scotland Yard early in World War II, had been known at the
time. During a visit to the Yard in 1942, I ran into one of the
greatest of all police man-hunts. A new "Jack the Ripper" had appeared, a sadist who had killed several streetwalkers with a knife.
The killings were all done in private rooms and no one had wit-
nessed any of them. In the latest the killer had left his knife—a

cheap, ordinary pocket knife—at the scene. On the knife there was a fingerprint so faint that it was almost invisible but, by the ingenious new photographic process, the fingerprint department of the Yard was able to bring it out clearly. There was nothing on file to match it, but for the next few weeks the print was compared with the fingerprints of all newly caught criminals. When a young Canadian officer implicated in a tavern fight was fingerprinted, his prints matched those on the knife; he confessed, and was duly hanged.

Fingerprinting is as a rule a dull, routine business. Once, however, we encountered a fingerprint case which must surely be unique and which cost us more work to solve than most murder cases.

I cannot even remember how the affair started, because it was so insignificant that in the beginning it was not brought to the attention of the Detective Division. Someone reported to a precinct station that a gold watch lying on a table in a room with an open window had been stolen. There were no clues as to the perpetrator, and the police captain in charge of the station eventually put it on his list of unsolved minor crimes. The number of thefts of this sort increased, however. They all had one thing in common—they were committed in the daytime in rooms with open windows, and generally only one single, bright object was stolen. An exception was an instance in which a lady had placed her false teeth on a table and left for a few minutes to go into an adjoining room. When she returned, the teeth had disappeared.

The police at first favored the theory that some youthful gang was committing the thefts. But many of them were committed on the second or even the third floors of houses, and this was hard to explain. There were so many losses that a detective was assigned to examine all the scenes of the thefts. One day he found a fingerprint on a windowpane; he at once had it fully stained and photographed. It was not like anything we had ever before seen. There was no pattern to the thing and all the ridges ran vertically. After a while, more of these prints were found at the scenes of subsequent thefts.

For several days, all the brain power of the Lyons police laboratory was concentrated on these prints. Every assistant got himself copies of them and, I believe, took them to bed at night and dreamed about them. At least, that's what I did. Locard was brooding over them. You could almost see from the mighty bald skull of Chevassus how his brain beneath was knotted under the pressure of his thinking. Had the thief been gifted with the most unusual fingerprints any human being ever carried?

Finally, Locard himself solved the problem. The prints, he declared, must belong to a monkey. He also hazarded the opinion, which no one has yet contradicted, that monkeys could be identified by their fingerprints as surely as their Darwinian descendants could. So, in a single memorable day, all organ grinders and other owners of monkeys (and they were not few) were brought with their monkeys to the laboratory. It developed that not all monkeys are willing to have their fingerprints taken. Some of them put up an ardent resistance, biting, scratching, and crying. Finally, by muzzling them and having two men hold their violently twisting bodies, we succeeded in fingerprinting them all. Locard was right. We found the criminal, a little monkey who belonged to an Italian street musician.

At first the man emphatically denied any guilt, but when his room was searched many of the stolen things were located. Thereupon the Italian confessed that he had trained the monkey to steal and that he had sent it into apartments which he thought might pay off. The monkey had been trained not to enter any room which was occupied. After the trial, the ingenious street musician had an opportunity to muse in seclusion for a few months about better training methods, and the monkey was kept snugly in the local zoo.

But fingerprinting is not the only means of identification. Anthropometry, the *portrait parlé,* and specialized descriptions of salient features, such as eyes and ears which do not change in the course of a lifetime, can also be used. This was brought out in one of the most famous cases of the early twenties—that of the woman who claimed to be Anastasia, Grand Duchess of Russia.

There are still many conflicting reports concerning the fate of the Russian imperial family. In 1917 Czar Nicholas II, his wife the Czarina Alexandra, their fourteen-year-old son the Czarevitch, and their four daughters including Anastasia, were placed under house arrest at Tsarskoe Selo, a suburb of St. Petersburg. As the fury of the revolution and civil unrest increased, they were taken to the Western Siberian city of Ekaterinburg (since renamed Sverdlovsk) and left in the custody of the local revolutionary junta.

In July of 1918, when Admiral Kolchak's offensive against the revolutionaries seemed to be making progress and there was a possibility that the Czar might be rescued, the local officials took the royal family down into the cellar and shot them. According to one account, the bodies were buried in a peat bog; according to another, they were placed in quicklime; according to a third, they were at least partially cremated by being saturated in gasoline and ignited. Nevertheless, when Kolchak's forces took Ekaterinburg the bodies of the Czar and Czarina were identified in spite of the fact that they had been partially consumed by lime or fire. Absolutely certain identification of the children's remains was impossible.

The Czar had left a fortune deposited in his own name in the Bank of England. The closest heir was the Grand Duke of Hesse, in Germany, but the Bank of England took the position that it could not turn the money over to him without irrefutable proof that no member of the imperial family was still alive. Such proof was extremely difficult to establish, and the matter rested for several years.

Then one foggy night a Berlin policeman, while walking his beat along one of the city's canals, saw a woman jump into the water. He promptly dove after her, succeeded in pulling her ashore, and took her to a hospital. There she lay for several days like a deaf mute. Since she was believed to be a mental patient, she was confined in the hospital at Dalldorf-Wittnauer. Finally she began to speak a little, in Polish.

To understand what happened next it is necessary to recall the atmosphere of Berlin after World War I—war-stricken, inflation-ridden, and despairing. Many members of the old Russian aristocracy and a number of courtiers from the former imperial retinue had taken up residence there, and they had never given up hope that some member of the imperial family might have escaped the Ekaterinburg massacre. Some of the people called in to try to identify the woman in the hospital noticed that she had a remarkable resemblance to the Grand Duchess Anastasia, the youngest of the Czar's daughters. More and more Russians visited her, and most of them marveled at the likeness they wanted to believe in. In a short time there was a large group of Russian emigrés who claimed the young woman was indeed Anastasia.

This was a role which the woman had no difficulty in accepting. True, most of what she said was in Polish and her Russian was halting, but it improved rapidly. Each of the former courtiers reminded her of some episode of her youth, and in a few months' time she knew enough about the Grand Duchess's childhood and background to be almost letter-perfect in it.

According to her story the execution had been carried out by a bunch of drunken sailors. She herself had not been shot but clubbed over the head with a rifle butt. Believing that the entire family was dead, the sailors began to carry the bodies away. When "Anastasia" regained consciousness she found that she was momentarily alone with one sailor. Noticing that she was able to move, and presumably on an impulse of mercy, he told her to run away and hide. "The others are so drunk they will never miss you," he added. So she made her escape.

After countless trials and tribulations she managed to find her way on foot across countless leagues of Russia and down into Rumania. The blow on her head had caused her to lose her memory of her native language and the details of her youth. In Rumania she had married a humble soldier, but she was never happy and one day she left him and trudged north to Berlin. In that city she found work in a factory, but the injury to her head was still severe, and even the details of her Rumanian sojourn had largely faded from her mind. Her situation frightened her. Troubled, confused, and sick, she had decided to commit suicide.

That was her story, and she stuck to it. As long as there was any possibility that it was true, the money could not be paid by the Bank of England. There was no easy way of refuting her account, but the Grand Duke of Hesse put heaven and earth into motion to have the woman's identity established. He was convinced that she was an impostor, but how was that to be proved?

It was not the custom to take fingerprints of Grand Duchesses, and the problem of comparing photographs was almost as hopeless. The young Anastasia had been photographed many times, but she had been an innocent and sheltered girl of sixteen when she was taken to Ekaterinburg. The haggard face of the claimant, etched with suffering, might or might not have a resemblance to Anastasia. Now, there is one sure way of establishing identity between a person and a photograph: the comparison of ears. Next to fingerprints, ears are the most distinctive features of any individual body. Like fingerprints, they remain the same from birth to death, and there are scores of details which can be used for identification purposes. Therefore the Grand Duke embarked on an implacable hunt for a picture of the ear of the original Anastasia.

Of the innumerable photographs, official and private, of the Grand Duchess as a girl, not one of them showed an ear. In the first decades of this century young girls decorously concealed their ears by long hair. In every single photograph, Anastasia's ears were hidden under her tresses. Then one day, when the situation looked desperate, an ear was discovered.

It appeared in a photograph which had been taken by a young French tutor to the Czar's children. While he was in Russia the four girls and the boy had all had scarlet fever, and in accordance with the belief that baldness as an aftermath of the disease could be avoided by the cropping of the patients' hair, the heads of

Anastasia and her brother and sisters were shaved. During their convalescence, the tutor had his hands full trying to amuse his bored and fretful charges, so one day he placed them behind a table, with only their heads projecting above it, and took a picture of them. The Czarina, a superstitious woman, became almost hysterical when she saw the photograph, declaring that it looked as if her children had had their heads cut off. She ordered every copy of the picture destroyed, but the tutor managed to save one and took it with him when he fled from Russia. In this photograph, one of Anastasia's ears was clearly visible.

This fateful picture, accompanied by photographs of the ears of the claimant "Anastasia," was taken to my learned friend, Marc Bischoff, head of the Institute of Police Science at the University of Lausanne in Switzerland. Bischoff compared the photographs and established with complete certainty that the ears were not identical.

16

DURAND AND THE DRUG ADDICT

After I had been studying under Locard for a year or more, several things about crime and criminology were becoming clear to me. The first was the endlessly recurring nature of criminal patterns. I began to understand the philosophical approach of the regular detectives toward their work. Duffaux, for instance, had not been convinced of the guilt of Mademoiselle Dubois in the poisoning of her aunt, although the probabilities, learned by long experience, had favored her guilt. Somebody was poisoned, and somebody else got the victim's money. If in this case there existed an exception to the general rule that crimes are committed by people who hope to profit from them, the endlessly patient routine of a police investigation could be relied upon to discover it. Therefore, it was necessary to arrest Suzanne Dubois and go to work. Out of ten such cases, the heir will be guilty in nine. Even in this particular case there had been two possibilities of guilt to one of innocence: she might have killed her aunt because she wanted the money, or she might have poisoned the old lady because M. Forgeot forced her to do it. A case such as hers stood out because it was one of the few interesting exceptions to the sordid rule.

The next thing I learned was a human matter mentioned much earlier in this book: crime is a tragedy to all the human beings involved. This tragedy is ugly, almost always permanent, and deeply poignant to any man, detective or not, with a skin thinner than the hide of a rhinoceros. Detectives are only human, and though they armor themselves psychologically against being hurt, they cannot wholly succeed. Thus, the Lyons police beat the pimps on Saturday because they had no legal means of coping with a vicious and evil institution and could not tolerate the daily impact of this evil. I mention this not to condone the beatings but to make the point that violence will beget violence, even in men who have learned to abhor it.

Depravity is a terrible thing when it is encountered at first hand. The courses of its various manifestations become hateful to men who have to deal with them. The wonder is not that policemen grow tough from experience but that they do not grow tougher than they do. They seldom seem to lose the human core, no matter how hard a shell experience has built around it.

In my second year at Lyons there occurred a case which summed up much of what I am trying to say. It was not important enough to merit a single stick of type in a daily newspaper, but it revealed poignantly both the toughness and the tenderness that a man must have to be successful in dealing with crime and depravity.

One day my friend Durand called me into the small, dingy office he shared with three other detectives. The others were out, but I found Durand confronting a young man, practically a boy, who was pleading with him. I picked a chair and sat down to listen.

"But she is really a good girl," the young man was saying, "and she is so beautiful."

An expression of distaste crossed Durand's broad face. "You are a young fool, my friend. The girl is a prostitute. If I started believing the sob stories prostitutes tell, I might just as well sign up now as a street sweeper." He turned to me. "This gentleman has had the bad sense to fall in love with a damned whore, and a dope addict to boot. He is a medical student and ought to know better." He swiveled back to the young man. "I'm practically willing to bet right here and now that there isn't a word of truth in what this girl has told you."

The youngster twisted his hands in anguish. "No! No! I have known her for nearly two months. I really know her. I have seen her child, who is living with a poor family close to this very place. I have seen her pitiful craving for cocaine, but you must believe me when I say I have also seen her remorse, and it is real. And," he added, looking out the window and speaking softly, "we love each other."

The look of scorn on Durand's face deepened. "You poor fool!" he said sharply. Then he leaned forward, and with a visible effort at calmness and control said, "In these last two months you have probably shared her 'love' with a couple of hundred other fellows."

The young man winced, but he shouted, "It is her soul I love!"

"Well," Durand observed, "I think that if you put that soul under a magnifying glass you wouldn't like what you saw." He paused momentarily and then went on. "I happen to know from my own experience a couple of romantic asses like you who married ex-inmates of brothels. They lived to regret it. As a business proposition, that's another matter. There's that one-time whore, the woman who has the bar in the Rue St. Nizier. She saved the money she earned as a prostitute in order to buy a place for her old age. When she retired from the profession, she married M. Pornin in order to get a business partner. That was a good and regular deal. But that you should throw your youth and probably your future away on a prostitute and a dope addict is outrageous. Go in peace, my young friend, and behave yourself. We're grateful for the information you've given about the drug business, and we'll attend to it."

His visitor perceived from the finality in Durand's voice that there was nothing more to discuss. He rose and left the room. Durand waited until the door had closed behind him.

"What a fool!" he said wearily. "Harry, sometimes I think the human race must be part jackass. Let me tell you a little something about this case. It's sad, in a way, but it's like a million others, and you will see just how silly that young man is."

Leaning back in his chair and looking up at the ceiling, he gave me the outline of the girl's life as he had extracted it from his visitor. Two years before, when she was eighteen, she was living with her uncle, both her parents having died. The uncle had some sort of small job, and she herself was working as a typist for a truck manufacturer in Lyons. She was unusually good-looking so, when the Paris automobile show opened that year, the truck company put her in charge of the company's information booth. Not far away was the exhibit of a luxury model of one of the great continental manufacturers, and their information booth was in the charge of the son of the company's president. He was an insolent, handsome youth of twenty-five.

Durand paused to light a cigarette. "That fellow's picture used to be in the papers all the time. He was a prominent figure in that international café society that the newspapers devote a lot of space to. That gang is an incredible mixture of half-wit film stars, phony princes, and crazy young heirs of moneyed families. They took our hero in as one of their own, and he reveled in it."

This Prince Charming noticed the beautiful girl in the information booth of the truck company and made her acquaintance. She became infatuated with him. He was the first man in her life; his sleek cars, his elegant bachelor apartment and English valet, his immaculate clothes, and his wealth turned her head, and he overcame her reluctance by promising to marry her afterwards. For almost a year they lived together in a mad whirl of parties and entertainments. Among other unpleasant things, the fellow was a cocaine addict, and he introduced his mistress to this vice. When the girl told him she was pregnant he kicked her out, apparently without the least scruple, merely giving her a few thousand francs.

"All this," Durand observed, "runs like a cheap magazine story. There is not much variety in these plots. Anyhow, the poor creature returned to her uncle and threw herself on his mercy. The uncle, probably a strait-laced old so-and-so, refused to take her back. In fact, he did the traditional thing and forbade her to enter his home again. Perhaps it wouldn't be so easy to recruit girls for the streets if there weren't so many parents and uncles like that," he added reflectively.

The girl found a cheap place to live, husbanding the pittance of francs her lover had given her and doing some odd jobs. The money did not last long because of her need for cocaine. Her desperate letters to the man who was responsible for her misery remained unanswered. By the time her child was born she was penniless. She gave the baby to an old woman to look after and became a prostitute. In a short time she had been rounded up twice by the police for failing to register. The present occasion would be the third, and under French law that meant a term of imprisonment.

In those days, the law required every street-walker to have a *carte jaune*, a yellow card issued by the police. A weekly sanitary inspection was required, and the card was stamped with the date. Girls who failed to register or who could not show the stamp of the week on their cards were hauled away to the hospital for examination. It is perhaps old-fashioned to observe that this regulation was a sensible piece of social sanitation. Legalized prostitution has since been abolished in several south European countries, but it is questionable whether the dignity of women has been enhanced or the venereal disease rate diminished as a result.

The life of the registered prostitute was circumscribed by many regulations. She was not allowed to walk near military barracks or near places of entertainment. Above all, she was forbidden to pick up clients either by speaking or by gestures. Violation of this rule was technically called *racolage*—crimping or soliciting—a word which is also used when a French barrister tries to attract clients by unethical means.

The Vice Squad supervised the brothels, which were divided into two groups—ordinary "houses" and *maisons de tolérance*. The ordinary houses were clustered together in certain streets, and the blinds of the windows on the street side were always drawn, as required by law. In the ordinary houses the girls were boarders, living half a dozen to a small dirty room under the eaves and sharing meals in the kitchen with the manageress. It was rare that the owner of such a house lived there. In many instances the house was one of a chain operated by a large company. Often the proprietor lived as a respectable citizen in a select neighborhood in Paris, sending his children to the best schools. The house itself was usually run by a manageress called *la sous-maîtresse,* generally a former prostitute with a head for business and figures. She was professionally gay, almost always fat, and usually dressed in black with plenty of costume jewelry.

The girls were on duty twenty-four hours a day and were literally prisoners, with one important exception. The law required the Vice Squad to visit each house once a week, line up all the inmates, and ask them if they would like to leave. This precaution was taken because at one time these establishments had sold clothes and cosmetics to the girls until they had large debts and were restrained by the management if they tried to leave. Now the law prescribed that no woman could on any account be kept in such a house against her wishes.

At the first inspection I made with the members of my squad, the *sous-maîtresse* invited us to have champagne and assembled the girls, whom she affectionately addressed by their first names and patted on their backs. I innocently asked the Madame what she thought of the white-slavery traffic. She laughed so hard the champagne almost went down her windpipe.

"White slavery!" she cried. "Why on earth should we deal with white slavery and risk years of penal servitude when every day girls knock at our door begging us for a chance to work here?"

Afterwards I learned that the woman was quite right. The white slave traffic in Europe was almost one hundred percent the fruit of journalistic fantasy. When I interrogated the girls individually, I discovered that they were all content. Each had a story about how she started upon her profession, but I didn't find a single one who wanted to quit it.

"Why," a strong young woman standing almost naked before me said, "we have everything we want here—drinks, as many as we like; men, as much as we like; and a nice living."

The *maisons de tolérance,* or "houses of indulgence," were higher class than the run-of-the-mill brothels. They were scattered through the business sections of the city and were supervised by the police, but not so closely. The girls often lived outside and didn't begin work until noon, when they received businessmen or commercial travelers who liked to be accommodated after lunch. Some rooms of these establishments in big apartment houses were designed exotically so that, as a *sous-maîtresse* once told me, "everyone can feel at home." There were Roman baths, ships' staterooms, Turkish seraglios, and so on. One contained, among other decorator's masterpieces, a farm kitchen with an enormous double bed.

This was the information in the back of my mind as I listened to Durand's story. Aside from the question of the girl's having to register, the basic police concern was, of course, how did she obtain cocaine?

"That fool of a youngster," Durand said, "believes that the girl will tell us where she gets the stuff if we catch her in a state of remorse right after a bout with the drug. He has promised to let us know when he finds her in that condition. I believe he will do so, because he is obsessed with his effort to save her. He wouldn't have come here otherwise. Well, we shall see. I'll let you know if anything develops."

The very next afternoon the young man telephoned to Durand to inform him that the girl was lying almost unconscious in her room in a small side-street hotel. Durand summoned me, and the two of us hurried to the place. It was the usual cheap French hostelry, a narrow, shabby building with a restaurant on the ground floor. Behind the reception room was a creaking old elevator which gave the impression that it might drop at any moment. When we asked for the girl's room, the hotel clerk informed us that she was living on the seventh floor but that the elevator ran only to the sixth.

"Those are our cheapest rooms," he said and shrugged his shoulders.

We came to the door of the girl's room, knocked, and a man's voice answered. When we entered, we found the young student sitting at the side of the bed, clasping the girl's hand. I had to agree with the student's claim that she was beautiful. She was in fact so remarkably beautiful that she brightened up the whole dingy room with its torn wall paper and shabby furniture. But she was also very thin and frail; there was no color in her cheeks, she was breathing heavily, and she did not even open her eyes at the sound of our entry.

"This is more a case for a doctor," said Durand, and he put his big hand on her forehead.

"No," the medical student replied, "I am doctor enough myself for this case. She is in no immediate danger, but we shall have to wake her up. I think she has taken a slight overdose."

The process of waking her was blunt—almost brutal. We stripped off her clothes. The student pulled the top sheet off the bed and soaked it in the wash basin. The three of us then wrapped her quickly in the sheet. The effect was nearly terrifying. As the cold wetness of the cloth surrounded her, the girl waked with a scream and almost leaped out of bed. After a moment we took the sheet away and wrapped her in a blanket. She sat on the edge of the bed and stared at us, saying nothing.

Her eyes asked for pity, but there was no pity in Durand's firm voice as he began to question her. Where had she been getting her drugs? What were the names and addresses of the cocaine dealers and peddlers she knew? How many other addicts did she know of? On and on, for a full hour he hammered at her. At the end of that time he had extracted the names of one big dealer and four small-time peddlers. The girl obviously knew no more. Durand relaxed and ordered up a bottle of wine and some sandwiches.

It was a strange sort of lunch. Between gulps of red wine and bites of ham sandwich, Durand gently drew out the girl's personal story. It was the same as the version which the medical student had given the day before, down to the last detail. Durand listened with an impassive face.

"All right," he said finally. "You, monsieur, and you, Harry, go wait outside in the corridor." Then he turned to the girl. "Mademoiselle, you will please dress immediately. It is not my habit," he said in an apologetic tone, "to stay in a room while a lady dresses. But once, years ago, in a case not too unlike yours, I left the room. The woman jumped out the window, and from that lesson I learned never to leave anyone alone when it is my duty to take her into custody."

He went over to the window and stood looking out of it.

"You mean I am under arrest?" she cried. "But I have done nothing wrong."

"Look here, little girl," Durand said in a fatherly tone. "This may be a mere formality, but it is a necessary one. We have to arrest all those drug-dealing friends of yours right away, and all of them at once. If we fetch in one first, it will be no soap when we go after the others. I can't possibly take the risk of your tipping off any of them. The same thing applies to your . . . fiancé . . . here. I'm sorry, but I shall have to lock you both up for a few hours. However," and his tone became more fatherly than ever, "I believe your story, in spite of all my experience, and as true as my name is Durand I am going to help you."

At this point he blew his nose to hide his feelings.

The medical student and I waited outside until Durand and the girl joined us. We took the young couple to jail. Personally, I hated to do it. Of all gloomy places, our jail was the worst. The cells opened off two corridors, and the only view was into a small, dismal courtyard with high walls crenelated by iron spikes. It was no place for lovers, but we had no choice. The day happened to be a Sunday, and when we got to the Palais de Justice we found all the cells crowded with the usual week-end riffraff. The most we could do for the young people was to tell the jailer to put them out in the court and keep them there until we got back.

Durand and I went at once to the Detective Division, where we reported to Sarbach, who immediately sent out four simultaneous parties of plainclothesmen to pick up the four peddlers the girl had named. He himself decided to go after the big dealer, and he assigned Durand, me, and two other detectives to accompany him. According to the girl's information, our quarry was a Swiss waiter in a certain *brasserie*, a form of beergarden, the only kind of place in France where meals can be bought outside the sacred hours of lunch and dinner. Usually a brasserie is open all day and late into the night. Such a spot would provide an excellent cover for anyone trafficking in narcotics.

On the way to the place we debated how to find out where our man was hiding his stuff. Almost certainly he would not be carrying it on his person. If we arrested him on the spot, we might very well have to tear the whole place apart to find his cache. Finally Sarbach hit on a plan.

"You, Santerre," he said, turning to one of the detectives, "go inside and try to buy some of the stuff while we wait outside. You look enough like a dope addict to be one!"

He laughed loudly, and even Santerre had to grin. Of course it was pure chance that the man did happen to look like an addict. And yet, one of the mysteries of police work is how often detectives do tend to look a little like the class of criminal in which they specialize. Perhaps long contact with a particular kind of offender results in unconscious resemblance. Anyway, one of the most successful heads of a narcotics squad I ever knew looked like a perfect example of an opium smoker or heroin addict, even though in his private life he was a middle-aged family man with five children and went to Mass every Sunday. There was also an elderly police inspector in Berlin who was in charge of police dogs and who looked like a Boxer. And it is remarkable how often there is a trace of foppish elegance about the members of the Vice Squad.

At any rate, when we got to this brasserie, Santerre went inside while we waited around the corner. Quite some time passed, but finally Santerre came out again, looking dejected.

"Nothing doing," he reported. "I got our waiter friend in a corner and asked him in a whisper where I could get hold of some dope. I told him I was desperate. He played dumb and said he knew nothing at all about any dope. I pretended to be almost beside myself, and flashed several big bills under his eye. The fellow not only refused but acted like injured virtue. Maybe I don't look enough like an addict!"

As we knew, the little act did not prove the innocence of the waiter. It would well have been a matter of sound business policy on his part not to sell to any stranger. The fact that he was a wholesaler might even mean that he would sell only to retail peddlers. There was nothing to do but arrest the man and search both the restaurant and his dwelling. The prospect disheartened us, because the stuff could be hard to find. Nevertheless, we trooped in and told the waiter he was under arrest. We took him into the office of the proprietor. While he kept protesting his innocence, we made him take off all his clothes, and we searched each article of apparel with minute care. We found nothing. We let him dress and then sent him off to the Sûreté with one of the detectives. The rest of us went back into the dining room and sat wearily down at a table for a glass of beer and some rather bitter reflection.

Our gloom was occasioned by the near hopelessness of the job ahead of us. Most dope peddlers are extremely ingenious, and the nature of the stuff puts a premium on ingenuity. A package no larger than an envelope can contain thousands of dollars' worth of concentrated dope. Despite painstaking searches detectives often fail to find the evidence, especially if it is in small quantities. Drugs can be concealed almost anywhere. They have been hidden in the hollow corks of bottles, in signet rings, in women's lockets; they have been concealed in the soles of slippers, in fountain pens, in flashlights, and under the felt lining of spectacles cases; they have been stored in a tube in a hole in the upper part of a door jamb, in a small pouch in a pair of underdrawers hung on a line, ostensibly to dry; behind a loose brick on the outside of a house near a fire escape; in an envelope gummed up under a mailbox in the street; in a waterproof box in the overhead flush tank of an old-fashioned toilet, and even under erasers on pencils.

The difficulty does not end with the discovery of the place of concealment. In the United States, when a drug addict is imprisoned, he often received so-called "satch" letters from his friends, each letter and envelope saturated with morphine or heroin. Prison guards who censor the mail, however, can feel by touch if a letter is "satch" and generally manage to intercept it. If such a letter does get into the prisoner's hands, he chews it up, piece by piece. If a drug addict is lucky enough to receive such a letter every week, he can stay happy in prison for any length of time.

Even at the time of our brasserie raid, I was moderately familiar with the headache of trying to locate the hiding place of contraband drugs. Since then innumerable instances of the same difficulty have arisen, but the most extraordinary method of concealment I ever encountered came to light in New York City, when I was working with the Police Department. The Narcotics Squad received information that there was a hop joint, or opium-dispensing operation, at a certain apartment house in lower Manhattan. The place was put under observation and, sure enough, every evening certain known addicts were observed calling at a particular apartment in the building. When some of them were picked up, they were found to be carrying opium "toys"—the small tins in which the gummy raw opium is packed and transported. These toys were ingeniously hidden under their collars, inside their hat bands, or in other accessible places. The police were thus absolutely certain of where the opium was coming from. Nevertheless, in the next five months, after raiding the place twenty-five times and endlessly interrogating its Chinese lessee, they failed to uncover a single toy, either on him or on the premises.

It was not a difficult place to search. The apartment consisted of only two rooms and a kitchen, all very poorly furnished. One night the two detectives working on this hopeless case climbed the fire escape and peered in through holes in the window curtain. They saw the dealer sitting in the kitchen, petting a tame ferret. This idyllic scene was soon interrupted by a knock at the door. The Chinese got up, opened the door a crack, carried on a conversation, and received some money. Then he walked back to his chair and let the ferret loose. The creature instantly disappeared down a rathole under the sink and shortly came back holding an opium toy between his teeth. He was rewarded with a piece of raw meat, and the customer was handed his purchase. When the detectives raided the place and arrested the dealer, they found thirty-nine toys neatly arranged by the ferret himself in the space beneath the floor under the sink.

The cunning of our Swiss waiter may not have been quite so deceptive as that of the New York Chinese, but the brasserie was a discouragingly big place. It had thirty or forty tables, at least a hundred chairs, and shelves around the walls on which there were plenty of small knickknacks, curios, and *objêts d'art*. When we began to make a reconnaissance survey, we found that there was also a big basement containing a kitchen, a cloakroom, and a pair of washrooms. The one for men contained a mammoth basin in the middle of the room with a brass rail around it and a sign above reading, *Pour les malades au mer*—for the seasick. It was quite a place, and our suspect waiter had had access to every part of it.

When we sat down again at our table, one of the detectives glanced around and cleared his throat tentatively.

"Look," he said, "I don't think it is necessary to search this whole huge place. The stuff must be concealed in such a way that the waiter can get hold of it quickly and without arousing suspicion. Perhaps I'm wrong, but I don't think it is in the kitchen because there would be too many people there to watch him. It must be either in one of the two staircases leading down to the kitchen or in the toilets in the basement, or, possibly, under one of the tables in the restaurant itself."

And right he was. When we examined one of the staircases leading to the toilets, we noticed that one stair board was loose. Underneath it we found a score of small packets containing a white powder which on analysis proved to be cocaine. Triumphantly we returned to the Laboratory.

The process of thought preceding this search and discovery is typical of the experienced detective. Bertillon once said, "One sees only what one observes, and one observes only what is already in the consciousness." This gift of observation reinforced by routine and experience is one of the outstanding assets of a good detective.

When we got back to the Sûreté, we found that the peddlers the girl had named had all been arrested.

The girl and her medical student fiancé were now brought to the Chief's office, and what followed was something virtually out of a fairy tale. A young *commissaire*, Muller, who was a married man, offered to take her into his home and have a try at bringing her back to a normal life. Several of the other detectives offered to contribute money for her upkeep, and the girl wound up by becoming a sort of "daughter of the regiment" of the Sûreté of Lyons.

For once, this well-meaning effort actually did succeed. Sarbach himself had a few straight-from-the-shoulder talks with the uncle, and after a short while the girl was able to return to his home. A year later, she and the student were married, and, as far as I know, they are still living happily together.

In an affectionate sort of way we used to tease Durand about this case.

"Well, maestro," we would say, "the way to reform prostitution is with a big heart."

"Nonsense," he would reply. "What you fellows lack is a simple understanding of human relations."

The drug traffic is properly a source of great concern in the contemporary world. Its close connection with crime and depravity is too familiar to require description; what was true in those Lyons years is still basically the world picture. For some reason, the bulk of the drug traffic is concentrated in the United States and Asia. There was not much of it in Lyons thirty years ago, and even today France ranks ninth in the per capita consumption of heroin, while the United States ranks third. The United States is tenth in the consumption of cocaine, while France is not even ranked, and the consumption of hashish, or marijuana, in which the United States is eighth on a per capita basis, is almost negligible in France proper, though French Morocco ranks fifth. Asiatic and Near Eastern countries account for a vast amount of the total "raw" narcotics (opium and hashish), while Western addictions are to the processed drugs, heroin and cocaine. A major reason for the necessity of international control of the drug traffic is that the plants from which really effective narcotics are derived grow in greatest abundance in southeast Asia. Only two are native to the Western Hemisphere: marijuana, which is found in Mexico, and the coca bush which grows on the mountain slopes of Peru.

A French friend once remarked that France's comparatively favorable showing in narcotics statistics could be accounted for by an abundance of good food, good wines, and beautiful women. However that may be, the Continent serves basically as a way station or middleman for drugs on their way from Asia to the United States, where the dollar market is so attractive. There is probably no field of criminal activity today in which a fortune can be acquired so speedily as by an enterprising man in the dope business. A short time ago, heroin—which is far from expensive to manufacture—was selling in New York for about six hundred dollars an ounce before adulteration. The adulterant, milk sugar, is mixed by the peddler in about the proportion of ten ounces of the sugar to one of the drug, and this mixture retails for two or three dollars per capsule of 1½ grains. At 7,000 grains to the pound, or 425 grains to the ounce, the adulterated stuff brings in at retail almost $8,000. No wonder the traffic supports a vicious criminal population!

The case of the girl in Lyons was my first experience with the traffic in illicit drugs. When I had been traveling in Persia I was often invited to smoke opium. At that time the drug was so commonly used among well-to-do people that it was served with tea, like muffins or cookies. Not wishing to offend my hosts, I never refused to smoke but always confined myself to a few whiffs, which did not affect me in the slightest. Later, in Indo-China, I found that many of the old French colonists were opium smokers, and generally they looked quite healthy. The use of opium in the East is so extremely widespread that it is remarkable what a small fraction of its users seem seriously affected by it. Perhaps it is like drinking. Most people have a tolerance for alcohol and drink it all their lives with no serious effect. Of course, the effects of opium, when felt, are infinitely worse, and the drug itself far more habit-forming than alcohol.

As for hashish—*cannabis indica* is the botanical name—my sole experience with it was in Persia. I was staying in the ancient city of the shahs, the romantic former capital of Ispahan, at a combined caravanserai and boarding house. I fell in with a young lieutenant of the local police who described in glowing terms the delights to be had from hashish. One evening he brought me a pill and I put myself to bed and swallowed the thing. Soon I was asleep, and about all I can recall of the effects of the drug is that I had most peculiar dreams compounded of color visions of triangles, circles, and stars gyrating. In the morning I woke very thirsty and with a bad taste in my mouth, and I never repeated the experience.

Heroin and cocaine are infinitely more vicious. They debauch their users; they lead to crime and depravity on the part of their consumers, and they support a wealthy and evil class of criminal. Until the whole traffic is controlled and kept within the bounds of licensed authority, these criminals will continue to generate festering sores in the body of society. But it will never be easy to control them, not only because the stuff is concentrated and hence easy to smuggle and hide, but because man's craving for enchantment, for getting away from the drab comonplaces of life, is so acute.

17

THE GLOZEL AFFAIR

Toward the end of my Lyons apprenticeship, I became involved in a case which I still regard as the most interesting investigation problem I ever came across. It was not, actually, a criminal case, although one of its cast of principal characters was murdered and another, possibly more than one other, might have been guilty of fraud. The affair is still not wholly cleared up, and perhaps it will never be brought to a close. Certainly my own interest in it continues, and more than anything else in my experience as a criminologist it has served to enrich my personal life.

One day I was summoned to Locard's office. *Le Patron* was leaning back in his chair and studying a letter.

"Sit down, Harry," he said. "I have an assignment for you." He smiled faintly. "An assignment very different from what you have been doing. You will be moving in most distinguished circles. Yes. Distinguished is the word."

Locard did not usually commence in quite this fashion. My anticipation began to be colored with something like wariness. I did not like the way he kept on looking at the letter instead of me.

"Anything you say," I replied.

"Well," he went on, "this is not a matter for inexperience. I shall have to send a good man." He laid the letter down finally and looked directly at me. "You have of course heard of the Glozel affair?"

Who hadn't? It had been a newspaper sensation for two years, and my heart sank as I heard Locard name it. The thing had started four years earlier in a small hamlet named Glozel, about twenty kilometers southeast of Vichy. Near Glozel was a farm which had been cultivated for some generations by a family named Fradin. One March day in 1924 Emile Fradin, then about twenty, was working in one of the fields when he uncovered two bricks which seemed out of the ordinary. After the day's work he went back to the field and did some more digging. His labors brought to light a shallow, oval pit about three meters long and a meter wide. The pit was lined with stones and the soil in it contained pieces of pottery. In general construction some authorities later considered that it might have been an ancient glass furnace of a sort not too uncommon in the region, but Emile was no antiquarian and knew nothing of this possibility. The next day he continued digging, perhaps in the hope of finding something valuable, and a few feet from the pit he came on another brick, or clay tablet. On this one there was a clearly visible series of markings.

Now the Fradin family had been working the farm since 1870, or over fifty years, without becoming rich in the process. The soil in this section of France is not so fertile as it is in many other regions, and Glozel was a small community with few opportunities even for the most diligent. Still, the Fradins were attached to their land. Both the young man and his grandfather, old Père Fradin, over seventy, felt excited by the thought that their meager acres might contain vestiges of some ancient culture. Certainly it was something to talk about in a community where every other topic had been talked out years before.

When Père Fradin told his neighbors about Emile's findings, a number of them began to make the farm the objective of their evening strolls. The more they came, the more they talked, and in a fortnight the matter came to the ear of a Mlle. Picandet, the schoolteacher of the parish. She took her pupils over to have a look at the excavations. By this time Emile had succeeded in unearthing additional brick tablets with markings on them and even the imprints of human palms, and a small stone hatchet.

Mlle. Picandet was much impressed with what she saw and made a report on it to her superiors. They in turn forwarded her letter to a Citizens' Committee which had been organized to promote tourist and business interest in the Bourbonnais region, where Glozel is situated. The Committee sent a representative to the Fradin farm, but the Fradins, whose field was a part of their livelihood, asked fifty francs for the privilege of two days' further digging. The Committee refused, on the somewhat specious ground that they had no funds for such a purpose. Things dragged along, and the Fradins began to discuss the advisability of plowing the field again. It had been lying in fallow pasture for several years and was now ready for another crop.

At his point Dr. A. Morlet intervened. He was a physician in Vichy and apparently a faithful reader of the reports of the Citizens' Committee. In the latest issue he had come upon an account of the Glozel matter. His own hobby was the archeology of the Gallo-Roman period in his region and, when he read that the Committee had refused to spend fifty francs for a dig, he went to Glozel himself to have a look at the site. According to his account, there was nothing Gallo-Roman about the artifacts. They were obviously far more ancient. He talked to the Fradins and learned one interesting detail from them. Clear back in 1870, the Fradins said, when their family had acquired the farm, the man who sold it to them had told of burying a dead animal in the field and uncovering an earthenware jar covered with strange signs. He had taken it home and put it on the mantlepiece, where it had remained for years. Many of the villagers recalled having seen it, the Fradins said, but after their family had moved in, it was thrown away.

This story and the artifacts themselves excited Dr. Morlet. Shortly afterward, Emile Fradin and his sister came to see him and told him that their grandfather had decided to plow the field. In antiquarian alarm Morlet offered to rent the field for nine years at two hundred francs a year, plus extra recompense to the Fradins for whatever work they might put in. He reserved the right of first purchase on whatever might be found and, even more important to such an enthusiast as he was, the exclusive right to reproduce and publish accounts of the discoveries.

So it was arranged, and from this innocent beginning there sprang a perfect tempest of controversy conducted with Gallic intensity.

When Dr. Morlet commenced his digging, he uncovered a great number of objects, particularly carved bones * and many more of the odd brick tablets with their indecipherable markings. These artifacts did not attract much initial attention, but one day the spade turned up a bone with the image of a reindeer on it. It was obvious that the carver must have seen a reindeer with his own eyes. Further digging brought to light some reindeer teeth and panther teeth.

To understand the resultant furor it is necessary to realize that paleontologists were agreed that there had been no reindeer in France since the end of the Paleolithic or Old Stone Age. At that time the sheet of glacial ice which once covered all Scandinavia and portions of the northern part of the Continent had melted and receded. For a long time, however, the climate was supposed to have been cold enough for reindeer to survive in central western Europe, until they too followed the ice and retreated to Scandinavia.

The second half of the Old Stone Age is divided into three main parts, of which the salt, or next to last if the Azilian be included, was the Magdalenian. In this era, in certain parts of France and Spain, the inhabitants were cave dwellers, primitive people with a magnificent talent for art. It was during their age that the great Dordogne, Altamira, and other similar cave paintings were made. The work was done with candor and beauty. But the Paleolithic gave way to the Neolithic, or New Stone Age, and the great cave paintings became a lost art.

* The drawings for this chapter were specially made for it by Mamie Harmon. They were prepared from actual Glozel artifacts.

At first Morlet judged that the artifacts he was bringing to light at Glozel were wholly Neolithic, but the reindeer discoveries and a number of other circumstances made him revise his estimate and date them at about the close of the Magdalenian epoch. This instantly threw him into conflict with established scholarship, which held that the descendants of the Magdalenians had lived on as primitives with a debased culture until more refined people, developing further East, had brought new light to the barbarian savages of the West. The finds at Glozel contradicted this established theory. If the great cave art had vanished, the descendants of the artists had at least shown great cultural vitality by inventing something which looked, on the evidence, to be a written language. Morlet was convinced that the rows of scratched marks on bones and bricks could be nothing less than the oldest known writing. Either Glozel was a hoax, or it was one of the greatest archeological discoveries of the age.

When Morlet advanced his findings in 1926, the battle was instantly joined. Some of the critics declared that young Emile Fradin was a forger and faker. The difficulty with that was to explain how a twenty-year-old, half-literate peasant boy could have invented a whole prehistoric culture and manufactured the approximately 1700 objects which were dug up at the Fradin farm. Where did he get the reindeer bone and the teeth? The critics claimed that the lad had copied the magnificent drawings out of textbooks in archeology, but there were no such books at the farm, and it seemed doubtful that Emile had ever read anything except his prayer book and an occasional newspaper.

Other skeptics contended that Dr. Morlet had not conducted

his digging in a thorough, careful, and scientific manner. There was a measure of truth in this. At the outset the excavating was conducted somewhat as a family outing and picnic. But the counterclaim to this criticism was also valid: a number of the critics were themselves guilty in this regard. Early in the operation, savants arrived at the site and demanded the right to dig independently to satisfy their doubts. Dr. Morlet had no choice but to comply, knowing well that any refusal on his part would make him suspect and subject to criticism. In consequence, dozens of more or less planless diggings took place.

After a barrage of scholarly articles—and a great deal of lurid stuff in the newspapers—the International Institute of Anthropology appointed a commission of scholars to inspect Glozel and render an opinion on what had been unearthed there. The world-wide stir which the case was occasioning also prompted the French government officially to declare the site one of scientific importance. This gave it the protection of the law, which began to find its hands full of Glozel problems. In early 1928 a surgeon who, like Morlet, had archeological leanings, but who was violently opposed to anyone claiming authenticity for these artifacts, went to the regional District Attorney and deposited an application for a formal finding of fraud committed "by person or persons unknown" at the Fradin farm. Guided by this gentleman, the police searched the farm and impounded about a hundred objects.

Eventually these objects were forwarded to no less a figure than Edmond Bayle, and at the time of my mission they were under analysis in his Paris Police Laboratory. Bayle issued no report for a full year. Meanwhile, scholars' passions and public interest were white hot. The background of the case and every least detail were matters of current journalistic prominence, and all this flashed through my mind as I listened to Locard handing this assignment to me.

"Sir," I said to him, "this is a very hot potato."

He avoided my eye. "The Lyons Police Laboratory has been invited to send a delegate to Glozel. There is to be an international committee to study it thoroughly from the standpoint of authenticity. Dr. Salomon Reinach who is, as you probably know, a world authority on prehistory and ancient languages, will come down from Paris. Then there will be Déperet from our own University of Lyons as the expert on geology and paleontology, and a number of others. As I said, you will be in distinguished company."

"I can see that, sir. But I think it would be wiser if you went. Your findings will surely carry more weight."

"Alas," said Locard, "it is impossible. There is the pressure of my duties here to consider."

This assignment was very different from merely going along with the police on criminal cases and conducting laboratory tests. While I suspected Locard of wanting to stay clear of the whole Glozel controversy and of selecting me to accompany the Committee because I was not only young and unknown but a foreigner whose future career would not depend upon French officialdom, I had also to admit that it was an honor to be chosen. The very uniqueness of the problem appealed strongly to me.

"Now, my young friend," Locard was saying, "let us talk for a moment of what it is you will be getting into. You know already how passionate these archeologists can get over their researches. They are supposed to be scientists with impartial detachment, but in actuality many of them are impulsive innocents of the first water. If a lot of them weren't so gullible, there would not be so many fakers preying on them. Indeed, sometimes scholars seem to be more foolish than any ignorant peasant. Let me tell you about the amazing case of the great mathematician, Michel Chasles."

In the middle of the last century Chasles was a professor of mathematics at the Sorbonne, a distinguished man who had discovered numerous techniques in analytical geometry. As a hobby he collected autographs, and in the pursuit of this interest he fell in with a dealer named Vrain-Lucas, a rascal who seems to have been only a clumsy forger at best. In seven years Professor Chasles bought from this fellow about twenty-seven thousand letters and autographs of famous persons. Vrain-Lucas' story was that the collection belonged to a nobleman who had drowned. The collection included everything—letters from Newton, Galileo, Mary

Stuart, Vercingetorix (the famous Gallic chieftain), Julius Caesar, and even Cleopatra. There was one letter from Cleopatra to Caesar which read: "My dearly beloved: Our son Caesarion is okay. I hope we will soon be able to endure the voyage from here to Marseilles." This was written on paper, not papyrus.

All these documents, in fact, were written on regular paper which had been treated with smoke. On close inspection it was even possible to make out the watermark of the modern papermaker. Out of the myriads of things which Professor Chasles bought, not more than a hundred were authentic. When Vrain-Lucas was brought to trial, he told the court that he only wanted to remind France of her great men and her great historic past, which she so often forgot. The court reminded him of some of the present statutes by giving him a sentence of two years.

No less remarkable was the discovery just outside the walls of Jerusalem of a chache of thousands of vases, urns, tablets, and statuettes, all modeled in clay and baked. These objects were alleged to be Moabite in origin and most of them were liberally covered with markings like the ancient writing of the Phoenicians. Amid this mountain of trash there was even the smoking pipe which had belonged to Astarte, the Syrian-Phoenician goddess of love and fertility. What she smoked in it was not clear, but it cannot have been tobacco which reached Europe and the East only after the time of Columbus.

Implausible as it may seem, a German scientist succeeded in talking the Prussian government into purchasing the entire lot at a stiff price. A famous German archeologist immediately commenced work on a tome about Moabite culture in the light of these objects, but a French scholar and diplomat, Charles-Simon Clermont-Ganneau, was able to prove that so far as the Moabite culture of the collection was concerned, it existed only in the imaginations of some illiterate Arab fakers.

This Clermont-Ganneau appears to have been a man of skeptical mind. Eleven years later, in 1883, he heard the astonishing news that the British Museum had secured an original portion of the Bible in manuscript. This priceless treasure was known as the Bible of Shapira, after its discoverer. The name Shapira rang a gong in Clermont-Ganneau's mind; he recalled that it was this same Shapira who had led the Prussian scientist to the hoard of Moabite fakes. The dauntless savant immediately set out for London to inspect this Bible, but the officials of the British Museum would not allow him to examine it. He had to do his inspecting along with the general public from the other side of a pane of glass. Even so, he quickly spotted the fact that it was another fake, written in ink on an ancient Torah scroll. Shapira fled to Rotterdam, where he blew out his brains.

"I could go on all day with stories like these," Locard said, shaking his head sadly. "There was that famous tiara that was supposed to have belonged to some Egyptian or Syrian queen. The Louvre paid a fabulous lot of francs for it. Seven years later it was proven to have been made by a gifted goldsmith in Odessa. And so on and on. Be on your guard at Glozel, Harry. There are fakers everywhere in this world—even on farms."

With these disquieting stories in mind, I took out our file of newspaper clippings on the Glozel affair to refresh my memory. As I read them at one sitting, I began to feel that I had been given a war correspondent's assignment. The controversy was incomparably the hottest ever fought. Like the American Civil War it had set father against son and brother against brother. Accusations and recriminations were thick as raisins in a pudding; public interest was at fever pitch. I began to feel definitely uneasy and, when my colleagues at the lab learned where I was going, their hypocritical condolences did nothing to console me.

What should I take with me when working on such a case? At the usual afternoon snack period, I got a good deal of advice on this point.

Old Chevassus said that I had better take a fingerprint outfit, adding, "You know, you never can tell if you'll have to fingerprint some of those fellows for our police files. Personally, I am very skeptical about the whole affair."

It was certainly not necessary, my friends thought, to take a pistol with me; archeologists are not known to shoot their way out or to resist arrest. Kindly old Grangeversannes, the police photographer, went so far as to lend me the smallest camera in the place, which was the apple of his eye, and he also gave me several packs of photographic plates. After much discussion, some small surgical instruments, such as scalpels and scissors, were added to my kit, along with a strong magnifying glass and a flashlight.

Finally I myself put a pair of handcuffs into the portfolio. Now, I find it hard to explain why I took those handcuffs along; perhaps it was merely to keep up my self-confidence as a detective. Then, too, the handcuffs had been acquired only the preceding day.

The day before that I had received a special delivery letter from Paris which said that the writer was a retired police officer who had invented a wonderful new handcuff which he called *les melonettes*, since his own name was Melon. This was a pleasant play on words, for the French word for handcuffs is *menottes*. M. Melon added that he would be in Lyons the following morning and asked me to give him an interview because he wanted to introduce his handcuffs to the Scandinavian market.

He proved to be a small man, burning with the inventor's zeal. In a bombastic manner he told me how superior his handcuffs were to anything that had been previously manufactured in this line. They were very light, being made of aluminum; very easy to apply; very difficult to pick; so dainty that no one should be ashamed to wear them. They sounded almost like jewelry as he talked about them. He ended his sales talk by presenting me with a pair and two keys. I did not want to get mixed up in the enterprise, but I gave him the addresses of a few Scandinavian wholesale houses which supply the police with this sort of thing. M. Melon went away apparently satisfied.

There were the handcuffs I put into my portfolio for Glozel.

The following morning I called on Professor Charles Déperet, Dean of Science and member of the Geology Department at the university. He seemed pleased to have my collaboration and told me we were to leave for Vichy, the nearest station to Glozel, the following day. Professors Roman, Mayet, and Arcelin were to accompany us.

Though I was not studying under him, I knew Déperet quite well because he was one of the most popular professors at the university. A tiny, frail, stooped man of seventy-four with a pointed mustache, he wore a bowler hat on all occasions. Earlier in life he had been a military surgeon, and only in his leisure time an amateur geologist. Incidentally, there are a surprisingly large number of such scientific amateurs among French military surgeons. Eventually, Déperet had become a full-fledged geologist, and a famous one. During the last decades of his life he concentrated on paleontology, and among his most famous discoveries were the prehistoric horse teeth at Solutré, not far from Lyons.

The expedition for Glozel left on the noon express. My learned companions and I had a compartment almost to ourselves; the only other passenger was an elderly lady who soon became as silently fascinated as I by the conversation of the four savants. It was really awe-inspiring. World-famous names flashed by our listening ears. Stretches of hundreds of thousands and even millions of years obviously were bagatelles to these men dedicated to studying the origin and development of the human race. The talk had a scale and a sweep to it which I found exhilarating. Nothing like it had come within my ken before.

It was a five-hour journey from Lyons to Vichy. I said practically nothing, but listened intently to my companions. Finally Dean Déperet turned to me and asked how my chemistry studies were coming along and about my work at the Police Laboratory. This led to some talk about fingerprints, and I opened my portfolio to show him my fingerprinting outfit. He examined it with interest. Catching sight of the *melonettes* lying at the bottom of the portfolio, I picked them up and showed them to him, explaining proudly that they were the latest invention in the handcuff field. Déperet asked me to put them on his hands, explaining that he wanted to feel for once what it was like to be handcuffed. I put them on him, and the instant those infernal things closed around his fragile wrists a fearful doubt swept over my mind. Had I brought the keys with me?

I had not. A minute search of my portfolio and all my pockets revealed this awful fact. When the truth began to dawn upon poor Déperet, his kind smile gradually became melancholy and his face grew haggard. In about twenty minutes' time we were due to arrive at Vichy, where scores of journalists, press photographers, and newsreel men would be waiting for us on the station platform.

What to do? What to do? A cold sweat broke out all over my body while I racked my brains as to how to get out of this situation. In French railway carriages there are always a few tools—at least a pickaxe, a small shovel, and the like—stored in a glass-covered case for use in emergencies. But a glance at delicate old Déperet convinced me that he could never endure harsh treatment. Next I thought of the locomotive. The engineer certainly must have tools, but he would be difficult to get to. Still, something had to be done. I was planning to perform the circus stunt of climbing over the fender to reach the locomotive.

The elderly lady, our fellow passenger, who had been observing the goings-on while busily knitting, suddenly said, "Why don't you try one of my hairpins? I have read in several detective novels that hairpins are very good for picking locks."

She drew a hairpin from her hair and handed it to me. God bless that clever lady! Contrary to the bragging of their inventor, those wretched *melonettes* were easy to pick. In a short while, I had opened one of them. And high time too, because the train was already slowing down for the Vichy stop. One of the cuffs was still around poor Dean Déperet's wrist. I tucked the rest of the gadget up into his sleeve and, to make assurance double sure, fastened it with a piece of string, also supplied by the amiable lady, who fished a length out of her big handbag. When I pulled the sleeve down, there was no outward sign of the handcuffs.

Smiling genially, we alighted from the train and were interrogated by the world press. The handcuffs remained out of sight, and the reporters missed a scoop. As soon as we got to the privacy of the hotel, I picked the other lock and freed Dean Déperet completely. I felt sure he would never again want to try on handcuffs. For myself, I still shudder when I think of what could have happened if that clever lady had not been in our compartment.

In Vichy, we met the great Dr. Reinach of whom I had never heard until now. That is not too surprising in the light of the fact that I had not hitherto moved much in the world of the liberal arts. Salomon Reinach, the archeologist, was the middle one and sole survivor of the three famous Reinach brothers who, around the turn of the century, played so great a role in French cultural life. When I met him in Vichy he was seventy years old, a small, fiery, gray-bearded man with piercing eyes and a high-arched nose. In spite of his age he was still active as Director of the Musée St. Germain in Paris and frequently contributed to journals in his special fields of philology and archeology. His wife was with him and I learned that in her youth she had been a Russian revolutionary. When she fled to France she met her husband, who was then studying medicine.

Our task force was much augmented at Vichy by a further constellation of learned gentlemen. There was the famous Professor Loth, at that time regarded as one of the greatest authorities on Celtic languages, and his son William, an engineer. Another member of the committee was M. Audollent, Dean of the Faculty of the School of the Humanities at the University of Clermont. He was a well-known Latin scholar, and I was informed that his specialty was the deciphering of medieval Latin incantations used by magicians. From Belgium the International Institute of Anthropology had sent Professor Bayet of the Academy of Medicine, an enthusiastic amateur archeologist. There were also Dr. Foat, an English specialist in Hellenic cultures; Dr. Arcelin, another French amateur archeologist; Dr. van Gennep of Belgium; and Professor Tricot-Royer of the University of Louvain, a specialist in the history of medicine. If the artifacts of Glozel held any secrets, I decided, this committee would surely bring them to light.

The committee assembled at once for a short preliminary meeting in a Vichy hotel room. It was up to me to define the precautions which would render our investigation immune to later criticism. I made my plan, which was approved by the group, as clear and foolproof as possible. My reasoning was that if the objects found in the farm soil were fakes, they would have had to be planted. I could not think of any way to plant the things except by disturbing the soil. Therefore, our digging must be conducted vertically, and no object found as a result of horizontal trenching or shovelling should be considered authentic beyond dispute. But if we first made a trench and then dug down vertically along its open walls, whenever we came upon an artifact we could study it as it lay in its own surroundings, *in situ* as the archeologists say. Such a technique, I felt, would expose any tampering with soil levels or other traces of fakery. All the members of the committee were in agreement that this was the way to proceed.

We were to spend four days at our digging. Late in the day though it was by now, we journeyed out to the farm to have a preliminary look. We were welcomed by the Fradin family, headed by old Grandpère Fradin himself. He was a small, old man with a drooping white mustache, dressed in a faded blue blouse, large, loose trousers, and wooden clogs. His grandson, then about twenty, was also short and slight, but his mustache was black and merely budding. He wore the same typical peasant garb. Grandmère Fradin seemed to me the most impressive member of the family, a woman of seventy with a face seamed and marked by a lifetime of drudgery but with the innate dignity of the French peasant woman.

The family led us to the field where the discoveries had been made. It was a small field and looked as if it had been bombed. It was pocked from edge to edge with the pits of the former diggings. It had taken a lot of work to make so many and such deep holes, and the field bore eloquent witness to the intensity of the scientific quarrel we had come to settle. The Fradins also showed us a sort of rough museum they had made in a barn. There, on plank shelves, were laid out hundreds of tablets, stone hatchets, carved and incised bones, and other artifacts. In the absence of the hundred specimens which had been impounded and sent up to Paris, the number of these surprised me then and surprises me to this day.

Next morning we selected a virgin piece of ground and set to work. First, a couple of laborers dug a trench about six feet deep and several yards long. When it was complete all of us could see plainly the anatomy of the Glozel soil. Its layers were as sharply defined as if they were layers of a cake. The top layer consisted of gray humus, a foot or foot and a half thick. Below was a layer of yellow clay mixed with small stones and sand, two to three feet thick, and that was the layer in which all the objects had been found. Innumerable roots of different plants penetrated deeply the layer of gray humus, reaching into this dark yellow clay. Below it was a stratum of more compact clay of a lighter yellow. I saw at once that if we came upon anything in the course of our vertical excavating it would be easy to ascertain whether the object had been deposited recently.

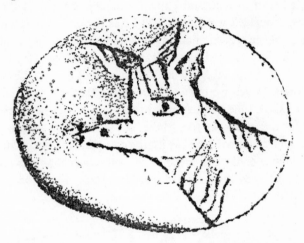

Luck was with us. In the four days at the site we found a piece of black slate on which had been engraved a running reindeer and some markings which looked like writing of some kind. We also came upon a piece of bone, highly fossilized, which was marked with similar signs, a small clay lamp, and a number of other objects. There was one clay tablet, the soil above it totally undisturbed, with the root of a bush penetrating it. That old dead root seemed to me an impressive piece of evidence. What better proof of authenticity could we ask? At least, if the artifacts had been planted, the fake was committed long, long ago. Even so, it was hard to see how such a job could have been done without marring the knife-sharp line of separation between the humus and the clay.

I also examined the contents of the museum and found baked into one tablet a fingerprint of its maker. I took the fingerprints of the whole Fradin family and of Dr. Morlet as well, but none was similar to the print on that brick. Subsequently, I published a paper about this fingerprint, which may possibly be the oldest in the world.

Every evening I spread plaster of Paris around our trench to prevent anyone from trying to dig near our excavation during the night. I also mounted guard. Late the second night, I took a taxi from Vichy to the vicinity of Glozel and walked out to the farm. It began to rain, and I spent a miserable night at the field. Perhaps, though, it was just as well I was there. The next morning a young college student named Vergnette came poking about the excavation. We ordered him to leave but he went over to the farm house and handed old Madame Fradin a small parcel addressed to Dr. Morlet. When we opened it we found that it contained some pieces of slate. One of them was carved and others bore cabalistic signs. In the package, too, there was a card on which young M. Vergnette had written: "With the compliments of the author." This evidence of the bitterness of the anti-Glozelians was an indication that the controversy had reached a stage where some of the parties had lost their reasonable restraint.

A few weeks later the committee published its report. As it had to do in the light of the evidence we had personally uncovered, the report affirmed that the Glozel findings were authentic. The anti-Glozelian faction received this report in the spirit in which a duck's back receives water. They were utterly unimpressed and continued their attacks unabated. Meanwhile, the whole scientific world was waiting for the report of M. Bayle, the head of the Paris Police Laboratory.

His report, when it came later that year, proved to be a stunning surprise. Locard read it without comment except for a slight, wry smile; I suspect he had a private opinion of its author which he never voiced. There had always been tension between the Lyons and Paris laboratories.

At this time Edmond Bayle was about fifty years old. He had been head of the Paris Police Laboratory since the close of World War I and was the almost direct successor of Alphonse Bertillon, who had died in 1914. For a few years the laboratory had been headed by a man named David, one of Bertillon's staff, but then Bayle had replaced him. His appointment was somewhat unexpected since he had been a physicist at the Pasteur Institute until then.

As might have been expected, Bayle placed great emphasis on the use of physical and optical analysis in police work. To him and an old German scientist named Jeserich goes the credit for introducing spectography to police science—the use of photographs of light spectra. In his own field he had a rather impressive reputation, but he was also known to be an overbearing and cynical man.

Bayle had taken more than a year to make his examination of the objects sent to him from the Glozel farm, and he claimed to have brought to light some remarkable discrepancies. In one of the brick tablets he had found a cotton thread dyed with an aniline dye (a matter which could be established by spectography, by the way), and in another he had identified a potato sprout. The bricks, he said, had not been baked but merely shaped and dried, which accounted for the survival of such vegetable matter.

The anti-Glozelians emitted loud sounds of triumph. As the *New International Year Book* for 1928 summarized the matter, "M. Bayle turned out to be an excellent detective. . . . Thus Glozel becomes a hoax and ranks among the most famous in history."

The faction which believed in authenticity was momentarily thrown into confusion, but it was unwilling to concede defeat. The immediate objection which they raised to the Bayle report was a criticism of the seizure of evidence which had resulted in the submission to Paris of the hundred-odd impounded artifacts. They pointed out that the Fradins had not been allowed to be present at this official event. Still worse, the objects had not, as the law prescribed, been separately sealed and wrapped and identified, but had been bundled up higgledy-piggledy and rushed off. A few of the weaker-spirited faithful discussed the possibility that young Fradin might have enriched the bonafide archaeological treasures with a few contributions of his own, but this defensive theorem never attained much currency.

Personally, while I sought to keep an impartial mind, I was not convinced by the Paris report. The matter of young M. Vergnette stuck in my mind as a small but ugly episode. I also remembered those clean-cut earth surfaces in our trench, with the objects still embedded in them. Bayle had not accounted for them, nor for the obvious characters of the Fradins themselves and the vast number of artifacts whose production would have required a small factory. The sweet and lovely lines of the reindeer drawings were an example of genuine artistic talent, it seemed to me, and who was the artist, or where were the books from which the drawings had been derived? What about the fingerprint?

The pro-Glozelians set to work to undermine the case of the opposition. Examination of baked bricks in many different places—Lyons, Brussels, Oslo, and Stockholm—proved that a clay brick might contain fossilized roots which had penetrated even after the brick had been baked. That weakened Bayle's point about the vegetable matter. In spite of a contention to the contrary, no evidence that metal tools had been used in marking the bones and tablets was ever established. Bayle claimed that there were traces of marrow in the bones, but experts claimed that the bones were definitely fossilized and extremely ancient. Unlike the famous British Piltdown case of recent years, the Glozel bones were very light in color and did not look as if anyone had attempted to make them look ancient.

A year later, while the controversy was still lively, an event occurred which provided fresh ammunition for the Glozel faction. On the 16th of November, 1929, Edmond Bayle was killed in the Palais de Justice of Paris by two revolver bullets fired by a man named Philipponnet.

The cause of the murder was relatively trivial: Philipponnet had paid 30,000 francs to the owner of a building in order to get a flat he wanted in it. (Even then, the housing shortage in France was acute.) Later, the owner of the house asserted that he had received only 12,000 francs from Philipponnet. A civil suit ensued, and an expert on questioned documents testified that the receipt had originally been written out for the full sum and that ink eradicator had been used to lower the amount. He added that with the aid of a powerful glass he could still see the original integers of the 30,000-franc figure.

The owner of the building thereupon took the receipt to Bayle himself for examination, presumably under the usual fee system for expert opinions. In a learned report, Bayle asserted that no ink eradicator had been used on the document and that the original sum had been 12,000 francs only. He regretted that in making his experiments he had been compelled to destroy that part of the receipt where the amount had been written. So great was Bayle's reputation in the Paris courts that Philipponnet lost the suit. His response was to shoot Bayle, who was immediately regarded as a martyr to the cause of justice and buried at the expense of the

French government. The Glozelians, however, smelled a rat in the destruction of the relevant portion of the receipt and set to work to scrutinize Bayle's whole career. Many peculiar matters were brought to light, but I am in no position to judge them. The matter will have to be left to the Last Court.

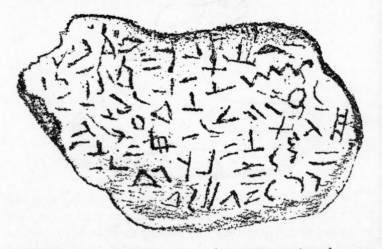

The Glozel case brought me something more precious than any fee. This was a friendship with Salomon Reinach and his wife. The childless old couple lived in a small chateau in the Bois de Boulogne outside of Paris, surrounded by books and flowers. I don't think I ever met another man who so thoroughly understood the art of living well in his old age. To sit with him and his wife, having luncheon on the terrace of the chateau on a mild spring day when the first green leaves were on the trees and the sun was shining as gently as it shines only in France, was something a man would never forget. Nor could one forget the luncheon, brought out from the house by the old cook, a very important member of the household.

In time I became so close a friend of the Reinachs that whenever I visited Paris during the early thirties I stayed with them as their guest. Salomon Reinach opened a new world to me, the world of the humanities. His opinions were an intermingling of indefinable French finesse, clarity of spirit, and humor.

But Salomon Reinach could be as terrible an antagonist as he was a good friend. His judgments were merciless. Once, when the Glozel battle was at its height, some specialist in prehistory expressed the opinion that Glozel was a fake, saying that prehistory was established on the solid base of sixty years' experience and the study of thousands of excavations. He asked, how could this pyramid of scholarship be overturned by the sole testimony of the doubtful Glozel? And he ended by saying that all specialists in prehistory resisted the Glozel evidence in the names of science and common sense alike.

Retorted Salomon Reinach: "This gentleman has a perfect right to speak in the name of the specialists in prehistory, who are just exactly that and nothing more. When a man knows neither Greek nor Latin, neither German nor English, nor yet Italian, when he does not know how to write his own language correctly—in one word, when he does not know anything—he turns to prehistory. The exceptions are very few, and there are hundreds of these specialists in prehistory to every good philologist."

In the years after I left France for Sweden, we kept up a correspondence. One day in the middle thirties I received a letter from France in a hand unfamiliar to me. In it were the tidings that Reinach had died suddenly and that his beloved wife had followed him the same afternoon.

They told me, Heraclitus, they told me you were dead;
They brought me bitter news to hear and bitter tears to shed.
I wept, as I remembered how often you and I
Had tired the sun with talking and sent him down the sky.

18

HOME TO THE NORTH

By the fall of 1928 I knew that the time had come to branch out on my own. I had graduated from the university's School of Science; my paper was a treatise on the identification of bullets and of cartridge cases fired from and by small arms—pistols and rifles. As a matter of fact, I had been on this project for about a year, collecting data on small arms ammunition from every part of the globe, and working on the spectographic analysis of powder residues. Like most police work, this research had nothing dramatic about it. Chiefly, it was a matter of collecting facts, sifting, and organizing the material. To my pleased surprise, the university faculty accepted the paper *magna cum laude*.

This gratifying estimate of my work may have been due in part to the more academic thesis which I was required to produce concurrently. I was a candidate for a doctoral degree and, in keeping with the standards of French scholarship, I was required to postulate (the correct term is "defend") two theses in order to gain my degree. This double requirement in France was a survival of medieval custom. The first thesis is necessarily a piece of original work good enough to be published as a book, but the second thesis had to be on a subject selected by the faculty. The story goes that in medieval times this gave the faculty an opportunity to reject an undesirable candidate.

Though this discriminatory purpose had been forgotten, the requirement for two theses remained, and the faculty had assigned for my topic an aspect of the diffraction of light, a complex point on which I should not wish to be questioned now. When the time for the public oral examination came round, I presented myself with only the usual amount of trepidation. It was attended by more than a normal-sized audience. Maître Locard was there, and so was most of his staff. I suspect their interest was more in my ordeal than in the refraction of light. Numerous members of the science faculty of the university were also attending out of a sense of academic propriety. The third element in the audience, the "public" representation, however, consisted of medical students who streamed into the classroom from adjoining laboratories and dissection rooms, bringing more than a whiff of formaldehyde. Their once-white smocks were stained with chemicals and blood, and their mood was hardly scientific. For the whole three hours of my examination they produced plenty of noise, had fun, and paid little attention to the diffraction and refraction of light.

Still, the examination went well. Before it was over, I had filled two blackboards with formulas and successfully withstood the interrogations of my professors. I passed. That evening, in celebration, I gave a large dinner in the private room of a favorite restaurant, *Filet de Sole*, for Locard and my colleagues in the Police Laboratory. Some of the details are hazy in my memory—perhaps due to the passage of time—but it was a very thorough party, and I do remember that Chevassus, Duffaux, Poux, and I wound up the night by having cheese soup and wine together at six the following morning.

On that glorious evening, many of the toasts pertained to my future. I had done a good deal of thinking about that. What was my future to be?

The suggestion which in one way appealed most to my sense of friendship and loyalty did not appear practical. Maître Locard had indicated that if I chose I could stay in Lyons at the Sûreté, on a salary basis. In time I might hope to become his principal aide. No more flattering invitation could have been imagined, but I was experienced enough to know that there was no real future in such a course. Already I had experienced some of the difficulties which any alien would be bound to encounter in the course of anything as essentially national as police work. The Glozel affair had showed me, by indirection, the sole advantage in belonging to another nationality, and there would not be many such chestnuts in the police fire. Certainly my French had improved enormously in the years I had spent in Lyons, but I knew that I should never lose my accent.

The saying goes that one has to live in France twenty years before losing his foreign accent and passing among Frenchmen as a native. I had had some small success posing as an Alsatian, of whom there were plenty all over France, but this was not an imposture I could hope to sustain all my working life. No, Locard's flattering suggestion was not really possible; in the long run the language obstacle would block my advancement.

There were still two other foreign proposals open to me, one from Chile, the other from Siam. The second was the more tempting in many respects. I had already seen the lovely country of Siam, and I felt a natural affinity for its kind and considerate inhabitants. The friendly sponsorship of Prince Vongsa Nirajara was not to be overlooked in this connection. The memory of his expense account alone was an inducement, and the title of Counselor to the Detective Division sounded important, even though the Detective Division was so far only a proposal on paper. The difficulty was that there did not seem to be a life's career in the job, and I felt that the time had come to embark on something permanent.

My other opportunity seemed to promise considerably more scope. The chief of the Chilean Criminal Investigation Department offered me a post under him. This proposal came about through my own marginal connection with a case involving two young Spanish anarchists who killed the Archbishop of Saragossa while that reverend gentlemen was walking in a religious procession. They succeeded in escaping to Chile. There they graduated into bank robbers and large-scale hold-up men. But when the Chilean police were ready to close in on them, they disappeared. Later, when I made the acquaintance of these gentlemen, I found to my surprise that they were two God-fearing, honest chaps who tried hard to support their old mothers in Spain. All the profits of their enterprises in Chile went to the treasury of the Anarchist Party, and they kept for themselves only enough for bare necessities. They were dedicated to the proposition that the world would be a much better place if it got rid of all kings, presidents, generals, and other officials.

One day in the late twenties King Alfonso of Spain was scheduled to make an official visit to Paris. The President of the French Republic was to welcome him at the railway station and together they were to drive through the streets of Paris in an open carriage, surrounded by the splendidly mounted Garde Republicaine. Naturally, all kinds of security measures were taken by the police, and in a last minute raid, made the morning the king was due to arrive, a rather peculiar automobile was discovered in a garage. It was a large and powerful convertible, and in its back seat was mounted a machine gun. There was a companion piece under the hood. The owners of the car were these two Spanish anarchists. When they were apprehended, they confessed willingly their intention to get as near as possible to the royal procession and kill the president and the king.

This was the first time the French authorities had been confronted with these two devoted anarchists. Under the law, their only offense was the illegal possession of machine guns, so they were sentenced to three or four months' imprisonment. The problem was, what could be done with them after they got out? One suggestion was to commit them to a lunatic asylum, but this was neither a pleasant nor a legal solution. Still, they had to be disposed of; so they were allowed to enter Switzerland, a country which in those days was a haven of refuge for political hotheads of all nations. Of course, it was almost as easy to leave Switzerland as to enter it.

So it proved in this case. One morning about six months after the two anarchists went to Switzerland, another Spaniard came to the Detective Division at the Sûreté to inform us that there were two of his fellow countrymen working in a truck factory in a suburb of the city and that he rather thought they were these two anarchists. Indeed they were. They were picked up and made no trouble at all. The only crime which could be charged against them was their illegal entry into France, and once again they drew four months' imprisonment.

But now both Spain and Chile were asking for extradition, and since the motivation for all their crimes was political, the notion of extradition and summary trials was unpleasant. The French authorities began to cast about for other possibilities.

The Chileans dispatched to Lyons a police delegation headed by Señor Mortega, chief of the Chilean Investigations Department. Their mission was to interrogate the prisoners as to their Chilean connections. Not much came of this, but the Chilean officers used the occasion to spend about a month in our laboratory, and therefore we became good friends. The two anarchists, having served their sentence, were allowed to escape to another country, and were never heard of again.

The episode apparently lingered in Señor Mortega's mind, for now he was tentatively proposing that I consider a post in his country.

Either one of these two opportunities could, I felt certain, be developed into an interesting job. The trouble was that they both had the same basic drawback as my staying on at Lyons with Locard had: the language barrier would remain, whether in Siam or Chile. To add to that disadvantage, both posts were far away from the intense European intellectual life which had become attractive to me. I felt either one would mean exile in a remote country.

There were, though, certain problems connected with going home to Sweden. Certainly no assured career waited for me there.

The Swedes are a nation of 7,000,000 people with old and deep traditions. They regarded their own institutions of higher learning as among the best, if not the very best, and there was some justification for this because Swedish academic education was—and is— really thorough. There might be no more geniuses per square mile in Sweden than elsewhere, but my fellow countrymen felt that there were more guarantees in Sweden than in most foreign countries that the geniuses would have suitable training. Most of my own higher education had been acquired abroad and, worst of all, I had just acquired a foreign doctorate. I knew that in Sweden foreign academic titles were regarded with suspicion.

To offset these drawbacks there were some strong inducements to turn my steps homeward. I had already made the acquaintance of Professor Nils Stjernberg, who taught penal law at the School of Law in Stockholm. He had promised that I could give a series of lectures in police science at the university, and this would mean a kind of official sanction of my foreign degree and training. To add to that, I was already known among the lawyers of Stockholm as an expert on questioned documents. I felt sure that I could earn enough money in that field to support myself.

Therefore the die was cast for Sweden.

I went to tell Locard about my decision. He looked me over with those wise eyes behind which there was always a trace of laughter, dug in the papers on his table, and brought out a few typewritten sheets which he gave me to read. They were a preface for my thesis, which was about to be publicly printed by a publishing house in Lyons. Locard had promised a preface, and here it was. I began to read, wondering what my mentor had found to say. His words were all that I could have hoped.

> Harry Söderman came from Scandinavia to study criminology in a French laboratory. I have followed, step by step, his clear intelligence, which is reinforced by a faultless tenacity and a strong love of work. Personally, I anticipate success only for those human beings in whom the

virtues of the spirit are allied to the merits of character. Harry Söderman is such a person. It is not a trivial circumstance that a young man who has devoted himself to an intellectual career began by traversing the deserts of Central Asia and hunting tigers along the Mekong. Nothing mediocre is to be expected from him. It is dear to my heart to have been a kind of godfather to Harry Söderman at the beginning of a career which I prophesy will be fertile, and to present to the public the first scientific work of a man for whom my estimation equals my affection.

Locard's words surprised and touched me; I felt wholly unworthy of such praise and support. The phrases of gratitude I mumbled were inadequate but, when we shook hands, speech was superfluous.

That farewell to Locard was my true departure from Lyons, but of course there were still many other hands to shake, much well-meant advice to hear, numerous bottles of Beaujolais to drink. Finally I packed two big suitcases, crated up my books in three or four wooden cases, and put myself on a train for Paris.

Two days later I stepped out on the platform of the central Stockholm station. In the whole city I knew only three or four persons at all intimately. Besides them, my assets consisted of my clothes, a couple of hundred scientific books, and four hundred Swedish crowns. A new part of my life was beginning, and it would need to commence promptly, before my money ran out.

STOCKHOLM AND NEW YORK

19

NATIVE LAND

It was early summer when I came home to Stockholm. There are people who have called it the "Venice of the North," but that seems to claim too much and too little in the same breath. Venice is a city which looks as if it rose from the sea (a flat, shallow sea at that), but Stockholm lies where rock hills slope to meet the salt water of the Saltsjö and the brackish water of great Lake Malar. It stands on spines of rock which run down into the water, and on islands which thrust upward above the level of the tides. There are countless such islands and numberless inlets, bays, and coves; still, Stockholm is a city of the land while Venice is a city of the sea.

And a deeper difference is apparent too. Venice has no real winter, but in Scandinavia winter is almost the normal climate. Even in summer it is impossible to forget that the green of the trees and lawns, the brilliant flowers, and the bright awnings of the cafés are to be seen for a few months only. As I left the station, I could feel a reminder of that in the gray of the old buildings, in the medieval part of the city where the narrow houses are huddled together as for company and warmth, and in the serrated ranks of the chimney pots above the roofs. On the sunburnished waters of the inlets and coves the shipping was clustered thick, but it was not composed of gondolas and *vaporetti*. Instead, here were coastal steamers, some of them not much bigger than tugs, loaded with every sort of produce, bustling about in the morning sun, manned by unsmiling skippers and deckhands intent on their occupation, rather than with Venice's serenading gondoliers. Stockholm, though it has its gaiety, is a serious city, a place where work goes on every day of the week.

But when I drove with my baggage to the hotel where I would be quartered for a day or two, I was thinking not of Venice but of Lyons. The years of travel and study were now over, and I was coming home to settle down and make a living in one of the most difficult of all professions. Criminology in France was an accepted science, and my degree from Lyons and my apprenticeship under Locard might have seemed to any Frenchman a springboard, but in my home country, Sweden, that was far from certain. In police science France was far in advance of the rest of Europe, and the citizens of small countries—particularly the Swedes—do not like to be told, much less shown, that they are lagging behind anyone else.

I knew there would be other difficulties as well. I had grown accustomed to the free-and-easy ways of Lyons, and the informality of the Sûreté, where protocol was often disregarded. Stockholm would not tolerate manners which might have seemed the height of punctilio in Lyons. Now I should have to dress according to my station, stay where I belonged, and comport myself with decorum. Onion soup in the market place as the dawn appeared would henceforth be a thing of the past.

These reflections did not dampen my delight in being back where I belonged, but they colored my approach to the future. I faced it without trepidation, however, possibly because police work was an old story in the Söderman family. As I unpacked my belongings, I thought back to my father's tales of his life as a police chief and decided that no matter how many difficulties I might have to confront, they could hardly be more rugged than those he had met.

In the eighteen seventies my father, Pehr Söderman, secured appointment as public prosecutor, tax collector, and police chief of the village and district of Delsbö. Each of the three aspects of his job was notably unpopular with the citizenry. Perhaps their objection to tax collectors was no more than a normal human reaction, but the police and prosecution facets of his job were actively resented. Delsbö was a tough district. The sturdy peasants who lived on the farms around its numerous beautiful lakes were not poor or underprivileged, but they had a name for—and pride in—preserving their ancient customs, continuing to wear their traditional costumes, and distilling their own alcohol without bothering about revenue regulations and licenses. They were accustomed to settle any difficulties among themselves without recourse to the processes of law. Most troublesome of all, the young bloods were the terror of county fairs, and few dared oppose them. Like the Hitler Brown Shirts years later, they recognized one another and stuck together in every fracas and brawl. Aside from these adverse factors, Delsbö had more than its share of Gypsies, who were equally proficient at using knives and stealing horses.

At the time when my father went to the region his task was regarded as something worse than thankless. The local saying went that there were only two possible courses of action for a police chief in the area—howl with the wolves, or perish. My father came close to perishing more than once.

For instance, his house was on one occasion blown up by a bomb, but the family escaped unscathed. There are conflicting family versions about Father's reaction. My half-sister claims that he cried out from the midst of the bedclothes in which he was entangled like Laocoon, "God have mercy on our souls!" On the other hand, my half-brother, a gay blade now in his seventies, always quotes Father as exclaiming: "Now everything's going to hell!"

In confronting this district-wide absence of enthusiasm for law and order, my father relied on help from the local constable, whose nickname was somewhat sinister—*Kniven*, the Knife. For years this man served faithfully under my father without the least irregularity, and they had several close escapes together. Once they had gone out looking for one of the illegal stills. Their information was

that the moonshiner was concealing his apparatus at the bottom
of a small lake in the middle of the forest. Father and the constable went to this lake and built a rough log raft, on which they
paddled out to fish for the equipment. While they were grappling
about, they were startled by a volley from the bushes along the
shore. Fortunately, the initial fusillade missed both of them, but
most of the farmers of that region were good shots, so Father and
the constable decided not to crowd their luck. They dived head-
long and sought refuge under the raft, sticking their noses up for
air now and then. Every time they made the least move there was
a fresh volley of shots from the shore. Eventually they made their
escape in the dark, long after sunset. Experiences like these made
the two men fast friends.

In his liking for Kniven, Father may also have been swayed by
pity for the man's unhappy past. Kniven had been orphaned and
reared at village expense. The boy was redheaded, and this made
him a natural target for the children as he grew up. They teased
him about his hair, his birth, and his lowly social standing. When
Kniven was old enough to do so he enlisted in the army. On his
return from service, he became the village constable, and his whole
character thereafter was built around his official function. The law
he served to the best of his abilities offered him protection against
the slights and scorn he had endured as a boy.

Unfortunately for Kniven, after some years my father left the
district to study law and advance himself in his career as a civil
servant. Father's successor at Delsbö did not like Kniven, and
Kniven was cashiered for the alleged embezzlement of a sum
equivalent to seventy-five cents. Thereupon the new superintendent
hired another constable, perhaps not wisely. Kniven was an experienced man and would not have been caught as the new constable
and the superintendent were when they went to arrest a young
cripple in a farmhouse. This fellow had a rifle hidden under his
bedclothes, and he killed both officers.

This dramatic event did not help Kniven. He had taken a small leasehold in the neighborhood and lived on it with his housekeeper. But he had a constant struggle to earn a living, for his enemies among the lawless made life unbearable for him now that he no longer had his office to protect him. He fell into somber brooding about the injustices inflicted upon him, and soon he became the leader of the ruffians of the district.

His only link with the world of decency was his housekeeper, who begged him not to become an outlaw. One morning he took her out in a rowboat on an island lake and threw her overboard. The report goes that when the poor woman tried to cling to the gunwale of the boat, Kniven took up a small hatchet and chopped off her fingers. With that murder he became a professional in the ugly business of killing. It was said that he would kill anybody for money, and that his fees ranged from a low of twenty-five dollars for an old woman to a high of seventy-five for a strong adult.

He and his gang also specialized in arson and other crimes, and for a time they were unchecked. But, as it always happens, in the end the organized forces of society caught up with this savage band. In an effort to escape punishment Kniven turned Crown Witness, and denounced his former companions. His confession put the police on the track of about fifteen serious crimes which were in preparation but which had not yet been committed. Since in Sweden the prosecutor has no power to compromise the final charge, Kniven found himself in jail awaiting the death sentence, which still existed in those days.

My father was by this time installed in a more northerly district, and Kniven wrote him a series of letters. Years later I found them in an old envelope case on which my father had writen in his bold and characteristic hand the single word *Knivabrefen*—the Knife Letters. Evidently Kniven had turned religious in the shadow of his execution; on the whole the letters made dull reading, like most tracts. His misfortunes he traced almost wholly to his having been unjustly discharged from service by my father's successor.

Kniven's story was a favorite of my father's when I was a boy.
Just what his personal verdict on it was I never knew, but there
was an ironic undertone as he told how the judge who had sentenced Kniven to the executioner's axe had persuaded Father, out
of humanitarian motives, to go down to Stockholm to present the
case to the King, the elderly Oscar II. Something about the story
must have moved the King, because he commuted Kniven's sentence to hard labor for life. All through this period Kniven re-
tained some portion of the piety he had acquired in "the death
house," to use an American term, but, when he was pardoned after
twenty-five years in the penitentiary, he found that his plot of
land had become valuable by reason of a new real-estate development. In his new affluence he abandoned his piety. However, by
then he had only a year to live.

Probably every young man thinks a good deal about his father's
experience at the moments when he feels his own career is at a
turning point. At least, that is what I did during those early days
in Stockholm when I was deciding just how to plan my future.
I felt sure that it would be impossible for me to be the kind of man
my father had been. Every son sees his father in part as a fragment
of history, if it is fair to say that history is everything that goes
before the conscious experience of the son. But in the case of my
own father, this view was perhaps more than ordinarily true. Pehr
Söderman was undoubtedly born a few hundred years too late, for
he had qualities which would have made a great adventurer in an
earlier century.

Certainly at Lyons no stress had been laid upon physical prowess,
for instance, and yet this had been a part of my father's equipment
essential for his survival in the kind of police work which his post
demanded. Another of his stories, recounted with relish and no
self-admiration, had to do with an occasion on which his life had
been at forfeit. The incident was a far cry from my own mentally
agonizing period of waiting until the detective squad rescued my
friend Savitch and me from that eternity of waiting in the Lyons
gambling salon over the bakery.

My father was in the habit of playing cards in the evenings at a tavern in the Delsbö district, near the railroad station. The walk to this place was only about a mile from his house by a road leading through a forest. Not infrequently one or another of his enemies hid in a ditch beside the road, intending to shoot him. For this reason Father formed the habit of going home through the woods.

One Saturday evening he forwent this precaution and followed the road. Coming round a corner, he met six or seven young toughs who saw a unique opportunity to eliminate their enemy. They seized him and threw him into a clay pit. Then, using a timber pole from a handy hay-drying hurdle, they set to work to pulverize him, like a substance caught between mortar and pestle. Father kept his head and managed to direct the end of the pole to one side of his body or the other. Eventually the cheerful bully boys decided that he must be dead and repaired to an illegal still in a neighboring farmhouse. There the gang put on a notable celebration.

Meanwhile, the fearsome Pehr Söderman managed to get himself out of the pit. Covered with blood, his clothes torn to rags, he was nevertheless inspired by a consuming rage as he ran back to the tavern. There he got a horse and sleigh and set out at once along the winding, snowy forest roads. He had recognized several of his assailants and had a shrewd idea where to go. Alone, standing upright in the sleigh and whipping the horses, he whirled toward the farm house on the hill.

He certainly made quite a sight standing in the door of the huge kitchen, covered with blood and surrounded by swirling snow. "I must have looked like a ghost," was the way father described the effect of his appearance on the celebrating malefactors. The fight was gone out of them, and Father had no difficulty in tying them, one after another, to a long rope. This he fastened to the sleigh and whipped the horse. They set off for jail in a long, stumbling train. It must have been a sobering run through that icy winter night.

However, the case did not end altogether properly. My father, the prosecutor of the district, was also the only witness in the case. This made conviction impossible, particularly as the young braves had mustered up courage again and denied their guilt individually and collectively. There were, in those days as now, circumstances known as "the law's delays," and though in the end they were freed, that was not until they had spent three years in jail awaiting "release." Whenever my father told the story, we youngsters felt that life imprisonment was the least those criminals should have received, but I am not sure that he felt that way. He used to tell us the tale on the porch at Kalarne, in the long summer evenings, and each time his blue eyes crinkled, and each time he roared with laughter as he described the long snake of culprits, tied to the rope, running for dear life along the icy roads, skidding, falling, and rising to run again.

Remembering the relish and gusto with which my father had lived his life and confronted the vicissitudes of a police career was good for my morale, but it was also urgent that I take immediate and prosaic steps to get established. A room in a small hotel was no base of operations for a beginning criminologist. True, the room, though small, was plenty large enough for my store of worldly possessions, which consisted merely of two suitcases, one heavy with books and another (which I wished were heavier) containing my clothes. There was no great burden of currency in my wallet, either. It behooved me not to let the grass grow under my feet.

After coming home from France, I found Stockholm almost a foreign city. I had to locate a flat large enough to house myself and my laboratory-studio, preferably also my younger sister, who had just graduated from junior college and had taken a temporary office job before continuing her studies.

Years earlier, in my travels to the East, I had made the acquaintance of Hugo Thörnblad, then in the Swedish consular service in Calcutta. He was now in Stockholm, representing the American advertising firm of J. Walter Thompson. I had called on him and outlined my plight, and he introduced me to a friend of his, Mats

Stenström, a newspaperman. These two friends may have left a few stones unturned in their efforts to help me but, if so, not many.

Within a few days Stenström got wind of a modern, three-room flat on the third floor of a brand-new building, and I leased it at once. The largest of the rooms was for my laboratory and studio, one smaller room for my sister, the other for myself. The kitchen had to do double duty as a dark room.

Next came the question of outfitting the place. Stenström was a designer of talent, and he drew up the plans for some inexpensive but attractive bookshelves and a laboratory counter. These I commissioned from a carpenter and painted red with black edgings, Very handsome they looked. I was also able to arrange a long-range credit with the famous German firm of Carl Zeiss, from whom I secured a good microscope and a micro-camera and essential accessories.

Thus settled and outfitted, I was ready for business, but the question of how to find it gave me a good deal of anxiety.

Under Thörnblad's friendly supervision I prepared some simple and carefully-worded advertisements which informed the people of Stockholm that Dr. Harry Söderman, consulting criminologist, was available to undertake the examination of physical evidence. Dr. Söderman especially solicited work in connection with disputed documents and handwriting comparisons.

Almost from the start, these public notices brought me in enough work for a modest living. It appeared that I had come to the city at an opportune moment; there were only two established experts in this field, and both of them were elderly men. The lawyers seemed to fancy my more modern training and French background.

Although I analyzed a certain number of suspected arson cases for insurance companies, most of my first assignments had to do with questions of authenticity in connection with sight drafts. Sweden was the country of the sight draft. In other nations, such drafts were almost wholly employed as commercial paper by business and trading firms, but in Sweden they had a vast circulation among all classes of the population. Any bank would accept a bill of draft from an individual if it had one or two co-signers of good credit standing. The due date was not of paramount importance. A draft could be renewed indefinitely if the interest was paid regularly and a modest payment made against retirement of the principal. This practice went to such lengths that it was said a good many university students financed their college careers on these sight drafts.

Today, regulations are more stringent, but my early months in Stockholm were greatly eased by this pleasant usage. The sensation of being established on my own was richly rewarding, though I did occasionally feel nostalgia for the Lyons days.

20

THE BEARD OF THE SAGE

Soon after my return to Stockholm I had the pleasure of being elected a member of the Travelers' Club, because of my journeys in Asia. Sweden is a small country as far as population is concerned, and therefore its citizens, if they travel any distance at all, are considered world travelers. This interest in the outside world provided one common bond among the members. Another was—and is—the fact that the Club does not regard conformity as the chief human virtue. The membership ranged from pure scientists and savants through adventurers to pure eccentrics. Under just which heading I was admitted is a point I have never examined too closely.

In any event, belonging to the Club was a delight to me. I did not join it to make advantageous business connections but rather for companionship and stimulus. There was plenty of both, and not long after I had been admitted I found also a link with my French years which resulted in an episode illustrating the diversity of character in which the Club abounded. The roots of the affair went back to the paleontological enigma of the Glozel farm and the Fradin family.

One of the voices in the noisy choir of scientists who were denouncing Glozel as the greatest archeological fake of the century belonged to a fellow countryman whom I shall call Count Claus von Gravling. In several violent newspaper articles von Gravling had asserted that Dr. Morlet and the Fradins were forgers and not even clever ones. I knew by hearsay that von Gravling was, among many other things, an amateur archeologist, and I also knew that he was a cousin of a friend of mine, another Count whom I shall call Hugo Taxenstern. Through the good offices of Taxenstern, an introduction to von Gravling was arranged.

Knowing Taxenstern, I was prepared to find von Gravling somewhat off the beaten path of human personality, and in this expectation I was not disappointed. It takes a number of collaborating circumstances to produce such atypical characters. First, they must be continental Europeans. Second, they must be descended from old families. Third, they require wealth to bring them to full flower. Not that they would have been obscure figures without wealth; these were both men of intellectual endowment, and without question they would have developed out of poor families into famous university professors. But their private wealth allowed them to apply sound scientific training against idiosyncrasies of personal leisure. They were both notable eccentrics, and in this regard it would be impossible to award the final palm to one above the other.

Taxenstern's interest in me sprang from my training in criminology, which appealed to him because he was a prolific writer of detective stories. Bitter necessity had forced him into this vineyard. His wife controlled the family estate, and she ran it in a hard-headed manner, with a rein much too tight to suit Taxenstern's tastes. He told his friends, however, that the climate of his ancestral acres was inimical to true cerebration. Whether his definition of the word climate was meteorological or social, he never bothered to explain. In any event, the climate of Stockholm did not hinder his unparalleled cerebration, either by day or by night. He possessed a fund of information almost equal to that of the Britannica, and every entry was always ready for use. He might be asked what sort of footgear was worn by the early Aztecs or for details of the latest advances in nuclear physics, and he could produce an immediate answer.

Taxenstern was a man of vast aplomb and assurance. It was believed in his own circle that only once in his life had he been caught at a loss. That was the day on which his noble beard turned violet and he was compelled to display this phenomenon to his cronies at a Club dinner. I have the story from an eyewitness, a journalist friend now long since dead, who used to recount the details with relish.

"It started with Kollan's fiftieth birthday," my friend used to begin, somewhat in the manner of Lord Dunsany's Jorkens. "Kollan was an art critic and a great friend of all of us, and the occasion certainly called for some special attention. Months and months beforehand Taxenstern, who admired Kollan in many ways, went to work on his golden jubilee gift for the critic and really put himself to the most enormous pains over it. The gift consisted of an elaborate genealogical chart, confected with the utmost skill and pains. On it appeared a complete set of imaginary ancestors for Kollan, clear on back to a spurious Roman senator named K. Collanius. That will give you some idea of the thought Taxenstern put into this friendly hoax; most people think they know that there was no K in Latin, but this is not quite true. The K had originally existed in the Roman alphabet, and though it was later supplanted by C in every other case, it was occasionally used in proper-name abbreviations. That kind of minute fact was the pride and joy of old Taxenstern's encyclopedic mind.

"Anyhow, from this non-existent Collanius the chart descended an endless staircase of feudal lords, medieval bankers, princes earthly and princes spiritual, merchants, captains, and Heaven knows what-all till it reached our friend Kollan himself. And that was not all. For every major entry on the chart Taxenstern had supplied the most plausible supporting documents and records. There were yellowed medieval parchments with huge wax seals, and even letters written in purple ink on a Cardinal's authentic personal stationery. It was magnificent, and Taxenstern must have put the better part of two years into its making. In the end he loaded the hundreds of documents and the chart into a big chest. Of course," my friend observed, "it was a practical joke. But it was also a labor of love undertaken to entertain an admired friend."

As I heard the tale unfold, I could not help reflecting that a man with Taxenstern's ingenuity and patience would hardly be likely to doubt that the Glozel treasures had been faked—unless by one of his superiors in the art, and it is to be doubted whether Taxenstern ever had a superior.

"Alas," my friend continued, "when the birthday celebration took place and the chest was presented to Kollan, he did not understand the joke. If not offended, he was at least indifferent. Poor Taxenstern was upset by his friend's lack of appreciation, but Kollan was a good-hearted man and, when he heard about Taxenstern's disappointment, he invited him—and me—to dinner the next evening. Before the dinner he made a short speech of gratitude for the unique gift; Taxenstern was much relieved and perked up at once. It was a convivial evening.

"Now Taxenstern and I happened to live not far from each other, so when the evening was over we set out for home together. When we came to the corner where our ways would part Taxenstern, now in high spirits, invited me up to his flat to sample some Rhine wine he had just laid in, but I was not feeling my best at the time and declined. While we were disputing the matter, a lady came up and greeted us. Perhaps I should say she accosted us." His face took on an expression of inner joy at this point in the narrative. "I recognized the woman at once. She was a seamstress of uncertain age but with an overdeveloped enthusiasm for the opposite sex. All of us in the district who came home late had encountered her roaming the streets in search of a man on whom to donate her favors. For the first time I was pleased to see her, because the argument with Taxenstern was getting out of hand. So I talked him into inviting her to share the Rhine wine. Somewhat reluctantly, she agreed. My conscience did not trouble me because I knew that in addition to the wine all she would get out of him would be a one- or two-hour lecture on some scientific subject. Then he would turn her out.

"At dinnertime next evening Taxenstern came into the Club without his customary air of assurance. Underneath his furious eyes and haggard face, that majestic beard flowed downward and outward as usual except for the fact that it was no longer white but a deep and startling violet. Of course none of us mentioned the matter for a while, but after the meal I took him aside and asked him what had happened.

" 'It's all the fault of that horrible woman,' he whispered in a husky voice. 'And, incidentally, your fault, too.'

" 'How so?' I asked. 'How could I have caused your beard to change color?'

" 'You got me mixed up with her. She came up to my place and stayed a good two hours. We had a couple of bottles of that Rhine wine you missed, and I gave her some really good advice about the care and feeding of Alsatian dogs. Then I recollected that after all she was only a woman and might not be interested in Alsatians, so I took her home and gave her a chivalrous embrace on her doorstep. Then on the way home I got to thinking about bacteria. That kiss could have transmitted several loathsome diseases. Unfortunately, the only disinfectant which I had in my home was permanganate of potassium. But the light had gone out in my bathroom and when I was mixing the permanganate the glass broke and I spilt the damned stuff on my beard. You see the result. I think I shall have to confine myself to my room for a few days till I can get rid of the dye.'

"But," added my journalist friend with relish, "for a long time afterwards Taxenstern's beard remained a shade reddish."

Whatever the shade of his beard, Taxenstern was an ornament to the Travelers' Club, and we became fast friends. Of our interests in common the Glozel affair was only one. My possession of a micro-photography camera played a larger role. Taxenstern had a private laboratory on his estate, but his symbiotic relationship with his wife did not extend to his being allowed the extravagance of one of these precision instruments. The object of his affection was a certain bacterium which was comparatively easy to photograph. Taxenstern spent the last years of his life studying this one-celled form of life, which was to be found only on the leaves of the potato plant, and he loved the thing like an only-begotten child. Life, however, seldom allows the luxury of a monopoly, and poor Taxenstern was plagued by some German who claimed priority in the discovery. He and this German battled it out in scientific journals. Who got the final credit I never knew, and with Taxenstern's death the affair dwindled into silence. But how often I helped him photograph his subvisible pet!

Taxenstern's enthusiasm for this botanical parasite brought him into direct conflict with his relative von Gravling. The two men were most unlike and, while I found it easy to enjoy Taxenstern's special eccentricities, von Gravling was somewhat harder to appreciate. He had started his academic life as a botanist and had earned a Master of Science degree. He made the acquaintnce of a young lady who was studying chemistry at the university, and the fact that she happened to be the daughter of a very wealthy mill owner did not dim his ardor. In a short time they married, but her father disapproved of the alliance, and the couple did not get a cent out of him as long as he lived. When he died, they came into a large fortune, whereupon von Gravling embarked upon the expansive life he preferred. In the midst of a fishing village in southern Sweden he built a small town of his own which included, among other things, a huge dining hall reinforced by an excellent kitchen, a complete library of cook books, and one of the best wine cellars in northern Europe. There were also guest houses, a botanical laboratory, a garden, and an archeology museum. Throughout the year, von Gravling maintained open house, some of his guests being the most famous scientists on the Continent. Like his relative Taxenstern, he too had a varied record of published books, including a manual of zoology for schoolteachers and a treatise on the history of Cuba.

Von Gravling had already put himself on record as believing that Glozel was a hoax, and I was extremely anxious to meet him since I did not feel that his published remarks constituted a refutation of the authenticity of the farm's artifacts. One night at the Club I explained my connection with the Glozel enigma, and von Gravling, out of pity for the benighted young man before him, invited me to his home for a full discussion.

The evening was a great disappointment to me. I had hoped for a scholarly refutation of the evidence. What I got instead was excellent food and drink and a great deal of pontification on the subject of credulity. This is not a commodity which criminologists keep in stock, and I am afraid we separated somewhat coolly, in spite of the hospitality. I found the evening unhappy in more than this respect; the man knew less about Glozel than I did, and he exhibited the preliminary manifestations of the palsy which was to end his life spectacularly. His wife was already living elsewhere—probably out of self-defense—and he looked as gross and domineering as the popular portrait of Dr. Samuel Johnson. His conversation was as dogmatic as the great doctor's was at its most crushing.

Not long afterward, von Gravling suffered a stroke which left him partially paralyzed. He was taken to a clinic where examination revealed that in addition to the effects of the stroke, he was suffering from a malignant tumor of the stomach. The doctors prescribed an operation and subsequent treatment, but von Gravling imperiously refused their advice. He declared that he trusted only French physicians, ordered a private car to be attached to the Paris train, took with him his trusted valet, Carl, who spoke nothing but Swedish, and off he went to gay Paris.

What followed was a grotesque cavalcade which still makes the conservative elements of his family shudder. At first he went around to different clinics in Paris but was turned away from one after another, partly because of his incurable condition, partly because of his violent temper. Then, sending Carl home because the man's inability to speak French made him useless, von Gravling abandoned Paris and started a tour of the famous French resorts. He was accompanied by two beautiful French nurses and was carried about on a stretcher. It was at this point that I was approached by his family, for the count was spending money at a speed which would quickly diminish their hoped-for heritage. The family supposed that my relations with the French police would enable me to have him deported from France to his native Sweden. But I declined to be mixed up in this kind of situation.

Von Gravling, however, got wind of the family's plot and had himself removed to Nice, on the sun-swept azure coast. There in one of the largest hotels he rented a magnificent room the size of a banquet hall. He hired two strong men, called for the sake of courtesy "private detectives," to protect him. No one could enter his room without scrutiny by one of these gentlemen.

Every evening this huge room was the setting for a feast unparalleled since those given by Lucretia Borgia for her father, Pope Alexander VI, in medieval Rome. Von Gravling's bed was in the center of the room. Around the walls stood supper tables, loaded with fine foods, wines and liquors. The guest list was less distinguished. One of the "detectives" would roam the streets and the waterfront to invite for supper every whore or pimp he could find. When the bottles had been drained, the floor of the room as well as the tables became the scene of lascivious proceedings. Immovable on his bed in the center, von Gravling silently watched everything.

Before the news of von Gravling's decadent mode of living reached Sweden, it came to the ears of the local Swedish consul in Nice, a religious and sedate man who felt that the honor of his country was at stake. After trying unsuccessfully to get in touch with von Gravling, he alerted the family. It was decided to send a distant relative, a well-known judge, to bring von Gravling home. This judge was a shrewd man. He knew that the count had not paid his bill at one of the private clinics in Paris. He therefore went to Paris, looked up the physician in charge of the clinic, and promised not only to pay the old debt but also to pay a handsome fee if the doctor would accompany him to Nice in order to break the resistance of the headstrong von Gravling.

They took the night train for Nice and, on arrival, walked straight into von Gravling's hotel and told the receptionist that one of them was a doctor who had been called because von Gravling was dying. After having gained admittance, they found the prodigal peacefully snoring and probably dreaming about the debauches of the night before. The Parisian doctor gave him a shot of a strong sedative and declared him to be in a dying state. In a few hours, von Gravling was snoring away in an ambulance car attached to a train for Sweden. Every time he tried to wake up on that forty-eight-hour journey, he was given a fresh shot. Thus, von Gravling began his nap in Nice and awoke in southern Sweden.

The family's commando operation was not wholly successful. Whether because of the development of his tumor, or because he had been subjected to too many narcotics, von Gravling did not respond to the purer atmosphere of Sweden. In a few days he died. The family then discovered that, with the consent of his wife, he had left his money to several institutions of higher learning rather than to those diligent relatives who had rescued him from his career of moral turpitude. Even the beneficiary institutions hesitated about accepting the money because of von Gravling's lurid end, but they finally found it possible and proper to do so.

After the deaths of von Gravling and Taxenstern I no longer saw or talked with anyone directly interested in the Glozel affair. In the career of any criminologist, the number of unsolved mysteries is not so large as popular imagination would have it, and probably the case never entirely faded from my mind. But when I came to set down the first draft of these memoirs, I felt an attack of something that might almost be called conscience. Salomon Reinach's death in 1932 had almost ended the matter for me, and I had not been abreast of the few developments that had followed. Yet here was a mystery far more intriguing than the solution of any particular crime, a mystery about the whole human story. My curiosity was roused again.

Almost a quarter of a century had passed. I did not even know whether Dr. Morlet was still alive after World War II. If this last great fighter for the authenticity of the Glozel artifacts had disappeared or died, it was a fair assumption that the anti-Glozelians, supported by Bayle's analyses, had said the final word.

Resolving to learn what had happened in the intervening years, while I was in the United States I went first to the New York Public Library. It is a credit to that library that Reinach's books on the subject were on its shelves. But those volumes had been printed in the days of the great battle. There was, it appeared, no more recent reference to Glozel in any scholarly dictionary or work of reference. Not even a monograph. *Vanitas vanitatum!* It seemed incredible that this affair, which had impassioned so many scientific minds and been the cause of so many headlines, could have been completely forgotten in a mere twenty-five years.

I wrote a letter to my old friend Marcel Sicot, the Inspector General of the French Sûreté, asking him to look into the status of Morlet and Glozel. Almost incredibly, the very day after I had mailed my letter, I received one from Morlet! He had sent it to Stockholm, and it had been forwarded to my house in Palisades, New York. What a coincidence! On the exact day I had started to think about Glozel again, old Morlet, still working as a doctor in Vichy, had broken the silence of twenty-five years!

In his letter he asked me if the Carbon 14 method could be employed in deciding the age of the artifacts of Glozel. The Carbon 14 test is one of the major new tools of scientific research. It is based on the fact that all organic material which is buried in the soil carries within it, from the time when it was part of a living organism, an infinitely minute quantity of a radioactive isotope of carbon called Carbon 14. This Carbon 14 loses its radioactivity at a certain established rate. For instance, half of the radioactivity will be lost after about six thousand years. Dr. Willard F. Libby, of the University of Chicago, demonstrated that it is possible to measure this loss of radioactivity by a sensitive Geiger counter and thereby establish the age of any appropriate object with surprising certainty. The margin of error normally amounts to only a few hundred years.

I replied to Morlet that it would be a great pleasure for me to aid him in establishing the age of the artifacts, and that I would get in touch with qualified American scientists if he would send me some objects to be analyzed. A few days later he airmailed me a small tin chocolate box. In it were a number of artifacts, most of them carved bones, wrapped in tissue paper and embedded in cotton.

It was with very peculiar feelings, and even emotion, that I un-wrapped those things. One piece of bone was covered with the mystical signs—perhaps alphabetical—which had once given rise to so many discussions. Another, and the esthetically priceless one if it should ever be declared authentic, was delicately carved with the shapes of galloping reindeer. As I looked at it, in my mind the persistent problem rose again: How could a twenty-year-old peasant boy, who had never displayed any artistic talents and certainly had never seen a living reindeer, not to speak of a galloping one, have made this beautiful and timeless image on a piece of fossilized bone?

There was even a second coincidence. On the evening of that same day, my wife and I had been invited to dine at the home of a famous surgeon, Dr. C. D. Haaginsen, one of our neighbors in Snedens Landing, New York. I knew that his daughter, young Mrs. Robert Gerard, was an archeologist, and that her husband, a geographer, also had archeological interests. I knew that they would be at the dinner, so I took the objects along with me. When the young couple saw the artifacts and heard my story they told me that I had not far to go to find a Carbon 14 laboratory. Only half a mile away was the Lamont Geological Laboratory, an affili-ate of Columbia University, where there is one of the foremost Carbon 14 laboratories in the United States.

For a brief moment I had hopes of an early and definite answer to the riddle of Glozel. These hopes were dashed by the discovery that the specimens which Dr. Morlet had sent me would not, in themselves, necessarily establish the age of anything except the bones themselves. Fossil reindeer bones from that part of France would admittedly be old, but the age of the carving could not be established by the age of the bones. For that, an artifact bearing some evidence of contemporary charring or firing would be required, so that the antiquity of the human workmanship could be established along with that of the bone itself. Now, such fragments, if there were any, had not been preserved at Glozel. Dr. Morlet and his supporters, if he had any in this twilight of the affair, would need to dig again and find specimens which could prove the case beyond any cavil. This new excavation would require careful authentication, and I did not know whether that would be possible.

Therefore the Glozel affair remains the most puzzling enigma of my experience. It ought to be of enormous importance to the whole civilized world. The fact that words such as "hoax" and "fraud" have been applied to the artifacts does not settle the matter. To a criminologist, the evidence seems too extensive and intricately perfect to be the work of ignorant and provincial French farm people. Even the far less intricate fraud of the Piltdown Man had been perpetrated by men of scientific training and background. If the Fradin family had labored, with an artistic genius equal to that of the painters of the Altamira caves, to perpetrate such an inexplicable hoax, what had they gotten out of it?

In any event, there the matter stands at the moment. Perhaps the Glozel story is not over; another such site may be found, an artifact may be uncovered which will permit the proper use of the Carbon 14 test, or, just conceivably, some scholar may some day decipher the magical runes on those ancient reindeer bones.

21

ANONYMOUS ATTACKS

My reputation as an expert on questioned documents continued to grow. I was able to increase my fees to the point where the Zeiss microscope became wholly my own. The time came, of course, when this increased volume of cases congested my small establishment, so I moved my work and equipment into a regular office suite. Although the expense disturbed me at the time, I soon found plenty of additional clients to cover the cost, and even to permit a gradual broadening in the variety of cases. The old reliable sight-draft cases, the arson investigations, and the forged documents began to be interspersed with cases of different kinds.

One of these occupied only fifteen minutes of a gray October morning. The office telephone on my new desk emitted the low buzz which meant that my secretary wanted to talk to me. I picked up the receiver.

"Yes?"

The secretary's voice was so muted that I could hardly hear her; I knew from that circumstance alone that she judged the matter was not an emergency.

"There is a lady here to see you. She says it is confidential and she can talk to no one else."

"So," I said. "Is she alone?"

"Oh, yes."

I sighed. Although any client is welcome when there is rent to pay and other expenses to meet, there is a certain kind of case which is unwelcome because it involves a larger element of human advice than skill. In my youth I once had an elderly professor of chemistry for teacher, and in a moment of exasperation he had uttered a truth which has stood me in good stead: "I have given out a lot of good advice, but no one has ever taken it." My immediate instinct was that the lady in the outer office had somewhere in her handbag a letter of a familiar kind.

"Send her in," I told my secretary with a sigh.

And in she came. One glance at her and my preliminary suspicion was strengthened. Her eyes were hot with anger, and she was blushing violently.

"Dr. Söderman," she said, without any preliminaries, "I have received a horrible letter. An anonymous letter."

"Sit down, Madame," I said. "Sit down and try to believe what I tell you."

Reluctantly she seated herself in the chair across the desk and began to grope in her handbag. "I have the letter here."

"Yes," I told her. "I am sure you do."

"Here it is."

I did not take the thing. "Madame, I asked you to try to believe me. Don't show me the letter. Here." I shoved the wastebasket toward her. "Tear it up and throw the pieces in there."

"But you can't mean it!"

"I do mean it," I replied. "Tear it up and throw the pieces away." I looked at her with what I hope was a sympathetic expression.

"But," she protested, "I thought you were an expert in forgeries and . . . and . . . things like that."

"Perhaps," I replied. "But anonymous letters are generally not worth bothering with."

She blushed again. "This one is. It says terrible things."

"About you and someone else," I told her. "Perhaps your husband, perhaps another woman, perhaps another man."

"Well, in a way . . ."

I told her about the professor of chemistry. "Look, Madame," I went on, "these things are very expensive to investigate, and they are not worth the expense. Whoever wrote that letter has already got what he or she wanted, which was to stir up your feelings. It takes a lot of strength of character and nobility of mind to resist the temptation to do exactly what the person who wrote that letter hopes you will do."

She kept looking at me with a sort of wondering doubt in her expression. "But I want to know who wrote it."

"Of course. That's only human. But it might cost a lot of money to find out. Whatever the letter says, and whether it is true or a lie, you can't possibly do yourself any good by investigating it. You cannot gain anything by exposing the writer, ninety-nine times out of a hundred."

She looked at the wastebasket. "But suppose there are more of these?"

"There are plenty of wastebaskets," I replied.

"This is certainly not what I expected to hear when I came to your office," she said uncertainly.

"I know," I said. "And if you insist, I'll see what can be done. But in most cases it's a difficult business to identify the writing. Even if there is a sure identification of the handwriting, the courts are generally reluctant to convict on that evidence alone. A trial of the case will drag you through exactly the kind of mire the writer had in mind when the letter was composed and sent."

"So there isn't any protection against this kind of thing?"

I shook my head. "Only within yourself."

Slowly and thoughtfully she tore the letter and put the pieces in my wastebasket. Then she thanked me, we shook hands, and she left. I watched her go with respect. Few people have the courage to confront a cowardly and ugly thing like an anonymous letter and face it down alone. Yet that is almost always the wisest course.

No normal person with a modicum of good character and a normal standard of judgment writes anonymous letters. In the many cases where the writers have been exposed, it has always developed that there was something or other wrong with them. It is hard to put a finger on some special spot and say that this or that makes a person write anonymous letters. The flaws seem to range from ordinary meanness and vulgarity through an ugly scale of hysteria and sexual deprivations.

If the letters are directed to, and apply to, only one particular person, there should certainly not be much ado about them at any official level. On the other hand, when the letters are directed to someone other than the person they concern and might do serious harm, the police give all the protection they can. But the police are often helpless in such cases. They have to confine themselves to collecting the names of suspects from the victim, securing specimens of the handwriting or typewriting of the suspects, and then turning the affair over to an examiner of questioned documents. But in most cases the victim will not be able to name a suspect. Then the only way is to ask the recipient of the letters to turn over any further letters to the police without opening them or at least without touching the interior. That preserves the possibility of finding fingerprints on the letter or discovering some other means of identification, though fingerprints on paper disappear quickly and haste is imperative.

A most extraordinary case dealing with anonymous letters came up in France. It began in 1917 and was not solved until the twenties. This was the so-called *affaire de Tulle*. Much has been written about it because it had many interesting facets. I had the inside story from Dr. Locard himself.

"*Il n'y a rien plus sale que le rêve d'un saint*—(There is nothing dirtier than the dream of a saint)," Locard began when he told me the story, and he was undoubtedly right.

Tulle is a medium-sized city, the capital of the department of Corrèze, in south central France. It has some importance as a provincial capital, but in the third year of World War I it was a calm, almost sleepy place. The young men of the town and even most males of middle age were fighting for France in the trenches, and in the sidewalk cafés the remaining *bourgeois* discussed the war news and food prices just as in happier and calmer days they had discussed the interest rate of bonds or the eternal squabble between church and government. In the parks the children played in the sand, and the only unusual aspect of the town's life was the presence of soldiers on furlough or invalided home.

But in the midst of this idyl something happened which put tongues to wagging. Toward the end of 1917 several prominent citizens, mainly civil servants, received by mail anonymous letters which referred to long-forgotten and well-buried scandals. One recipient was informed that his grandfather had been a swindler and forger, another that his grandmother had had a child before she married, a third that one of his cousins had died in the penitentiary fifty years ago, and so on.

Most of the recipients of these letters did not complain. Then came a wave of letters dealing with contemporary events and directed to civil servants or their wives. Men in the trenches were informed that their wives were indulging in debauches in their absence and that the latest baby had nothing but its name in common with the husband. Wives were informed that their husbands went on short leaves from the front and did not pay much attention to their vows of marital fidelity.

Tulle began to hum like an aroused hive. There were many theories about the origin of the letters and the identity of the writer. It seemed almost certain that whoever wrote them had some connection with the provincial government, because the victims were for the most part government employees. These suspicions were strengthened when a man who shortly was to be appointed Governor of the Province received a whole series of obscene anonymous letters. At that time his prospective appointment was known only among certain inner circles of the provincial government.

In the beginning the letters arrived by mail, but with time it

appeared that the writer feared, and correctly so, that the mail-
boxes were being watched. Letters were left on sidewalks or staircases or were tucked in the door jamb of the victim's home. A
juvenile delinquent one day found on a bench in the park a long list
itemizing the most prominent citizens of the town and their supposed mistresses in one column, and the wives and their supposed
lovers in a second column. The youthful hoodlum pasted this list
on the billboard of the local theater, and the whole town had read
it before the police tore it down.

Another day, when a priest was taking a walk he noticed on the
threshold of a pharmacy a letter addressed to the proprietor. His
first impulse was to put the letter back again because the apothecary was known as a member of the anti-church group. But his
kindness conquered, and he entered the pharmacy smiling and delivered the letter to the apothecary. He told himself that he would
show this wicked man how forgiving a servant of Christ could be
toward an enemy. The knowledge that the apothecary brewed an
excellent cordial with which he treated his friends may have somewhat fortified the priest's decision.

In any case, the apothecary, moved by the kindness of the priest,
invited him to sit down and have a drink. But the priest was polite
and in no haste and asked the apothecary to read the letter first,
in case it contained something important. The apothecary opened
the letter and, after reading a few lines, turned white, then red.
He howled aloud and jumped at the priest, who was so surprised by
this behavior that at first he could not defend himself. But presently he put up a good resistance and there was a heroic battle, accompanied by the clanking of broken pill jars and medicine bottles.
When neighbors arrived and separated them, the pharmacy was
almost wrecked. It developed that in the letter this very priest
was accused of having intimate relations with the apothecary's wife.

The letters continued to exacerbate the city after the Armistice
and on into the early twenties. An atmosphere of suspicion and
ill will spread. The unhappy people who were named by local
gossip as the originators of the letters were driven to despair. At

one time the wife of a civil servant was looked upon as the instigator. When her husband heard this rumor, he lost his entire mental balance from frustration and despair. Ultimately he had to be committed to an asylum, where he died. As late as 1922 the stream of letters had not ceased, and the *affaire de Tulle* had achieved international notoriety.

The police of Tulle had not been napping. On the contrary, they had followed every possible clue, but in vain. At last some civil servants in the provincial government headed by a M. Jean Laval, a supervisor of one of the bureaus, wrote to the attorney general of the province and asked him to have the affair thoroughly investigated. The attorney general appointed a grizzled and experienced assistant district attorney named M. Richard to the job.

By the time Richard started to work there was one faint clue. A certain M. Moury, also a supervisor in the provincial government, had recently married a Mademoiselle Fioux, the daughter of a wealthy ironmonger. Mademoiselle Fioux had previously been employed as a typist at her husband's office. Now, this M. Moury was the only person in the provincial government who had never received an anonymous letter. On the contrary, if anything good was said in any of the letters (which rarely happened), it always concerned Moury or his wife. This anonymous appraisal of the two certainly made them suspect; they were quickly judged in the opinion of the town as the most probable culprits. The life of the poor couple became almost unbearable. When the civil servant who went insane died in the asylum, the wrath of the populace was so great that a mob tried to wreck the shop of Madame Moury's father, and all the police of the city had to be called out in order to restore order.

The dramatic solution of the mystery finally came about by pure coincidence. M. Jean Laval, the supervisor who headed the group of civil servants asking the attorney general for an investigation, had a sister, Angèle Laval, who had also been a typist in M. Moury's office. M. Laval was very interested in the progress of the investigation and often conferred with M. Richard about it. One

Wednesday he told Richard that a certain Mademoiselle Leynac had just received a very obscene letter. He said that he had got to know this through his sister, who was a friend of Mademoiselle Leynac. On Saturday the same week, Richard met Mademoiselle Leynac and in the course of conversation mentioned that Laval had told him about the letter on Wednesday. But Mademoiselle Leynac insisted that she had not spoken about the letter to Angèle Laval before Friday. How could it be, M. Richard asked himself, that on Wednesday Mademoiselle Angèle Laval had knowledge of a letter about which she was not told until Friday?

Richard sent for Angèle Laval and interrogated her himself. She denied emphatically having had anything to do with the letters. Richard sent Dr. Locard in Lyons a batch of letters, about three hundred in all, to be compared with the handwriting of Angèle Laval. Specimens of her mother's handwriting were also sent him since the two ladies lived together. The anonymous letters had been hand-printed in block characters, so Locard found it necessary to go to Tulle to watch Angèle Laval make block letters while he dictated to her. The dictation took most of one day.

Angèle Laval went into hysterics twice during the morning. She was a nervous woman about thirty-five years of age, very slim, with a dark complexion and big, black, intelligent eyes. She was willing to write block letters, but it took her ten minutes to write the first line, for she changed and improved every letter until the line was finally a jumble of ink stains and retouches. But in that first line there was a Y which looked like a V with a sort of serpent's tail on it, and this peculiar letter was exactly like the Y's in the anonymous letters. She also made a very unusual G just like the G in the letters. The identification was complete, therefore, from the first line.

Without betraying the least pressure or intensity, Locard informed her that she would have to write several pages, and after that announcement she made no more changes. After a few lines, however, she began quite a different sort of writing. After a few more lines, she developed and stabilized this new writing until it filled several pages. In the afternoon she became tired and fell back into her old writing which in all its details and similarities was the same as that of the anonymous letters.

Among the more than one hundred letters there were also some in ordinary handwriting, and Locard was able to prove that these had been written by the mother of Mademoiselle Laval. The assistant district attorney now had enough evidence to prosecute the mother and daughter.

The two women chose death rather than the coming court ordeal and decided to drown themselves in a neighboring reservoir. The mother jumped into the water first and died instantly, perhaps of a heart attack. Angèle Laval hesitated for some minutes but finally jumped too. However, some woodcutters arrived on the scene and saved her. On account of her attempted suicide, she was examined by a psychiatrist who found that, though of a very nervous disposition, she was fully responsible for her actions. She was sentenced to two months' imprisonment and fined 500 francs. Cheap indeed in the light of the consequences of her acts!

The story of Angèle Laval tempted Locard to create a new name, "anonymograph," for this sort of person. Anyone who writes only an anonymous letter or two is not an anonymograph. The difference between the ordinary, mean little writer of one or more anonymous letters and an anonymograph is that the first writes his letter with some positive goal before him but the latter writes letters merely for the sake of sadistic pleasure. The average writer of anonymous letters does so perhaps only once, and then because of jealousy, revenge, or a similar feeling. But in the life of an anonymograph such letters are an important part of his being. He writes them by hundreds or by thousands. In some respects the psychopathic writer of anonymous letters can be likened to a drug addict.

It is all very well to say that the writing of such letters is a psychopathic act. That very description, however, shifts the focus of attention from the victim to the perpetrator, who is certainly among the most contemptible of all forms of criminal. A public accusation, whether made in the form of a libel or slander, is at least actionable. The victim has a recourse against the pain and injury he has suffered. But he has almost no recourse against the unknown author of the filth that comes to him through the mail, and even if the writer is unmasked by investigation the odds are against any legal satisfaction by way of redress.

Criminal law is mostly concerned with offenses of physical violence or against property. To many people the writing of an anonymous letter may not appear as heinous as a burglary or an assault with a deadly weapon. Possibly that is true because the violence is in the mind and heart of the victim, the recipient of such a communication. A case like the one in Tulle which involves a lot of people over a long period of time is a rarity, but the amount of concealed anguish and destroyed happiness which such letters occasion every day and all over the world must be very great indeed.

The lady who brought her ugly letter into my office and thus testified to the hurt she had received was probably in the minority. My guess would be that the greater proportion of anonymous letters are destroyed by the recipients without mention. It would be interesting to know how many of the victims think the problem through for themselves and follow this procedure. Perhaps the number of private citizens who do so is large, but it has to be admitted that the decision is much more difficult for persons in public life, and that sometimes even the most disciplined self-restraint is not enough to deal with the crisis.

The case of a high official in the provincial government at Lyons during the 1920's, one which Maître Locard himself investigated, illustrates the difficulty of remaining silent past a certain point. This man, whom I shall call M. Berthin, returned to Lyons one morning after an extended trip. Pasted on the front door of his house he found a large sheet of paper inscribed with the worst sort of accusations against his wife and daughter. It was even illustrated with a picture of M. Berthin himself wearing the traditional horns of cuckoldry. After an inner struggle, M. Berthin had the offensive thing washed off his door and tried to forget it.

The anonymous slanderer was not satisfied. A fortnight later there was a second such sheet, even more obscene than the first, and the day's mail contained a letter of the vilest sort repeating the same accusations. Each new day's mail brought another of these epistles, and the situation became intolerable. M. Berthin finally laid the matter before the Sûreté.

Locard was assigned to the investigation, which on the face of it was almost hopelessly difficult. All the anonymous writing was in block letters, and M. Berthin could think of no one who wished him ill. Thus there was no convenient list of logical suspects to winnow. At first, the investigation made no progress, but finally the anonymograph made a slip. On one of the sheets—this one also pasted to the door—one of the words was not spelled out in block letters but consisted of printed letters pasted together. The letters obviously had come from some official form, and M. Berthin recognized that the printing was characteristic of that on a certain form used in his own office. It now appeared reasonable to concentrate the search on the staff members of the victim's own bureau, but this did not turn out to be so helpful as Locard hoped. For one thing, there were scores of people subordinate to M. Berthin; for another thing, he had a reputation as a severe taskmaster, and many of the people working under him were known to resent the discipline he enforced.

Fortunately, the perpetrator of the poisonous notes made another error. Similar letters about M. Berthin began to be received by the man's friends and acquaintances, and one of these letters was typewritten. Since no two typewriters are wholly identical, Locard proceeded to examine every machine in M. Berthin's bureau. In the end he found that the letter had been written on one located in a room to which only two employees had access—a father and son. They may as well be called Thevenet. Thevenet *père* was a thin, shabby man who had spent his whole life as a petty official at a low salary out of which he somehow managed to give his only son a good education. The sacrifice seemed to have been worth while; young Thevenet was a refined man with a university education. He was already a novelist of promise, and he was next in line to become chief of the bureau. His father had become his secretary. The two were interrogated individually and together; indignantly they denied any knowledge of the letters and posters.

Locard reasoned that if someone writes on a wall, his tendency is to do so at about eye level. The same rule might apply to the pasting of a sheet of paper on a door. Père Thevenet was short as well as slight, while his son was exceptionally tall. The height at which the sheets had been posted on M. Berthin's door suggested that it might be the father who had fastened them there, but this was a long way from proof. Locard felt himself stymied in the absence of positive evidence.

At this point, a routine police precaution paid dividends. Locard had requested M. Berthin to bring to the Sûreté any new anonymous letters unopened, so that the police laboratory could examine them for fingerprints. Several fresh letters came in, and on one of them the technicians discovered a fingerprint. Immediately the Maître requested permission to fingerprint the two Thevenets. Both refused, the father flatly, but the son with high-flown indignation.

"Shall I," he said among other things, "a lawyer and member of the bar, a Master of Arts and a novelist, the friend of a great Cardinal and of a great author, have my fingerprints taken like a common thief? No. Decidedly no!"

Locard explained that the simple process would free him of all suspicion.

"Again, no. Do you think I wish to have my fingerprints filed along with those of despicable *apaches*?" He enlarged his refusal by pointing out that some diabolical villain might have forged his fingerprints. "Besides," he added, "I am a Freemason, and the statutes of my order forbid the giving of fingerprints."

Although young Thevenet's protests had to be heeded and his

fingerprints could not be taken, somewhat to Locard's surprise the father finally did consent to be fingerprinted. It was immediately clear that the print on the anonymous letter was not his.

Still the anonymous letters continued to arrive. But now their tone was changed. They were serious, well written, and addressed to the attorney general, to the local judge, and even to the Minister of the Interior. The letters defended the Thevenets; in one of them another civil servant was named as the instigator. However, the Thevenets were now being watched day and night. One day the father was observed putting a gray envelope in a mailbox. The envelope turned out to contain only a blank piece of paper, but the address was block-printed in the same way, as in the anonymous letters. A search warrant for the Thevenets' house was now issued.

This search resulted in an unexpected discovery. In the drawer of a desk was found unused stationery with authentic letterheads from several official sources, including the provincial legislature, the Magistrate, the Governor, and the Chief of Police. There were even several correspondence cards of the kind used by the Mayor of the city for his personal notes. Some of this official stationery was already prepared with anonymous messages ready to be sent off in an attempt to confuse the investigation.

The Thevenets were arrested. They defended themselves with energy, but their arguments were so fantastic that no one believed them. Why did old Thevenet put an envelope with the same paper and the same writing as the anonymous letters in the mailbox? The answer was that an unknown friend, who was the true instigator, had warned them by mail that they were suspected and that he could not bear to have the innocent prosecuted. He had seen that the police were trailing them, and he had advised them to put a blank letter (which he would furnish them) in a mailbox. The police would then understand that they were innocent. The answer on the next question was just as convincing. How had they come into possession of the official stationery found in their house? Reply: A political enemy had put it there.

The Police Laboratory found a fingerprint in the mucilage on the last sheet which had been pasted on M. Berthin's door. It was blurred, but by a special photographic process eleven characteristic "points" were restored, and it was identified with the right index finger of young Thevenet. With eleven points there was one chance of a mistake in 4,194,304. Young Thevenet tried to explain away this disturbing fact by furnishing the theory that M. Berthin's daughter could have stolen the paper from his room, filled it with obscene accusations against herself, her mother, and her father, and then pasted it to her own door. The theory in itself could not be overlooked, but there was one small flaw in it. Young Thevenet's fingerprint was *in* the paste and not *underneath* it, as would have been the case if Mademoiselle Berthin had been degenerate enough to satisfy this defense.

The defense attorney cast some doubt on the fingerprint identification when the matter was brought to court. As mentioned earlier, in France, twelve similar points are required if a fingerprint is to be used as identification. The defense therefore insisted that the fingerprint on the poster be examined also by the Police Laboratory of Paris. The result was that two additional similar points were spotted, and the identity was thus established with certainty. Because young Thevenet denied his guilt to the end, Locard never found out whether this particular sheet had been pasted lower down on M. Berthin's door by the son at the father's eye level out of consistency with the earlier postings, or whether out of sensitiveness about his own height.

The Thevenets, father and son, got exactly the same sentence as Angèle Laval had got—two months' imprisonment and a fine of 500 francs. Young Thevenet, the lawyer, author, and humanist, had to go to prison, and all his father's untiring efforts to make him a career had been in vain.

The Berthin case had several obvious points of similarity with the affair at Tulle. In each, the motives were vague, and not substantial enough to justify either the underlying viciousness or the vast amount of pains taken to implement it. There was the same mass fabrication of letters, though M. Berthin was the recipient of the majority of them and was the sole target of the operation. There was also a family collaboration, this time father and son. The different element was the extraordinary factor of the authorship— a cultivated and promising young man, a novelist, and a civil servant with a reasonably assured future. That such degenerate, obscene stuff should have come from such a source is not easy to believe, even for a case-hardened policeman.

22

MURDER WILL OUT

According to Shakespeare's most tragic of princes, murder will confess itself. Hamlet observes that "though it have no tongue" murder "will speak with most miraculous organ," and he goes on to express the belief that it is conscience which will proclaim the crime. This would certainly be a great convenience to the police forces of the world if it were true often enough. Unfortunately, the consciences of most murderers are atrophied. The more hardened can—and often do—remain silent for the rest of their lives. The most common accuser of the guilty is not conscience at all, but the corpse of the victim.

As a rule, murder itself is not a difficult crime to perpetrate. The creature called man is fearfully vulnerable, and there are scores of easy ways to deprive him of life. But no sooner is he killed than the dread question arises in the mind of the killer: what to do about the body? How many times has a murderer looked down on the motionless body of his victim and racked his brain for a means of getting rid of it! No doubt there have been successful solutions to the puzzle, all too many of them, but the number of failures is very high.

The human body is made up of a lot of substances. Some, like the teeth and bones, are very durable. Others, which might at first seem easy to dispose of, persist no matter how carefully the mur-

derer attempts to tidy up the scene of his crime. Blood, in particular, offers the criminal a fearful problem if it has been spilled,
especially indoors.

Now, blood is a most remarkable liquid, not simply from the
medical point of view, or the literary one, but also from the criminologist's. Most people know that it has, in its complex structure,
a great many identifying characteristics. Human blood cannot be
mistaken for animal, and within the human race it is possible to
subdivide individuals by their blood type into comparatively small
groups. This complexity makes blood a valuable instrument of
proof in a prosecution. But it becomes more so when the fact is
taken into account that even extremely small amounts of it can
be used for analysis. Moreover, blood is a liquid which, in a crime
of violence, seems to have an uncanny capacity to hide itself, only
to reappear at a fitting moment and testify against the murderer.
Blood will creep under the tiles of a floor, into the cracks of boards
and the grain of wood, under fingernails; blood will linger in the
water trap of a basin where the killer has washed his hands. It will
cling beneath the top of a table where fingers have been thought-
lessly wiped. It splashes on clothing and into hair.

So the body and its vital fluid are a formidable part of the problem that confronts a murderer. It might be supposed that an intelligent man, especially one with technical training, would hesitate
to commit a murder unless he were confident ahead of time that
he could dispose of the body itself. But this is not the case, and
even in my years of apprenticeship at Lyons I was given a dramatic
example of the kind of paralysis of the will and intelligence that
committing murder seems to induce.

The victim, M. Alphonse Martin, was a dealer in horses and
cows. He had a quite comfortable house in one of the suburbs
of Lyons, and the stables where he kept the animals were in the
courtyard. I saw him only after he was dead, but he must have
been a fairly ordinary-looking man, with light graying hair and black
mustache, a trifle portly and in his early forties. This M. Martin
was married but had no children. His wife was several years older

than he and not very attractive. Gossip claimed that her dowry had enabled M. Martin to start his business.

Everyone in the neighborhood, including Madame Martin herself, knew that, whatever merits M. Martin had, fidelity was not one of them. He could almost be described as a satyr, a kind of suburban Casanova who did not discriminate among women. Young or old, good-looking or ugly, all women were the same to his insatiable appetite. One day the inevitable result of the life he led occurred, so he went to a doctor.

This doctor, whose name was Jean Thevin, had an excellent practice in the same suburb. Each day his waiting room was full of patients for he had a good personality, always saying some comforting word for a patient. He was about forty-five, happily married, and the father of three children. In every way, including faithful church attendance on Sunday, the Thevin family was a model of respectability.

M. Martin's worst suspicions were confirmed by Dr. Thevin. The patient needed a weekly injection, and the course of treatment might have to be continued for several years in the then-obtaining body of medical knowledge. M. Martin, repenting his sins, sighed, and obeyed orders. In time the two men became well acquainted, and M. Martin often confided to the doctor many things he did not speak of to anyone else.

About a year after the treatment began, M. Martin came for his injection later than the appointed time. The nurse ushered him into the office and, while he was taking off his coat and rolling up his shirt sleeve, he told Dr. Thevin that he was late because he had been able to sell a dozen horses at a very advantageous price.

"And I was paid in cash, too," he said. "I don't like to keep so much money on me, but it is too late now to go to the bank." He pointed to the bulky wallet in his coat.

The doctor stared at him a moment and then made a characteristic joke about money never being too heavy to carry. He pressed a button on his desk and, when the nurse entered, told her, "You have been working hard all day, and I have been thinking lately that you need a little fresh air. There will be no more patients this evening, so you do not need to return until tomorrow."

M. Martin sat in a chair, his naked arm ready for the syringe, but the doctor continued to talk. After a few minutes, the door slammed as the nurse went out. Then the doctor said, "Today I shall not give you one of the usual ampoules. There is a new medicine which they say works wonders. We'll have a try with that."

He went into another room and soon came back carrying a syringe which contained a crystal liquid. He rubbed a small section of the skin on M. Martin's arm in the usual way with a piece of cotton soaked in alcohol. When the syringe entered, M. Martin closed his eyes because he did not like the pricking of the needle.

He was never to open them again. The doctor had injected cyanide into his veins; there were a few convulsions, a slight groan, and M. Martin was dead.

Dr. Thevin took the wallet out of M. Martin's jacket and looked at the contents: It was much more than he had imagined when he had gotten his sudden impulse to kill. But what to do with the body? Dr. Thevin decided that there was time enough later to solve that problem. To be relieved of the body temporarily he carried it, with great effort, into his waiting room where there was a big, empty closet. He placed it inside, locked the door, and put the key in his pocket.

The explanation for this incredible act by a well-known and respectable physician was simple, yet intricate. The doctor was a kind of Dr. Jekyll. By day he was the learned physician and the good family man. By night he frequented night spots and gambling places in the company of a red-haired prostitute. This woman had charmed him so completely that he had spent a lot of money on her. At the time of the murder, he was desperately in need of cash.

The next morning the nurse told the doctor that the closet where she was accustomed to hang her cloak was locked and the key had disappeared. Irritated, the doctor answered that he had put some of his own stuff in the closet and that she should hang her cloak elsewhere. It was a hot summer day. By the time the nurse left in the evening, she noticed a faint, unpleasant odor in the waiting room.

There was still time for Dr. Thevin to try to solve the problem of getting rid of the body, but something held him back. (Later, when he was questioned, he could offer no explanation for this inactivity.) By the following day, the odor was still more apparent, and the nurse told the doctor that the patients had complained. The doctor suggested that it must be some animal, perhaps a rat, which had died under the floor, and he ordered the nurse to spray with oil of wintergreen. He received his patients as usual, making his small jokes and giving his gentle bits of advice. He told many of them that he would have to get a carpenter to take up the floor in order to get rid of the smell.

This went on for several days. The disappearance of the horse dealer had been reported to the police but, as M. Martin had never told his wife of the treatment he was undergoing, there was no clue pointing to the doctor, who continued his life as usual, spending his days in his office, his evenings with his family, and nights with his red-haired mistress.

On the eighth day after the murder the number of Dr. Thevin's patients had diminished and the neighbors had begun to complain. Dr. Theven still did nothing, although he must have known by then that his frightful deed was very near to being discovered. The nurse had localized the odor to the closet, and it began to dawn upon her that something awful was hidden there. On the ninth day, there were only two patients, and the doctor left early in the afternoon. The nurse, who had remained to tidy up, was by this time almost hysterical. Whenever she had to pass through the waiting room, she ran and didn't dare look at the closet. Feeling she could not stand it any more, she went sobbing to a neighbor, an architect, who was one of those who had complained about the odor. The architect went with her to the waiting room and succeeded in picking the lock of the closet. When he opened the door, the swollen and already half-putrefied body of the horse dealer fell out.

The same afternoon Dr. Thevin was arrested and confessed willingly. He was sentenced to hard labor for life, in French Guiana. Here was a clear case of a murderer so hypnotized by his own deed that he did not so much as try to get rid of the body, in spite of his knowledge of anatomy.

Dismemberment, though, is not a sure way of disposing of a body. The detective division in Copenhagen, headed by my friend Thune-Jacobsen, was once confronted with a case which suggested that Dr. Thevin might never have succeeded in covering up the traces of his crime.

The Copenhagen case did not at first seem to be a murder. It began with the discovery in one of the city sewers of the leg and foot of a woman, cut off at the knee joint. A search of the police records contained no entry for a missing woman, and the detective division was inclined to believe that this grisly piece of anatomy represented a jape on the part of some medical student at the university. Such practical jokes had been played on the police before, not only in Copenhagen but elsewhere, when medical students had deposited some part of a dead body in a city sewer or on a street corner.

However, the first discovery was followed by others. Within a few days so many different parts of a body had been collected from the sewers that they could be pieced together in the office of the medical examiner. They were seen to be the body of a woman of twenty-five to thirty years of age. Only the head was missing and this, in fact, never was recovered.

The detectives, in collaboration with the medical examiner, made a minute search of the body. Sticking between the fingers of one hand was discovered a small piece of newspaper, which contained the letters Q-U-O. The inference was that this probably constituted a part of a movie advertisement for D. W. Griffith's grandiose film, *Quo Vadis*. It was quickly discovered that the type did not come from any Copenhagen newspaper. Now began a painstaking search among all the provincial newspapers, of which there are a good many in the highly literate little state of Denmark. After a whole month of research it could be said with certainty that the fragment of newsprint had come from a certain provincial newspaper which had been printed about ten days previous to the finding of the first leg.

In the meantime the remains of the body had been X-rayed. It appeared that the woman had a tubercular congestion in the right lung. In the hope that she had been recently X-rayed in some clinic, a search was made of all Copenhagen clinics for women of that age who had recently been X-rayed and shown to have such a mark in the right lung. At the same time all subscribers in Copenhagen of the provincial newspaper were scrutinized. There were not many of them. One, however, was a pimp, well known to the police. While this man was being investigated, in one of the clinics an X-ray plate was located which corresponded to the plate taken of the body. It belonged to a certain Bodil Knudsen. It developed that Bodil was a prostitute who had lived with the pimp, but she had disappeared a few months earlier. Since she had no relatives, her disappearance had not been reported to the police.

The pimp, when interrogated, made a kind of confession, saying that they had had a quarrel and that she had tried to hit him on the head with a bottle. While defending himself, he had caused her to fall and she had hit her head on an iron oven. She had died, he said, almost instantly. He had been so frightened by this accident that he hadn't reported her death but had decided to dispose of the body. Since he had been a butcher's apprentice, it was an easy task for him to dismember the corpse.

The court had to accept his story, and he was sentenced to five years of hard labor for murder in the second degree. It might be judged what sort of person this pimp was by the fact that when he was released from prison he went home and killed his old mother because at the trial she had given a not very favorable report on him.

A classic way of getting rid of a body is to cut it into convenient pieces, put the pieces in a suitcase and deposit this valise in the cloakroom of a railway station or send it off to an imaginary address. Some murderers abhor the nasty business of cutting up the body; instead they put the whole body into a trunk, from which comes the well-known expression "trunk murder." The murderer hopes to remain anonymous, for he certainly does not leave his visiting card in the trunk.

The police start by establishing the identity of the victim. Murder is for the most part a very personal matter, and as soon as the identity of the victim is established there is a fair chance of identifying the murderer as well.

Many years ago, in Lyons there was an old and amorous bailiff named Gouffé who was known to carry large sums of money. A prostitute named Gabrielle Bompard stands high in the annals of crime not only because she committed the first trunk murder but also because she killed her victim in a peculiar way. She induced him to think that she was infatuated with him, and old Gouffé was proud as a rooster about this, for to gain the true love of a prostitute at his age is indeed unusual. One night Gabrielle invited him to share her old-fashioned four-poster, with beams connecting the posters and curtains all around it. Over the beam at the headboard she had slung a strong silk cord, one end of which was made into a noose hidden inside the folds of the curtain. The other end went down to the floor, where it could be managed by her pimp, who was lying underneath the bed.

The amorous old Gouffé came at the appointed hour, undressed, and placed his thin and frail body in the bed. He was followed by Gabrielle, who embraced him passionately, while she slipped the noose over his head. On a signal, the pimp began to haul at the cord and Gouffé was swiftly hanged. The pair then deposited his body in a trunk, took it to the railroad station, and directed it to Paris, thereby inaugurating the "trunk murder."

Fire has been used many times to burn a murder victim, but the cremation of a whole human body in a stove or even in a coal furnace is not so easy as it seems. It takes a long time and attracts attention by the stench of burnt flesh. Still, with much patience and care the thing can be done: witness Landru, the famous French murderer, who was guillotined some time after World War I. This man had murdered about twenty women, spinisters or widows, with whom he had made contact through advertisements. No bodies were ever found, and Landru never confessed, even when confronted with overwhelming circumstantial and other evidence. The police, suspecting what his method of disposing of his victims must have been, burnt horseflesh in his stove of the same weight as an average woman. This test proved that it could be done. Of course, the bones and the teeth would not have been destroyed in this way, but they could have been got rid of in one way or another.

It is a curious fact that if much publicity is given to a crime which has been committed in a spectacular way, inevitably it will be repeated elsewhere by less ingenious souls. In the late twenties, a Parisian diamond dealer called Mestorino killed and robbed a man called Tryphene, put the body in his car and drove out to the country. In a lonely place, he deposited the body on the ground, soaked it thoroughly with several big cans of gasoline, and set fire to it. In this case the few remains of the body were finally identified and Mestorino was arrested, sentenced, and executed. This method of disposing of, or at least disfiguring a body so as to make identification well nigh impossible, spread like wildfire. In Lyons alone in the following months we had two ordinary murder cases where the body was soaked with gasoline and burnt. We even had a case where a man soaked the still-living body of his mother-in-law with gasoline and burnt her to death.

In the last twenty or thirty years there have been a few so-called acid murders. The first one happened in the late twenties in Marseilles and, peculiarly enough, did not attract much publicity.

An old Englishwoman, a Mrs. Catherine Tinker, lived alone in a suburban villa. She was robbed and killed by a couple who lived in a neighboring villa and who were members of the Marseilles underworld. This couple, named Dentu, carried Mrs. Tinker's body to their house one night and put it in their bathtub. They had bought several big carboys of concentrated sulphuric acid, which they poured over the body. It is said that poor Mrs. Tinker dissolved very slowly. Every day the Dentus carried buckets of used acid to their garden and buried it there, in holes which they had dug. Gradually the whole garden became poisoned, the grass and plants in a wide circle around the burial place of Mrs. Tinker died, and finally there was only a huge black spot. When the garden of a neighbor was similarly affected, he began to complain, and an investigation was commenced. The mysterious disappearance of Mrs. Tinker was known to the police, and it did not take long for them to unmask the murderers.

An almost endless list of other ways of disposing of the bodies of murder victims has been tried. It is said that gangsters have seated their enemies with their feet in tubs of wet concrete, allowed the cement to harden, and thrown the still living victim overboard into the sea. There have been buryings of every sort, concealment of bodies in lonely woods and lakes, and the leaving of corpses in all kinds of out-of-the-way places such as wells and abandoned houses. Sooner or later, though, the crime is apt to come to light, and enough remains of the victim are found, if only teeth, to give the police some clue. The body of the victim, his blood and teeth and bones can protest for decades the violence that has been done.

There remains one form of murder in which the disposal of the body is not a problem of the crime but the very end and purpose of the deed itself. The reader with a delicate stomach may well wish to pause at this point in the present chapter. There is no way of making polite or civilized reading out of the business of killing human beings for their own flesh. Such monstrous murder as this occurs, of course, very rarely in times of peace and reasonable prosperity. But it is not uncommon in periods of chaos and hunger.

In the early twenties there was a hot-dog vendor plying his trade at one of the railroad stations in Berlin. His name was Grossmann and he had once been a butcher. Grossmann was about fifty years old, a thin, insignificant little man with a haggard face and a sloping mustache. About twice a month he used to spend a day on the platform where long-distance, slow trains with cheap fourth-class carriages stopped. If he saw getting out of one of these carriages a girl who looked as if she were coming to the city to hunt a job as a housemaid, he would approach her (provided she was fat enough), politely lift his cap and inquire whether he could be of any assistance. During the conversation he would drop a remark that he was in need of a housekeeper for his bachelor household, and that she could have that job if she wanted. He paid well, he used to say, and there was not much work. Often a girl accepted, and any who did would not be seen again.

Grossmann kept each of these girls for a couple of days, then murdered her. He cut up the bodies with a butcher's skill, kept the flesh, and disposed of the balance in some sewer. Then he pickled the meat, ground it and put it in his sausages, which he later sold at the railroad station.

This constant stream of girls into his flat finally alerted some neighbors, who put the police on his track. Bundles of female clothes were discovered in the closets, and finally Grossmann confessed.

A few years previously an old, retired schoolteacher in Silesia, near the Polish border of Germany, had committed a series of hair-raising murders, apparently with the financial side of the business in mind. This man too was a bachelor and lived in a house situated on the outskirts of a small town near a highway. It was his custom in the afternoons to sit peacefully at the side of the road and smoke his pipe. In those days there were, and no doubt still are, many young apprentices and artisans walking the roads of Germany in order to see the country and learn more of their professions. When the old schoolteacher saw someone he thought would suit his purpose, he would speak to him and inquire if he would like to earn a few cents by writing a letter for him.

"Because," he would explain, "I have hurt my right hand and cannot write."

Usually the boy was willing to earn such easy money. The old man would take the boy to the house, put him at the writing desk in his drawing room, and start to dictate a letter. While doing so he stood behind the boy and suddenly picked up a hatchet and killed him.

This went on for quite a long time. It was difficult to obtain meat in Germany in those days, but this old man was one of the foremost black-market dealers in the town and, owing to his supposed connections with farmers in the surrounding district, was known as a man who could always produce a veal steak when desired.

One day a lusty young apprentice came walking up the road whistling, his belongings in a little bundle dangling from a stick which he had slung over his shoulder. He was approached by the old man, who gave his usual story. The boy agreed to write the letter and went into the room to the fatal writing desk.

Probably inspired by the healthy and somewhat stout boy, the schoolteacher began his dictation with the words, "You thick sausage!"

This the boy found so funny that he laughed and turned his head to look at the old man. At that very moment the old man swung the hatchet and the blow went into the writing desk instead of into the boy's head.

A brief and terrible struggle followed, but the boy was too strong for him and succeeded in getting away.

When police seached the house, they found in the cellar whole barrels full of pickled fingers and toes.

23

MORE OR LESS PERSONAL

The School of Law of the University of Stockholm invited me to give a series of lectures in police science and circumstantial evidence, and in 1931 I was appointed to the faculty as Assistant Professor in Police Science. Two of my sponsors were the late Professor Sven Thunberg, whose field was history but who was better known as the genial *Rector Magnificus* of the University—a position somewhat like that of Provost, but rather more refulgent—and the University Director, Axel Simon Edstrom. These two good friends arranged it so that along with the appointment I was given two rooms in a building in the old portion of the campus. These were fitted out and used as demonstration and research laboratories.

Partly as a result of this work at the University, I began to receive a measure of official recognition. The Swedish government asked me to organize the first course in police science offered to district attorneys and sheriffs. This course also seemed to go well and was followed by others each year until 1939. These stamps of approval were doubly welcome, not only for the reassurance and recognition implicit in them, but because they were likely to open many other doors. Indeed, to anticipate my own chronology a little, these appointments led eventually to my becoming the first director of the Swedish National Institute of Technical Police, as well as to many challenging assignments in various foreign countries.

Meanwhile, of course, my private practice of criminology expanded. I testified in innumerable cases involving expert analysis of technical matters. The growing extent to which expert testimony was becoming a part of court procedure resulted, as early as 1935, in an endowment by the combined Swedish fire insurance companies of an Institute of Criminology and Police Science at the University of Stockholm.

In spite of the rapid progress I was making in the capital of my native country, I was not wholly content, for my years in France and the Far East had given me a taste for travel. I began to cast about for some way of seeing still more of the world. The Swedish-American Foundation every year gives a group of scholarships to Swedish citizens who wish to go to the United States to study. The roster of applicants is always large and ranges from young students to assistant professors such as myself. It seemed to me that I had nothing to lose by trying, and in 1933 I applied for a special fellowship to travel to the United States and study police methods. To my satisfaction I received a grant of $2,000.

My introduction to the problems of American criminology began before I even set foot in the United States. The Swedish steamer on which I was to cross the ocean sailed from Gothenburg. While she was still at the pier, and just before the gangplank was hauled aboard, I noticed a short, enormously fat man rushing aboard. He was wearing a white raincoat and a sports cap, and was followed by a panting porter loaded like a camel with a formidable mound of luggage. Soon the word went round among us that this character was a Norwegian-American real-estate broker from New York.

In the first few days of the voyage, the same grapevine reported that he was enormously wealthy and was presumably on his way back across the ocean to add to his treasure. It was a February sailing out of Gothenburg, and in consequence there were only a few first-class passengers. Our wealthy and important realtor was therefore seated at the Captain's table, next to a Mrs. Smith, an

American woman about fifty years old who was married to a golf-club manager somewhere on Long Island. I also had a seat at the Captain's table, courtesy of the steamship line and the Foundation, and could not help making the acquaintance of the real-estate man, whose name turned out to be Halvor. He was always boasting about his money, and this did not especially endear him to any of us.

The night before our arrival in New York the customary Captain's Dinner was given. Though there were few passengers in the first class, the second class was overcrowded. Several amateur talents had been spotted among the second-class passengers, so they were asked to give the evening's variety show. The arrangement was that the first-class passengers would go to the second-class quarters after dinner to attend the show. This was not altogether wise, because on board a passenger ship those in the less expensive sections are apt to look at those in first class as arrogant capitalists.

Among the second-class passengers was a woman from Chicago, a professional singer, who had been in Scandinavia giving radio concerts. She was accompanied by her husband, a small Italian who looked like a brother of Al Capone.

When we went down to the second-class salon I noticed that Mr. Halvor and the golf-club manager's wife were missing. The rest of us took our seats and there followed some musical entertainment. Then the diva from Chicago came forward and started to sing. At that moment Halvor entered and pushed himself noisily to the first row.

When the singer had finished he cried loudly: "You repulsive bitch, you are singing like a cat in March!"

The impact on the audience was terrific. There was a moment of awful silence, and then the Italian husband of the singer ran up to Halvor and punched him in the face. In a moment many passengers were struggling with one another for an opportunity to hit Halvor. Now, there is an old rule that if you are attacked by too many people at once you have a fair chance of escaping. It was so in this case.

ABOVE My friend the late Chief Inspector, John J. O'Connell, then head of the New York Police Academy and one of the best policemen the United States has ever produced.

BELOW The author lecturing in 1934 at the New York Police Academy. The audience was composed of police captains and inspectors.

At the desk in my first office at the University of Stockholm. The building in which I worked was nicknamed "the haunted castle."

The major clues in the Gerd Andersson case, with which this book opened.

At the LEFT is a magnification of dog hairs, and ABOVE is Gerd's blue trench coat with the dog hairs and jute fibers adhering to it.

The massive Halvor succeeded in getting out of the room by crawling between the legs of the fighting people. Standing in the corridor he succumbed to a fit of hysterical rage and attacked a big, glass-covered key case, cutting his hands so badly that the ship's doctor was summoned.

When I managed to work my way out into the corridor I saw Halvor sitting on the floor, the ship's doctor binding up his gashes. It was a fantastic scene, with the noise of the brawl in the background to give it an accompaniment. Suddenly a white-faced and frightened steward scurried down the corridor to the doctor and whispered something in his ear.

Giving a final tug to one of Halvor's bandages, the doctor rose and came over to me. "Will you please follow me, Mr. Söderman?" he said in a low voice. "This steward reports that Mrs. Smith—you know, the golf-club man's wife—is lying dead on the floor of her stateroom."

"Certainly," I agreed.

In the cabin Mrs. Smith was lying naked on the floor. She was marble-pale and showed no sign of life. Neither was there any sign of a struggle. The stateroom was in order; on the table stood an almost empty whisky bottle and two used glasses. The doctor went down on his knees and examined the woman. Then he shook his head disapprovingly.

"The only trouble with Mrs. Smith is that she is very drunk." He pointed at the two glasses. "She has undoubtedly been drinking with Mr. Halvor, and when she became too drunk for him he went his way." He shrugged his shoulders. "I will have her carried out to the ship's hospital and will give her appropriate treatment. But what on earth could she see in that fat old scoundrel to induce her to put herself in such an awkward position?"

Two stewards arrived with a stretcher. Covered with a blanket, Mrs. Smith was carried away.

A few days later, in the New York Police Department, I was looking through the files. Impelled by a low curiosity, I went to the drawer marked *Ha*. Sure enough, there was a record of my fat friend Halvor. The dossier mentioned not a word about Brooklyn real estate, but it had plenty to report on the man's career as a check swindler, known and sentenced from coast to coast. He was just out after a long stretch in Sing Sing.

Mr. Halvor was the first American criminal I had met, a thorough rascal worthy of his counterparts in Europe.

I immediately got in touch with two gentlemen whose acquaintance I had already made in Sweden. The first, Bruce Smith, was a well-known expert on police organization. The other, Leonard Harrison, was then employed by the Rockefeller Foundation. They in turn introduced me to General John F. Ryan, the newly appointed Commissioner of Police, and to John Sullivan, at that time Chief of Detectives. I started by going over the department in the usual way of foreign students. In a few days' time I arrived at the Police Academy, which was in a former factory on Broome Street. There I met for the first time my unforgettable friend John J. O'Connell, then deputy chief inspector and head of the Academy. He invited me to give lectures at the Academy on scientific methods in criminal investigation.

Out of this lecture experience came the idea of organizing a police laboratory within the New York City Police Department. This proposal was heartily approved by Ryan and Sullivan, and in about a month's time I was transferred from a student's status to that of the department's technical advisor. The new laboratory was inaugurated by General Ryan in the presence of the top members of the legal profession in New York.

Alas, nothing is permanent in this world. In August of 1934 I went home to Sweden for a month. When I returned to New York, I was met at the pier by my friend O'Connell and two detectives who had worked in the laboratory from the very beginning, Francis Murphy and Patrick Hartnett. They were hollow-eyed and sorrowful. A disaster had come upon our cherished laboratory. The disaster was named Fiorello H. LaGuardia, mayor of the city.

One day, while inspecting the police department, he had asked to whom the building on Broome Street which housed our laboratory belonged. The place had once been a candy factory, but the firm had moved elsewhere and rented its old building to the Police Department. When LaGuardia heard the name of the candy company, he darkened, for it was known for its connections with Tammany Hall. As bad luck would have it, the lease was just running out, and LaGuardia ordered that the lease should not be renewed, and the police to vacate the place immediately.

What followed must have been a grandiose spectacle. In this big, five-story edifice covering a whole city block, every conceivable square foot was in use for some police purpose. All the cars of the police department were housed there, all the miscellaneous stores, all the files of criminals, the police laboratory, the Police Academy, and even the undercover squad.

In a few days the building was clear, but at enormous cost. The officers of the candy company, enraged, cut off the electricity so that the elevators did not run. It was necessary to make a kind of bucket brigade of cops in order to get the paraphernalia out of the building. The adjoining street was closed to traffic and filled with the equipment. The whole time this evacuation went on, it was raining. The cars and their spare parts were crowded onto an empty pier. The instruments and equipment of the police laboratory were transferred to an old police station in Brooklyn which was empty because it had been condemned as a fire trap. The worst problem was with the heavy steel file cabinets. The candy factory had been singularly well suited for the files because it was built to carry heavy machines. No ordinary structure could support the enormous weight of those hundreds of thousands of files, so they had to be put in different places. The story went that the Letters A through H were in Manhattan, I through N in the Bronx, and so forth.

Well, it was a case of roll up the shirt sleeves and start all over. But I don't think such a thing could have happened in any country but the United States where the approach to problems is more impulsive than anywhere else.

24

TO GET RICH QUICK

My months of work with John O'Connell and my other friends in the New York Police Department reaffirmed a conclusion I had reached long before—that one of the great appeals of crime is the hope of easy money, the dream of getting rich quickly without the disadvantages of honest toil.

So it is that the usual experience of most people with crime is in the form of an attack upon property. In that guise, a crime lacks even an anecdotal glamor for the victim. His car is taken, his home is burglarized, his safe is blown open, his warehouse is pilfered, his merchandise is lifted from the counters of his store, his pockets are picked, or his cash register is plundered. Even an addicted reader of crime fiction does not get much entertainment out of these crimes when they happen to him.

Neither, of course, do the police. Investigating such crimes is drab, sordid work. The element of novelty and the quality of surprise are conspicuous by their absence. And yet . . . well, once in a very long while there is a fresh twist, something different enough to make a case stand out. One such case came up while I was in New York.

Now, burglary constitutes one of the main categories of a detective's practice, and he does not expect to be surprised in the course of its investigation. The pattern, indeed, is monotonous.

Burglars work at their trade in certain areas and almost always each one employs the same technique. Describe the crime, and the police files automatically yield a small group of suspects, among whom may be found the perpetrator of that crime. In a number of cities today known criminals are identified on mechanized accounting and indexing machines, the cards being punched in such a way that the selector can be set to the characteristics of the reported crime, and thousands of criminals' cards can be sorted in a few minutes. Out will come a few cards which constitute the known burglars of the area, type, and technique exhibited by the crime. The rest is routine.

In this instance, which happened to be before the punch-card era, the case began normally enough. The wealthy tenant of a penthouse in Manhattan reported to the police that his place had been entered and that the thief had got away with $8,000. The New York police immediately bethought themselves of an old acquaintance who specialized in penthouse burglaries. He had given as his reason for preferring this sort of roof-top job that "as a rule, you always get something valuable and easy to carry." Detectives interrogated this specialist. He readily confessed but became annoyed at the mention of $8,000, for he seemed to feel that was a slur on his operation.

"Eight thousand dollars, hell!" he retorted. "I got a cool thirty thousand, and all of it hidden behind the wall paper."

The victim did not seem pleased by this testimony. Emphatically he denied losing more than the specified $8,000. It is, of course, possible that he was thinking about the internal revenue department.

The police were in a delicate position: Was the victim more likely to be honest in his testimony than the burglar?

Aside from the unexpected disagreement between victim and criminal anent the amount of loot, this case illustrated another aspect of police work which needs to be mentioned. The burglary, even if only $8,000, was a sizable one. That is one reason it was investigated at all, let alone solved. It is true of police departments everywhere, no less than in New York, that the bulk of detective work consists of looking into thefts, burglaries, and swindles. In even the smallest police department, no day passes without some loss of property, yet the larger part of such crimes are only cursorily investigated. Police forces are undestaffed and can usually take care of only the big cases. The smaller losses are noted, filed, and brought to the attention of pawnbrokers and second-hand dealers by means of lists which the police circulate.

Except in some rural districts where the local policeman has time to look after even very minor losses (although not always with success because of his lack of training), ordinary thefts and burglaries have never had the attention they deserve. This situation is universal. Perhaps it is inevitable that the same effort cannot be made to solve the abstraction of ten chickens from Mrs. Smith's backyard as to the theft of $100,000 in a safe cracking. Even if a commissioner were to plan a very liberal staffing of his detective division—and I never saw such a liberal plan drawn up—he would certainly not expect petty crimes to be as thoroughly investigated as the big ones. No one knows how large a detective division supposed to deal thoroughly with every reported crime, big or small, ought to be. But the fact is there: the public is not getting all-out protection against the very sort of crime which occurs most often.

No police anywhere ever "break" more than twenty-five percent of burglaries committed. Many a police force is reluctant to publish the bald statistics of failure in this branch of detection. Yet statistics on burglaries are the best means of testing the efficiency of a detective division, since the identity of the burglar is, as a rule, unknown at the beginning of an investigation. The performance failure is concealed by a mixture of figures on other crimes and offenses. Suppose a police department shows, on paper, a batting average of seventy, or even eighty, percent of all reported crimes as solved. This may look impressive. But in the majority of crimes reported to the police—such as forgeries, embezzlement, and the like—the perpetrator is usually potentially known from the beginning because his name is given as a suspect when the crime is reported, and his apprehension is routine work.

It is a pity there is usually no time to investigate thoroughly minor crimes against property; they present exactly the same aspects of criminal investigation as major crimes and so are an excellent school for young detectives. These petty crimes exhibit the same patterns of human character and quirks of mentality and offer the same opportunity as the larger felonies to use all the clues and techniques which modern police science affords.

It is impossible to discuss stealing without discussing receivers, the people who purchase and resell stolen goods. There is an old saying that if there were no receivers, there would be very little crime against property. Certainly the existence of receivers of stolen goods is responsible for a good proportion of the crime against property. Many youths committing first crimes, as well as professional criminals, would be totally discouraged if there were no means of disposing of their collections. The big receiver is a businesslike person who never deals with criminals directly but delegates such sordid affairs to a lieutenant. Even this lieutenant often deals through a third man.

I use the word "businesslike," for the receiver has to be a wholesaler or retailer who needs quantities of furs, watches, drugs, or other salable material. He informs his lieutenant as to his requirements, and professional burglars are informed, perhaps even with a hint as to where the acceptable commodities may be found. A warehouse is then pilfered, and the goods are delivered to the lieutenant, who removes the means of identification, makes payment, and arranges for transportation to the receiver.

The small-time receiver has a more hazardous career. In the first place, he often connives with the thieves and is in danger of being blackmailed. If a thief is imprisoned, the receiver may have to take care of the wife and children under threat of exposure. Technically also, the small receiver is worse off than the big-timer, because he cannot afford to specialize in certain goods but must buy miscellaneous items. Of course he passes these on as quickly as he can. Nevertheless, he is often apprehended with identifiable objects still in his possession.

The aristocrats among burglars are the safe-breakers. A good safe-breaker possesses countless bits of information: the size and the make of the safe, the time when cash is left in it and the amount, the best method of access and escape, the habits of neighbors, patrolmen, and watchmen.

There are several methods used in opening a safe. In a "ripping job" the door is ripped open by a jimmy after a hole has been made with an electric drill, exactly as an old-fashioned can opener is used. This is a petty, small-business job.

Then there is the "punch job," where the dial is knocked open with a sledge-hammer and, after some manipulation, the lock is released. This method works best with old safes, and it is surprising how many old safes are still in use. Many of them are family heirlooms, not worth much more than an ordinary steel cabinet.

For a "burn job," as it is known to the criminal fraternity, ordinary tubes of acetylene and oxygen must be carried to the safe. The lock is cut out by the torch flame. This is an easy and quick method widely used today. It is of course difficult to transport the gas tubes, but this can be overcome. I remember a case from my days in Lyons where, in the daytime and during business hours, two gas cylinders were brought into a bank by a couple of workmen and placed in the hall, together with some other paraphernalia. The "workmen" did not say anything, and the employees of the bank assumed the delivery was in preparation for some construction work. In that instance, though, the burglars were caught by the night watchman. Sometimes the victim himself furnishes the gas, especially in a small workshop or garage where gas cylinders are a part of the equipment.

Even simpler are the "carry-away" jobs, in which the safe, if it is small enough, is boosted onto a truck, delivered to a hide-out, and opened at leisure.

Farther up the scale are the "combination" jobs in which a safe with a combination lock is "picked." To the public this activity has been glorified by literature until "combination" burglars are thought to be amazingly clever. Well, yes. There are some in the United States today who are supposed to be able to open any combination lock in a comparatively short time. My friends in the New York Police Department estimated that there were not more than four of these characters, three of whom were currently in prison. One had been known to use a small device which looked like a fountain pen. Under the screwed-on tip, instead of a pen there was an almost microscopic steel rod. After a hole had been drilled in the safe above the lock, the rod could be inserted to aid in the manipulation of the tumblers.

Usually in a "combination" job the safe has not been properly locked or else the burglar has the combination to help him. Often he has only to examine the desk of the chief executive or cashier and, more likely than not, will find the combination pasted to the side or bottom of a drawer. Of course, it is possible to open a safe by the exercise of special knowledge. Safe manufacturers generally have on their staffs a few men who are able to open a lock without the combination. This is done mathematically and takes several hours for an experienced man. But these expert employees are not supposed to be safe-burglars.

Finally, there are the "blow jobs," where explosives are used. This operation is almost extinct in the United States but is still used in other parts of the world, especially Scandinavia. The American safe-blower must, in his day, have been a spectacular figure, for he used nitroglycerin, which he called "soup." Nitroglycerin is a sensitive liquid which is likely to explode on the slightest provocation, and this is especially true when it is home-brewed and the acids employed in making it are not washed completely away. The safe-blower carried his soup in a rubber hot-water bottle under his coat, but even these bottles sometimes exploded unexpectedly.

The modern Scandinavian counterpart of the safe-blower uses dynamite and very often in such large quantities that the contents of the safe are destroyed. Some years ago a dynamite burglary took place in the flat of a wealthy banker in Stockholm. The burglars wrapped the safe in what they could find in the flat to deaden the sound of the explosion: in this case Oriental rugs. Those carpets were worth several thousand dollars, but the burglars found twenty dollars in the safe.

The most successful safe-burglar of all time remains Max Shinburn, who operated in the United States at the turn of the century, the golden age for this felony, when safe designs had not caught up with the amount of money available to put in them. My friend Robert Heindl once told me Shinburn's story, which has hardly been surpassed.

Shinburn seems to have been a poor boy who emigrated to the States after having served his apprenticeship as a mechanic in Germany. He was first apprehended as a burglar in St. Louis and served a sentence. But in those days he was still a novice and had not realized his gifts. He graduated into big time by opening a bank vault in Boston; after that he operated only on safes and vaults. It was said that he could walk into any bank as if the doors had been opened for him, since there was no lock then in the world he could not pick.

Over the years Shinburn ransacked a great number of banks and acquired enormous sums which he threw to the wind. He lived in the most expensive hotels, always moved in good society, and was to be seen at horse races and theatrical premières. He was an assiduous patron of gambling halls and lost enormous sums. After many years he was betrayed by an accomplice just when he had successfully burglarized a bank of $200,000. He was arrested in Saratoga, and society was temporarily deprived of one of its most ingenious members.

But Shinburn did not stay long behind bars. He knocked down a prison guard, grabbed the keys, and walked out to liberty and more safes. He was caught again but again escaped, and each time he made a bigger and better haul. Finally Pinkerton himself, the master sleuth, arrested him. To prevent his escape this time, he was handcuffed to two of Pinkerton's best men, and all three were put in a secure room for the night. Probably Pinkerton's men slept, because in the morning Shinburn was not there. He had picked the locks of the handcuffs with his stickpin.

The peculiar thing about Shinburn was that he did not share the fate of almost all habitual criminals by ending his days in prison or the workhouse. He fled to Europe. He did return to the States long enough to pillage the Ocean Bank in New York of several hundred thousand dollars. So far as is known, this robbery was his last. He retired to Brussels and lived there until his death as a respected *rentier*.

There have been others who were also clever but did not have the luck of Shinburn. Once, while I was visiting my friend, Thune-Jacobsen, the Chief of the Detective Division of Copenhagen, he took a toothpaste tube out of a drawer in his writing desk.

"Here is a fine example of why nothing should be overlooked," he said. "This tube ended the career of the Sass brethren."

I looked curiously at the thing. And I could not help laughing when I remembered these two bank "directors," the Sass brothers, who were currently behind bars in Copenhagen. They had been the two most daring burglars of the twenties, and there was not a detective on the Continent who had not heard about them. I could imagine the brothers' dismay at being caught by their own clumsiness after they had defied the police of many countries for a decade.

The Sass brothers were Germans and, at the time of their capture in the early thirties, lived in Berlin. Outwardly they were the respectable owners of an auto repair shop in a suburb. This gave them an opportunity to possess all kinds of tools, acetylene torches, and power drills, without arousing suspicion. They undertook only big jobs. As time passed they concentrated on banks and could really have been described as vault-burglars. On one occasion they acquired nearly $200,000 worth of gold bullion from the vault of the Dresdener Bank. They had rented a place across from the bank and dug a tunnel under the street to the vault.

But it was in Copenhagen that they carried out their master-piece. One of the largest banks of the city was building new head-quarters, and when the foundation was laid, a big vault was begun in the basement. The huge steel door leading into the vault was the work of a famous German maker. This door was a most impres-sive object, being about thirty-six inches thick, made of glistening armor plate, with a part of its complicated lock mechanism dis-played under plate glass at its back. Because of the size and weight of the door—it weighed several tons—it was delivered and brought into the cellar before the construction of the first floor was begun, and it remained in the excavation for several months.

Not long after its arrival two innocent-looking German tourists arrived in Copenhagen. One night they descended without diffi-culty into the unfinished cellar, screwed the door open from the rear and took out parts of the locks. They did this in such a way that the locks continued to function but could be opened with almost any key. This done, the Sass brothers returned to Berlin and calmly awaited their time.

After the bank building was completed and the door of the vault installed, every morning at 9:30 two bank directors, each carrying a different key, ceremoniously opened the vault, not know-ing that it could have been opened practically by a hairpin.

When the Sass brothers decided that the vault was ripe for harvest, they set forth again as tourists, with visas entitling them to stay in Denmark for a fortnight. On board ship bound for Den-mark, fate intervened in the form of two shapely Danish sisters in whom the brothers became quite interested. They invited the sisters to a seaside resort, where they had such a good time that they overstayed their visas. It was a simple matter to have any tourist visa extended. It was necessary only for them to go to the Alien Section of the police and get another stamp. But the brothers, who had an innate shyness where police were concerned, did not wish to enter into any official explanations, so they changed the date of entry to Denmark on their passports. The forgery was immediately discovered in the Alien Section, and they were arrested for this reason.

Of course at that time the police had no suspicion of their criminal activities. Purely as a matter of routine, their hotel room was searched. In a toothpaste tube was discovered a little roll of thin paper showing a sketch of the vault mechanism. The Danish police immediately guessed that these were not small fry and, in conjunction with the German police, uncovered the career of the Sass brothers. After serving their sentences in Denmark, they were returned to Germany, where new convictions awaited them.

One obvious moral of this story is that the doors of vaults should never be left alone when a bank is being built.

Modern vault doors, in cases where cost and weight are no object, are completely burglarproof. The contemporary burglar, therefore, never undertakes to go to the door when trying to force his entrance into a vault. Instead, he tries the walls. In a modern vault the walls are constructed of special concrete and reinforced with manganese-steel bars. But with time, patience, good tools, and an acetylene torch, a hole can sometimes be made. Even the vault builders, if occasion arises and an entrance into a vault has to be forced, prefer to go through the walls.

Therefore, in order to be absolutely burglarproof, a vault has to be surrounded by a gangway from which the area underneath the floor and the top of the roof can be inspected. And there should be such an inspection several times every night. But this is an ideal which few banks attain. As a matter of fact, many vaults with imposing doors are easily accessible because of the poor quality of the walls. There is one bank I know which has a vault with a most impressive door, so heavy that it is swung out in the morning and put in place in the evening with the aid of a crane. And yet the walls are built of bricks, in some places not more than two layers thick. Any chain is only as strong as its weakest link.

In Stockholm in the middle thirties we had a burglary which almost amounted to the perfect crime. (Incidentally, I have never come upon the perfect crime. The criminal may be very shrewd and calculating in every detail, and the execution of the crime may be perfect so far as his own actions are concerned, but there are so many imponderables in the surrounding world, over which he has no power, that it will always remain pure chance if any crime is left undetected.) In this case, the criminal gave himself away. His name was Berglund. He came from a good family, had some education, but had always lived as a ne'er-do-well of the more harmless type. At the time of his crime he was earning his living as the concierge of an apartment house, where a part of his job was to attend to the central heating. Because of this chore, he had access to a little mechanical workshop. Several years previously, he had been employed briefly at the tax collector's office and was well acquainted with the times of the year when the safe in that office was stuffed with money.

Berglund managed to perform the almost incredible feat of gaining access to the tax collector's private apartment, entering the bedroom where he was sleeping with his wife, and stealing the keys from his trousers pocket. He then went home, made a duplicate of the one to the safe, and returned the keys to the collector's trousers. On a suitable night, he went to the collector's office, gained easy access, but found that he hadn't copied the key exactly enough and that the safe would not open. So he repeated his feat, and for the second time stole the keys from the tax collector's trousers and returned them.

This time, the duplicate key functioned and he got away with about $100,000 in small bank notes.

An innocent clerk in the tax collector's office became the suspect of this burglary and was held under arrest for a short time. This probably did not burden the conscience of Berglund but, like most people who come into easy money, he started spending freely and went to Copenhagen on a spree. He behaved so peculiarly in the hotel there that the clerk reported him to the police. Under questioning he confessed.

This might have been the perfect crime: Berglund had been unknown to the police. If he had gone into some small business and given the appearance of earning money, he would certainly have gone scot free. He had left no traces, no clues, no fingerprints.

Ever since the introduction of insurance against burglary, there have been simulated burglaries as well as real ones. The explanation, alas, is that sometimes it is easier to get money for the goods in a store or warehouse from an insurance company than by selling them to ordinary customers. By the same token there are always burglars willing to undertake a soft job in the interests of an insurance collection, but it is not easy to get in touch with them. So in many instances the merchant has to rely on his own wits, and this leads to trouble. It is not so simple to make a burglary look authentic in the absence of a professional, and many imitation burglaries have been exposed by a wrong move.

The first case of this sort which I ran into was of an almost classic type. One day in Lyons a M. Alphonse Berthier reported to the police that his jewelry shop in the Rue de la République had been burglarized. He claimed that thieves had entered the cellar of the house, made a hole up through the floor of the shop, and stolen jewelry worth about $20,000. His story seemed plausible enough, but as a routine assignment I was sent from the Police Laboratory to have a look at the scene. That the police considered the affair *bona fide* could be deduced from the fact that I, a young foreign assistant, was the one sent to investigate. Yet the event taught me that small crime is not without merit as a training exercise.

I had with me the standard outfit, consisting of a pocket fingerprint kit and a piece of molding clay for making casts of the marks of the burglar's tools. Arriving on the scene, I introduced myself to M. Berthier and his wife, who proved to be a typical French little-business couple. He was a small, nervous, rabbit-like man who served the customers, while she was a Junoesque woman in black who acted as cashier. M. Berthier told me that he had been asked by the police to leave everything as it was until the scene had been examined.

The building was a couple of hundred years old, with the thick walls of its period. As the thief was supposed to have entered the cellar, I went to the basement. Down there was a long, dark corridor with many rough wooden doors leading to individual storerooms, each allotted to a tenant. One of these doors was open, its rusty old lock dangling by a single screw. The hasp was of the hinged type which covers the screws that fasten it to the jamb and the door proper. I examined the door with my flashlight; on the outside of it I could easily observe the marks of a jimmy. So far so good. The burglar had evidently used his jimmy to loosen the lock. Three of the screws were on the ground. Leaning over, I picked them up and examined them in the palm of my hand. One was bent and the thread was full of minute particles of wood; this screw had evidently been torn away by the impact of the jimmy. But on the other two there were the marks of a screwdriver, and the thread on each was clean and glistening.

I felt that indescribable sense of joy which I suppose a bloodhound has when he first snuffs the trail. It is this feeling of success in solving the mystery, this warming up of the blood, this comfortable feeling in the stomach, which compensates for so much frustration in the life of a policeman. I turned and looked at M. Berthier, who was watching me with anxious eyes. Not a word was exchanged, but I could read defeat in his eyes.

In continuing to follow the course of the alleged burglar, I entered the almost empty storeroom. In one corner there was a heap of bricks and rubble clearly originating from the hole which had been made in the ceiling. It was through this hole that the burglar was supposed to have entered the store. It struck me that the burglar must have had an uncanny knowledge of the layout, since the hole was in a free place, away from counters and cabinets. I played my flashlight on the hole and saw hanging there several pieces of loose plaster which would certainly have fallen down if someone had forced an entrance. I was now certain that the burglary had been simulated. Berthier kept watching my movements with the eyes of a hypnotized chicken.

When I had finished in the basement, I went up into the store, where an examination of the floor confirmed my findings. The floor was covered with tiles, and the tiles around the hole bore jimmy marks which proved that they had been attacked from above.

I asked the wordless proprietor and his wife if I might use the telephone to call Headquarters. I then asked to have a man sent down to the jeweler's store. While I waited, I placed myself at the door and watched the Berthiers, who by now were very uneasy. In ten minutes, the detective came, and I whispered into his ear what I had found.

My theory was that M. Berthier had arranged a simulated burglary in his shop. Because of his knowledge of the building, he chose the exact place in the basement ceiling where a hole could be made into a convenient spot in the shop. But when he started to break open the door in the basement, he found that the lock was too resistant. Thereupon he unlocked the door, took a screwdriver, and removed two screws in order to facilitate the task. Then he closed and padlocked the door again, broke it open, and began to cut the hole in the ceiling. Now, to make a hole in an old-fashioned brick ceiling almost one yard thick is a very hard job, and it was easy to imagine M. Berthier working and perspiring with dust and small pieces of plaster falling into his eyes. When he was half through, he probably found the job too strenuous, so he went upstairs and commenced to dig his way down, after having measured out exactly the right point.

The headquarters detective arrested the pair, charging them with fraud. They were taken to the Sûreté, where they confessed.

25

LOST ARTS AND NEW CRAFTS

My study year in New York came at a time when some of the more usual techniques by which many criminals supported themselves were beginning to become lost arts. Not that I found the detectives full of regret about this technological obsolescence, but there is, for any policeman, a certain irritation at having to learn afresh what the boys are doing now. Tourists to the France of a few years ago may remember a sign, enamelled on metal and as typical of the country as the sign that informed them that today the elevator was not, *hélas!*, marching. This sign read:

MESSIEURS ET MESDAMES
MÉFIEZ-VOUS DES PICKPOCKETS

and tourists and citizenry alike were thereby warned that they should look out for pickpockets. I know that even today there are still a few gentry of this profession operating at times and places like New Year's Eve in Times Square, and perhaps in the subways of New York and London and Paris, but the tradition of Fagin is gone, and Dickens would have to look elsewhere, and in less agreeable places, for an introduction to the schools of crime. Violence is taking the place of dexterity.

Perhaps this change is due to a habit of carrying lesser sums of money in the average pocket; perhaps to a development of the vicious practice of mugging; perhaps, indeed, to many changes in the structure of society too subtle to measure against a single alteration of the law of cause and effect. But the elevator operators of the *Tour Eiffel* no longer drone out their warning message, the enamelled signs have gone, and the wallet is no longer so often abstracted with finesse from the pocket of an unconscious moneyed victim. In short, the art of picking pockets has almost disappeared.

It is as if this non-violent method of separating a citizen from his bankroll had been superseded by more vicious and overt methods, and that the picking of pockets, like other crafts of dexterity, could not survive in the machine age. Gone are the days when a fatherly friend would teach eager pupils the best way of getting a wallet or a watch out of a pocket without the owner's knowing about it. Gone also are the massaging of the fingers and the art of using the index and middle fingers as a forceps to pull something out of a pocket. It is rare to find in the modern criminal trade a trained, adept gentleman possessing these specialized qualities.

Such artists are nowadays found only on the stage, where they will, before the very eyes of the spectators, take the suspenders off an innocent burgher without his knowing what is happening. I once knew a retired sheriff in California who, in a restaurant, could life the wristwatch, the suspenders, and the bowtie off a waiter. He certainly had all the professional qualities of the old-time pickpocket but, of course, he used his art only to amuse his friends.

Along with certain types of confidence men, the pickpocket belongs more or less to the Gay Nineties, the age of bowler hats, mustaches, tight-fitting trousers, and starched collars. Nowadays a thief employs cruder and more brutal methods when he intends to relieve someone of something. The bag-snatcher is a typical example of the modern practitioner. The hold-up is also a standard technique. The old-time pickpocket was usually a man of gentle nature who would not have dreamed of hurting his victim. The hold-up man of today has been admirably described by old Chief Sullivan of the New York Detective Division: "If you are ever the victim of a hold-up, hand over everything you have, even the watch of your dead father. Otherwise, you will be dead too."

In talking with pickpockets I have learned of their irresistible craving to steal. I know that certain social reformers do not believe in this compulsion, but every experienced detective could tell them the same. Whatever the psychological explanation may be, it is true that there actually is the kind of person who cannot resist stealing and who will steal for the sheer joy of stealing. From the viewpoint of society, these are obsessive cases.

Many years ago I was compiling a dictionary of the Swedish argot of criminals. My collaborator was an old thief. The general word "thief" correctly described him because in a small country like Sweden he had not become so specialized as he might have become in a large country. In order to make a living, he had to be a jack-of-all-trades, ranging from pocket-picking to safe-burglary.

One day when we had an appointment, he arrived a little late and came to my office with an air of excitement. His face was noticeably flushed. When I asked him what had happened, he said that on his way to see me he had stoped in at his favorite beer garden. After the waitress had brought him his glass of beer, she stood by his side a moment, and he noticed that the leather purse she carried slung over her shoulder was half open.

"And you know, there was a hundred-crown bill protruding from it. I could not resist taking it. It was too easy money. And so I took it. When I finished and came out on the street, however, I remembered that the waitress was an awfully nice girl who on several occasions, when I was out of cash, had staked me to beers. So I went back, ordered another glass of beer and put the hundred-crown bill back in her purse."

He looked at me, hoping to find signs of admiration for his noble deed.

And why not? It *was* noble. I am not sure that some of the sharks in the financial world of the time would have done a parallel thing for one of their innocent victims.

In 1940 at a line-up in the New York Police Department I encountered one of the very last of the kind old pickpockets. During the endless procession of criminals of different brands, an elderly and dapper little fellow was brought to the platform and stood there blinking in the strong light.

The police captain who was conducting the line-up barked at him, "Your name is Isaac Ahasuerus. You are seventy-two years of age. You were caught in a Presbyterian Church, by the side of one of the church elders, an engineer, who carried $500 with him. The money disappeared while you were sitting next to him. Do you confess?"

"No, sir," the old man answered humbly.

"How does it happen that you, a Jew, were in a Presbyterian church?"

"Well, sir, I worship God in all forms."

Later I had a little talk with him. "Of course you took that money," I said in a low voice.

"Of course I did," he whispered. "But there was no witness. I have been arrested twenty-seven times in my life, and if I confess that will be the end of me."

Then, rather foolishly, I asked, "Don't you think you are too old to go on stealing?"

He whispered back. "There are no pensions for people like me." Then he added proudly. "I have always made a nice living. I never bought a pair of shoes under forty dollars."

Of course, the old boy was released, as he had been often before. A smart pickpocket always passes on his loot at once, and there was no evidence against him except that he had been arrested many times and had been sitting next to the Elder. He was one of the last survivors of the fine, old pickpockets of New York who, though not so famous as those of London, were once regarded as the best in the world.

Generally swindlers are the most interesting criminals, for they are almost the only ones who put sharp brain-work into what they do. They are also likely to be excellent actors who perfect their impersonations with great patience and skill. A pair of confidence men, for instance, will commence work on a selected victim who is an absolute stranger to them, and within a short time the victim will regard at least one of them as the best friend he ever had, a noble and trustworthy character. Soon he will almost plead with the con man to take care of his money.

The United States cannot be called the native land of the confidence man, but there is something in the trusting air of that country that seems to develop some of the finest flowers of the species. One case in New York impressed me as a minor masterpiece of the actor's act, and, incidentally, of the victim's talent for credulity. Naturally, in order to evoke that credulity the con man had to be a master actor, a scoundrel whose talents might well have been put to better use. It began with an elderly man walking down a main avenue shortly after ten in the morning one fine day. Coming in the opposite direction was a young fellow in shirtsleeves, and somehow they struck up a conversation. One word led to another—the slackness of business, the ingratitude of customers, the lost opportunities. Anyhow, the older man confided that he had once been a locksmith—and isn't this weather unseasonable?—and here was a new patent lock he was trying to sell.

And so the game was on, a game which is known as the "switch" —in this case the more precise term, "the handkerchief switch," would be appropriate. The young man and the older strolled on together for several blocks, exchanging confidences. By and by they noticed an old man who seemed bewildered and lost.

"I wonder what's the matter with that old man?" the young fellow observed.

The other went over to the old man and inquired, "What is the matter?"

"I just arrived from the West where my brother has just died and left me $10,000 in insurance," the stranger replied, sighing heavily. "If I return home with all that money, my mother will wonder where I got it, and she'll soon realize that my brother, whom she loved so much, is dead, and I don't want to grieve her so. The trouble is, I don't know what to do with the money. I'm a stranger here and I'm afraid to trust it to anybody."

Tears dripped from his eyes as he held the inside pocket of his overcoat open, revealing a small canvas bag such as might hold money.

It soon developed that the old man was a native of the same state as the locksmith, and the locksmith immediately took a neighborly interest. He arranged with the young fellow then and there that they should be the old man's guardian. After all, they were businessmen and knew the dangers of a big city.

The old man, still in tears, listened to this conversation. "But how can I be sure that you are honest people?" he inquired.

The young fellow turned to the locksmith and asked him if he had any money on his person.

"No, not with me, but I have a bank account," was the reply.

The young fellow turned back to the old man. "We will show you how to keep your money safe by demonstrating to you how a bank operates."

The old man, delighted to meet honest people, wiped away his tears and promised them the good pay of $25 a day for guarding him and his money.

On their way to the bank, the old man expressed amazement at the large buildings and asked many questions about landmarks and city life. He held the locksmith's hand, caressing it, and with tears of gratitude kept repeating his obligation to such honest folk.

At the bank, the locksmith withdrew a thousand dollars and showed the old man the money to convince him that he was a man of substance, and to quiet this fears. The young fellow in shirt-sleeves then suggested that the old man put his money in a package with the locksmith's thousand, so that the locksmith could safely deposit it in the bank. The three of them left the bank and stepped into a doorway nearby. Then the locksmith took his own thousand dollars in cash and placed it in a handkerchief. The old man thereupon placed his money bag in the same handkerchief, which was then tied with knots at the four corners. While they were doing this, the young fellow kept cautioning the locksmith to be careful with such a large sum. With much ceremony, he unbuttoned the locksmith's vest, talking all the while about the necessity of caution.

It was during this maneuver that the poor old man switched the handkerchief and substituted another, without the locksmith's noticing the exchange. He then exclaimed excitedly, "You got safety pin, I got safety pin, here, here, place it so!" And he pinned the handkerchief to the inside of the locksmith's vest, buttoned the vest, and then the coat.

When the locksmith returned to the bank, he discovered that the handkerchief contained newspaper clippings cut in about the same size as paper money.

The coin matchers have a different sort of confidence game. About twenty years ago I knew a young Swede who fell victim to this piece of chicanery. He had been sent to the United States by his father, a wealthy manufacturer, to study production methods. He was about twenty-five years of age, well bred, well educated, and possessed of normal intelligence. In spite of all this, he lost a thousand dollars and in doing so showed himself to have a bit of the crook in his own mentality. The peculiar thing about most switches is that they play on that small amount of greediness and wickedness which is in nearly every human being and which comes to light when the occasion arises.

This young Swede, staying at a prominent New York hotel, was walking near Times Square when he was approached by a man who asked him where the Museum of Natural History was located. The Swede replied that he was a stranger in the city and was unable to furnish the information. The man then asked the Swede where he was from, and the Swede told him. The stranger expressed surprise and said that he was of Scandinavian descent and was more than glad to meet a fellow countryman. He invited the Swede to attend a show as his guest.

After the play, they walked north on Broadway. They were approached by a man who asked them—some years too late in point of history—where he could find the Hippodrome. They said they were strangers and did not know. The newcomer said he was from the South, had been in New York only two days, and was finding it a very unusual city: everyone he spoke to proved to be a stranger and nobody could direct him to any place he wanted to visit. The Southerner confided that he had been left a large sum of money by his mother, who had died recently, and that he had come to New York to spend part of it having a good time. He said it was hard to get acquainted in New York and proposed that the three of them go to dinner.

They all entered a cigar store and bought cigars. The Southerner insisted on paying for them, and an argument arose on the subject. They finally decided to match coins to determine who should pay. The Southerner lost and paid for the cigars, but he remarked that he had bad luck every time he gambled and pretended to be sore. He then suggested that they match for five dollars. The three continued to match, and the Southerner continued to lose. The more he lost, the angrier he got.

They then continued their walk north on Broadway and reached Central Park. The Southerner excused himself to go to the lavatory. His confederate said to the Swede, "Let's work together and get this fellow's money." The Swede refused at first, but finally consented when the swindler agreed that they would return the money after winning it.

When the Southerner rejoined them, they resumed matching. The Southerner lost approximately a thousand dollars and the Swede about the same. A noisy argument arose between the Southerner and the Swede's acquaintance, the Southerner claiming that the other two were playing in conjunction with each other to swindle him. He threatened to call the police and have them arrested. The Swede became excited and pleaded with them to be quiet. He implored the confederate to return the money to the Southerner and settle the argument.

The confederate refused, and told the Swede to leave the matter in his hands. "Go on to your hotel," he said, "and I'll meet you there later."

The Swede left. After waiting at the hotel two hours or more, it dawned upon him that he might have been swindled. He referred the matter to the Swedish Consul General, who phoned me about it. This was at the end of my year of study in New York, the day before my departure for Sweden, but I managed to find half an hour to see the young man. He told me his story in the presence of a police inspector and was taken down to the Rogues' Gallery, where he was able to identify the two men almost immediately. But it was not so easy to catch them because, although they were well-known swindlers, they had already left New York. A few weeks afterwards they were arrested in Palm Beach and confessed. The two of them had been making a nice living from suckers such as the Swede.

During the year of my visit to the New York City police, the door of the office assigned to me at Headquarters carried the curious inscription: INTERNATIONAL WORLD POLICE. This had nothing whatever to do with my grant from the Swedish-American Foundation or the fact that I was, in the language of a university, a sort of Visiting Fellow. The inscription had come about in quite another way and, when I first learned its background, I had no premonition that later in my life I would be closely associated with the idea that had given it birth.

The man who was responsible for the legend on my door was one who could have emerged only in the United States, and then only in his own day and time. He was the late Baron Collier—Baron being his name and not a title—and he had been born in the border state of Tennessee less than a decade after the close of the Civil War. He once listed himself in *Who's Who in America* as a capitalist, and that description was certainly accurate enough in that he had made a lot of money. At the age of seventeen or eighteen he had gone into the advertising business, from which his extraordinary genius led him into a number of other fields. He became a banker, a Florida real-estate operator, a transportation expert, a corporation executive in a dozen companies including hotel and typewriter firms, and, along the way, a gifted amateur in police work. He had held the posts of Special Deputy Police Commissioner in New York City, Deputy Sheriff of Westchester County, and, not listed in the schedule of his honors and attainments, that almost unknown human post, benefactor of police. It is, in fact, hard to think of anyone else who has ever felt the way Mr. Collier did about the value of police to our society.

This fondness for police and police work had led Mr. Collier to the inspired idea of uniting all of the world's police forces in a coordinated fight against crime. He put much money and effort behind this proposal, being aided in it by my friend and future collaborator, John J. O'Connell, who was at that time, as I have said, Deputy Chief Inspector of the New York Police Department and later, shortly before his death, its Chief Inspector.

Aided by O'Connell and paying all the expenses, even the fares of the delegates, Collier invoked in the early thirties an International Police Congress in New York. He invited the heads of various European police forces to attend, but in those days the International Police Commission of Vienna was in operation and Collier's idea of a World Police did not appear to be necessary. The only outcome of the Congress (except for a beautiful volume containing all the proceedings and the speeches of the delegates, paid for by Collier) was that he received some Continental decorations. For several years, however, one of the rooms on the first floor of the New York police headquarters on Center Street continued to serve as the office of the World Police, with a full-time secretary.

At that time Collier was an honorary police commissioner of New York, had a badge to display, and was entitled to a siren on his car, all of which gave him innocent pleasure. If anyone ever merited such distinction, it was certainly he.

Behind Baron Collier's idea of a World Police was a great deal more sense than was realized in his own day. Criminals are not prone to sentimental nationalism; this is particularly true of swindlers, whose activities are as often aided as thwarted by state boundaries. Only by international cooperation could such characters be brought to book.

As bizarre a figure as ever came to my official attention was a certain Ivan Dimitroff (as I shall call him, out of respect for the name he most often employed). Very possibly it was his real name, but he had lived in so many places and so deviously, and his past was so clouded, that I am not sure even he himself knew what his true name was.

I ran into this Dimitroff not long after my return from New York. At that time he styled himself a movie agent and was living in Paris in an elegant bachelor's flat not far from the Champs Elysées. His crime of that moment was swindling a major Swedish motion picture importer, and his accomplices were the Paris representatives of that importer plus the head cashier at the importer's main office in Stockholm. Dimitroff supposedly acted as agent for French motion picture producers. With the Swedish representatives of the Stockholm firm as intermediaries, he charged the importer several times the film rental actually quoted by the French producer of the film. He got away with this by the use of faked invoices, and his other accomplice, the head cashier in Stockholm, paid out the exorbitant rents without blinking an eyelash.

That head cashier was a tragic case. She was an elderly widow, an impoverished descendant of old Swedish nobility. She became a tool of Dimitroff in order to give her only son, a dashing young cavalry lieutenant, enough money to keep a stable of thoroughbreds and to live in conformity with his idea of his station in life. When her deceit was discovered, she committed sucide. As for the Swedish Paris representative, he was small fry, an elderly alcoholic, a former journalist who had been hired largely because of his knowledge of French.

When I came to Paris at the request of my client, a Swedish movie importer who was an old friend of mine, I went at once to call on Pierre Mondanel, then the head of the Sûreté. Mondanel assigned me a *Commissaire* by the name of Le Falle, to aid me in the investigation. We spent several days hunting for Dimitroff, whom the Swedish ex-journalist representative had already identified to me as the head man of the swindle.

Commissaire Le Falle, a man of small stature with dreamy brown eyes and a black mustache, had just emerged from the Stavisky case, one of the most peculiar of the financial scandals which shook France in the thirties. The case had involved the ruin of thousands of people, the mysterious death of the magistrate handling the case, the downfall of Cabinet members and, finally, the suicide of Stavisky.

(I think it is fair to call it a suicide, although a part of the French press hinted that he had been murdered by the Sûreté in order to close the case. There was also a hint that Le Falle, who had tried to arrest Stavisky at the moment of his suicide, had instead deliberately shot him on orders of his superiors. Now, this theory was madness, as anyone would have been sure if he had known Le Falle. He was very indignant when he told me about the circumstances of the arrest of Stavisky. Let me add that there is no institution in France which has been so shamelessly and impudently criticized by newspapers as the Sûreté, in spite of the fact that it is composed of as fine policemen as can be found in the world.)

However, when we got to know each other more closely, Le Falle confessed that he was a Communist. This was the only time in my life that I met a policeman, and especially one with such a high rank, who admitted to having this particular delusion. I attributed the fact partly to his poverty, since he had a very low salary. Moreover, this was in the time of the "Front Populaire," those years before World War II which were so disastrous for France. Whatever the reasons for his politics, Le Falle is dead now, but the picture of him as a confessed Communist, holding a trusted position with the police, has often haunted me.

Anyhow, we started our investigation quite simply by taking the tram and going to the flat of Dimitroff. A valet, who looked like Sam Weller in *The Pickwick Papers*, eyed us suspiciously and informed us that his master had not spent the night at home and he did not know his whereabouts. We had a glance at the apartment, which was stuffed with antique furniture and pictures, and left. Next, we went to Dimitroff's office, but his secretary only shrugged her shoulders. By questioning the janitor of the office building, Le Falle learned the name of the garage where Dimitroff kept his expensive sports car. When we got there a mechanic told us Dimitroff had been round a few hours earlier and had taken out the car. He volunteered further that Dimitroff had made a telephone call from the garage and had told someone that he was going to the Montparnasse section of Paris. The mechanic added in a whisper, "I think I heard him say to meet him at a place called *Au Cent Femmes Nus.*"

This was at least a lead. We spent the whole day searching up and down Montparnasse, even forgetting about luncheon and dinner, but eventually we did find him. By nine o'clock we were seated in the dreadful establishment named by the garage attendant. The hundred naked women were there, all right, but when we came in the only customer was an old man who looked like a drunken taxi driver. Those hundred women had not much of a target for their affections.

After we had waited until midnight, Le Falle got hold of the proprietor, took him in a corner, flashed his badge, and told him he knew that a gentleman who looked thus-and-so was somewhere in the house. The frightened proprietor replied at once that he had such a client in a private room but that he was busy for the moment with a girl. We asked the proprietor to show us to the room.

The door was locked from the inside, but Le Falle knocked discreetly and whispered through the crack that he was the waiter, that he felt ill and was going home, so couldn't he have the bill paid? Dimitroff fell into this trap and opened the door. He was a powerful man with a dark complexion, about forty-five years old. In the background lurked a dusky and only half-naked woman, obviously a native of Madagascar. On the table were empty champagne bottles.

Dimitroff was extremely annoyed, but there was nothing he could do about it. We let the woman go and started to interrogate him. He told us that this was a mistake that would cost us dearly. He knew M. So-and-So and M. Thus-and-Such, and he would see to it that Le Falle lost his job at once.

Le Falle let him rant on for a few minutes, then said coolly, "You may do what you like tomorrow, Monsieur, but I am going to interrogate you here and now. You are not a Frenchman, are you?"

"No, Monsieur," answered Dimitroff. "I am a Honduran."

With those words, he produced a brand-new passport which had been made out by the Honduran Legation in Paris.

At that time the small Central and South American countries kept only one legation on the Continent, in Paris. Their ministers were badly paid and sometimes added to their income by selling citizenships.

Le Falle asked calmly, "And can you name for me, Monsieur, the capital of Honduras?"

This was a small matter which the clever swindler had not prepared himself to answer.

"Were you not a Swiss before you became a Honduran?" Le Falle asked.

Dimitroff's dossier at the Prefecture had provided us with some details on his career. He was probably Russian and had supposedly fled Odessa, in South Russia, in 1919 when disaster overcame General Wrangel, a leader of the Whites. It was known that the Swiss Consulate at Odessa was burglarized of several blank passports and obviously one of them had fallen into the hands of Dimitroff, who proceeded to France.

In Paris he prospered until, in the middle thirties, the Swiss Government required every Swiss living in a foreign country to obtain a new passport at the nearest Swiss Consulate. He did try to buy a new passport from a clerk at the Swiss Consulate in Paris, but he was denounced to the police. Dimitroff was in a tight spot, especially when it was discovered that he had never paid any taxes since entering France. For this peccadillo he remained under arrest a few days, but then was freed. The affair ended in a *cul de sac* because, at the bottom of his thick dossier, there was a slip of paper on which was boldly written in red crayon, "*Affaire fermée. Recommendation de M. Xéridat, Député, dans les couloirs de la Chambre.*" I do not know what had motivated M. Xéridat to cover up for this scoundrel, but there it was.

At this particular midnight Le Falle and I got a sort of half confession of the current swindle, Dimitroff blaming the Swedish representative and declaring that he had only thought to do the man a service. Next day, it was decided to drop the case because, owing to international complications, it would be difficult, almost impossible, to prosecute him before a French court.

I then did something which I have never done before or since, in the light of my opinion that fiscal matters are not necessarily police business. I encouraged Le Falle to report to the income tax authorities on Dimitroff's antique furniture, the paintings, and the sports car.

Gypsy musicians enlivened the lighter moments of the 1936 Belgrade meeting of the pre-war International Police Commission.

My friend, Heinrich Tandler, head of the new German Police Laboratory, organized with my assistance by the postwar Bonn Government.

Chatting with one of my farmhands; the family manor
house in the background.

The Söderman family at the farm in 1955. The heart
is where home is.

26

RAPE AND WORSE

From the very beginning of my studies as an apprentice criminologist, it was borne in upon me how powerful a role sex plays in the whole tragic drama of crime. Out of all the seven deadly sins, lust and greed are the ones which cause almost all the criminal violence human beings perpetrate upon each other. In a city such as Lyons, prostitution, with its attendant corps of pimps and maquereaux, provided the foundation for the organized criminal structure. But even in many crimes committed by non-professionals, the sexual aspect was predominant. I can think of no way to talk about the subject in a manner suitable for tea-table discussion, and yet a criminologist should not profess to write about his experience with crime and then out of decorum omit this central aspect.

Before now I have reminded the reader that crime is an ugly business. Its nastiness, at least in the case of crimes of violence, does not seem susceptible of gradation. Perhaps it is possible to feel some indulgence toward rascals, scoundrels, safe-breakers, and pickpockets, but whether a murderer is more or less revolting than a rapist depends upon individual opinion. Neither seem to me to be in any degree tolerable. If there is a reader of this book who feels that crimes of sex are beyond the admissible literary pale, this chapter is not for him or her.

Even as mild a manifestation of aberrant sex as the Peeping

Tom is unattractive, to say the least. The kind of prurient curiosity such fellows exhibit may be nothing more criminal than a vicious invasion of privacy which is, perhaps, partly understandable because there is nothing which seems to arouse human curiosity so much as sexual matters. Considering the tremendous role which sex plays in normal private life, this urge to explore it may be considered logical. But people whose most intimate moments become the source of sexual satisfaction to a clandestine observer are sure to feel a sense of personal outrage if they learn they have been spied upon.

The French police used to call these deviants *voyeurs—Peeping Toms*—and at the Sûreté we used to hear that many a French commercial traveler carried a sturdy little brace and bit in his valise, even if he was not a hardware salesman. With the aid of this tool, he could arrange a peephole into a neighboring room occupied by a couple. Presumably this was an economy—no need to waste money on a ticket to the motion-picture palace. It was certainly a fact that a good many of the smaller hotels had peepholes through the walls or decorations of their honeymoon suites into the adjoining rooms.

Moving one scale down the unpleasant ladder of prurient interest in the mechanics of sex, there is the recurrent question of the filthy motion picture. There are so many references in contemporary fiction to the notorious *cinéma bleu* of Marseilles that readers may be tempted to assume that indecent motion pictures, like bouillabaisse, are a specialty of that city. Not at all. It is true that France was the great producer of these entertainments, if they may be so described, in the years before the Second World War. But the French had no monopoly on the raw materials for the market. When France was occupied by the Germans, these articles were absorbed by the customers at hand and so disappeared from the export market.

In Sweden, as elsewhere, the supply of such films ran short. To meet the demand, a small-time photographer in Stockholm decided to make one. Generally, such a movie needed only two actors, the man and the woman. This particular photographer already had the woman who, oddly enough, was not a professional prostitute. At least, not all the time. By day she was employed in a haberdasher's shop in Stockholm. To find an actor for such a movie is generally more difficult, since the role entails remaining in readiness for hours, and under the sharp eye of a camera. The producer-photographer and the actress must have stood in the studio scratching their heads over the problem of finding a suitable actor, when they heard the faint sound of a violin in the courtyard below. The photographer looked down and saw a young street musician scraping away at a fiddle. He was a well-built youngster in his early twenties, obviously with a dash of gypsy blood in him. The photographer promptly ran down the stairs and asked the astonished musician to follow him to his studio for an important business proposal. Then and there the thing was settled. The musician was to have a handsome fee and free gin in payment for his performance. Free woman was implicit in the deal.

And so the movie was produced. It was not a bad one from the photographic standpoint, and the performances of the musician were really remarkable. But by the time the film was processed and ready, the photographer was short of cash and could not afford to wait to market it through the usual channels. So he began to show his masterpiece in secret to schoolboys, who gladly paid a few crowns' entrance fee. After these clandestine premières had gone on for a few weeks, a parent got wind of the business and reported it to the police. The film was seized and the photographer prosecuted. He got two months in prison.

This story had a peculiar aftermath. The confiscated film was brought to the Police Museum, where it was appraised as one of the best items of its category ever impounded. But, in prison, the photographer repented and asked that the film be destroyed, so one day I ordered one of my men to go with a can of gasoline to a city dump and burn it. The order was carried out, but the photographer had not vouchsafed to us the interesting detail that there was another copy of the film in the possession of the actress.

Meantime, this women had got hold of a young man who became smitten with her somewhat tarnished charms, and they became engaged. In a moment of candor she told her fiancé the story of the film and about her copy of it. Not unnaturally, he became furious and ran to the police with the film. The story, as reported to me, makes me believe that he never saw the film projected; he could never have married the girl if he had seen it. Anyhow, this second print was not a part of the record in the case, and I have no information as to its ultimate fate.

One of the criminologist's most valuable stocks in trade is his memory of earlier crimes, derived either from experience or from the record. Some years after I had become established in Stockholm a case arose in which the memory of another, a hundred years earlier, helped to provide the solution, though not of the kind we had expected.

Late one night the Stockholm police received an agitated call from an elderly, wealthy businessman whom I shall call Anderson. This Mr. Anderson was a bachelor; he employed as his housekeeper an orphan girl named Lisa, the daughter of one of his deceased friends. The girl was about twenty-two, a graduate of an excellent woman's college, and a shy, good-looking creature whom the merchant looked upon almost as his own daughter. They lived in an eight-room flat on the second floor of a large apartment house. Several rooms separated Mr. Anderson's bedroom from Lisa's.

On the night of the call to the police the girl had awakened her employer. She was weeping, and her nightgown was torn. Between sobs, she told Mr. Anderson that a man had entered her room through an open window and raped her. Then he had disappeared through the window again. She had been so terrified that she was unable even to cry out, but she was able to give a detailed description of the man.

Mr. Anderson immediately called the police, as well as his old family physician. Both arrived in a short time. The police could find no trace of the perpetrator of the rape, but they noticed that anyone could easily gain entrance to the room by means of a drainpipe and balcony. After a hurried manual examination, the doctor's report was that Lisa was no longer *virgo intacta*. The police promised to do what they could, but there was faint hope of getting hold of the man, whom Lisa described as a swarthy fellow about thirty-five years old, with a handsome face and bold, dark eyes, wearing a light blue suit.

Mr. Anderson had to leave on an important business trip and, in order not to leave Lisa alone, he invited a young couple to stay in the flat during his absence. Late the next evening, while the young people were having a cup of tea and playing the phonograph, Lisa excused herself to answer the telephone in the next room. She returned in an almost hysterical state, explaining that the rapist had phoned, asking her to meet him the next day at a certain street corner. She said she had agreed in order to set a trap for his capture. The police were informed, and Lisa appeared at the street corner at the proper time, watched by a squad of detectives concealed in shops and doorways or pretending to be innocent passersby. No rapist appeared, and after an hour it was decided to abandon the watch.

Lisa reported that immediately on her return home she received another telephone call, in which the rapist said he had seen the policemen. He then made a new appointment for a week later.

After Mr. Anderson returned home, he came to see me personally. He told me that life in the flat was nightmarish because of the possibility that the rapist would return some night. He slept with a pistol at his side and left all the doors open so that he might hear the slightest disturbance.

I asked Mr. Anderson to send the girl alone to my office, and when she came she blushed upon being pressed for details of the crime. Reluctantly she described everything: how on that eventful evening she had made her preparations for the night, including that ritual which ought to scare off any rapist—smearing her face with cold cream. She said that she had left the window open because it was warm, put on her nightgown, and got into bed. After reading a French novel for about an hour, she had fallen asleep and was awakened by a sound. When she opened her eyes, she saw the dark man perched on the window sill, looking at her by the light of the full moon.

She said she was so frightened that she couldn't move a limb or cry out. The man slowly lowered himself to the floor, undressed, and got into her bed. He caressed her for a moment and then the frightful thing happened.

"And then," I asked. "What happened afterwards?"

"He got out of the bed, took a comb from the bed table, and combed my hair."

"Couldn't you cry out by this time?"

"No, it was just like a spell on me," the girl answered.

"And what happened when he had combed your hair?"

"He raped me again," she replied with tears in her eyes.

A most exceptionally virile fellow, I reflected.

My mind immediately produced, like a reference file, the unhappy story of Lieutenant Roncière le Noury and young Mademoiselle de Morell, a story almost a hundred years old but still a classic of its kind in police annals. As I talked with Lisa I recalled the details of that ancient case.

In the year 1834, at the French Cavalry School at Naumur, there was stationed a dashing young cavalry lieutenant named La Roncière le Noury. His commanding officer, the Commandant of the school, was General le Baron de Morell who had a sixteen-year-old daughter. He and Madame Morell invited the young lieutenant to their home a number of times. On such occasions the young man behaved with suitable gallantry, but no more.

Soon, however, the General began to receive anonymous letters, signed only with the initials "E.R." Then Madame Morell and several of their acquaintances as well started to receive these epistles. Each letter dealt with the love which the writer bore for the General's daughter, the fair Mademoiselle de Morell and, though they commenced in the flowery romanticism fashionable at the time, they became increasingly passionate in tone. Finally, in the most violent of all the letters, the anonymous lover declared that he proposed to take by force what he could obtain in no other way. The writer went on to describe the forthcoming rape in considerable detail.

The girl's family took suitable precautions, but to no avail. One night the household was aroused by screams from Mademoiselle de Morell's room. When they reached her, it was already too late; the rape had been committed, and the criminal had disappeared. The young victim declared that she had recognized Lieutenant Roncière le Noury as her assailant, even though the room was very dark. She was believed at once, the more so because the anonymous letters pointed in the same direction.

Le Noury was placed under immediate arrest and prosecuted for rape. He denied the whole thing indignantly and violently, but circumstantial evidence and the girl's identification of him brought about a prompt conviction. He was sentenced to ten years at hard labor.

Still, as time passed, Mademoiselle de Morell behaved strangely. Gradually it became clear that she was extremely hysterical, and in one of her outbursts she confessed to having written the letters herself and simulated the rape. It was never explained whether she did so out of unrequited love or only in order to make herself the center of attention. Whatever the reason, the lieutenant was released from prison and reinstated. He went on to a good career and eventually became Governor of a French archipelago in the Pacific.

So went the hundred-year-old story. But the case now confronting me was somewhat more complicated. There were no letters to work on, for one thing. (Mademoiselle de Morell's hysterical forgcries would never have stood the scrutiny of modern handwriting analysis.) Even more difficult was the report of the Anderson family physician that Lisa was no longer a virgin. As I turned the matter over in my mind, a doubt began to form. Was there a possibility that the doctor could have been mistaken? The more I speculated, the more I felt that this possibility had to be eliminated before we could proceed further.

Asking the girl to stay where she was for a few minutes, I went to an adjoining room. Quickly I telephoned an old friend, a gynecologist who was the head of a large maternity hospital. "Is it possible to determine," I asked him, "if a girl is a virgin by manual examination only?"

"If you are very experienced, yes," he replied. "However, it is easy to be deceived. Even I would prefer to have a girl on my examing table before I could pronounce on the matter with certainty."

I arranged for Lisa to be examined in his office right away and went back to my office.

Lisa consented to the examination quite meekly and in less than an hour after she had left my desk, the telephone rang. My gynecologist friend was on the wire.

"The girl is as virgin as a National Park forest," he said.

Of course, most rape cases are not the figments of hysteria. As distinguished from seduction, they are very often the work of habitual sex offenders. The prosecution of such a case is complicated by the fact that there is usually no witness, and by the difficulty in proving that it took place without encouragement from the victim. Yet an experienced policeman is generally able to judge by the attendant circumstances.

In an unpleasantly large number of rape cases, the proof is simplified because there has been more than one rapist. Gang violence, especially among juvenile delinquents and young hoodlums, seems to be on the increase. Perhaps this is because of the greater freedom allowed young people by modern parents, or perhaps it is a symptom of the tension of our time. Perhaps both.

One form of sexual deviation has recently been attracting an unprecedented amount of attention. This is homosexuality. Particularly in the United States, the postwar fear of the Communist conspiracy has occasioned an hysterical demand for the elimination of "security risks" from military or government posts, key defense industries, and similar responsibilities. Homosexuals are considered bad security risks because they can be blackmailed through fear of exposure, possibly into the revelation of military, political, and scientific secrets. And it is certainly true that fear of exposure has a kind of panic intensity for such men.

This deviation from the norm is probably older than man's history as *homo sapiens*. Zoologists and students of animal behavior have reported sexual activity between members of the same sex in many species of mammals. The phenomenon was ancient in the days of the Greeks who took a tolerant attitude toward it. It is known in every country of the world and in many primitive tribes. The antiquity and the universality of homosexuality have made the matter one which most police forces disregard unless the aberration results in violence, treason, or some other criminal manifestation. Under the laws of most Western countries, homosexuality is a serious offense, far more so if a minor is involved. In some few countries like Sweden the practice, if it is confined to adults and if no public nuisance results, is not a legal crime. Even this much latitude, however, creates plenty of work for the poor—and usually disgusted—policeman. Just as normal men often like young girls below the age of consent, so the homosexual frequently prefers boys. Therefore many young hoodlums make a nice, easy living from unhappy older men whom they threaten to expose.

An old friend of mine in Stockholm, an architect, telephoned one day to request an appointment. He asked to meet me outside office hours, and I finally consented to call round at his bachelor apartment after work that afternoon. I found him outwardly as always—a remarkably good-looking man in his middle thirties, with light hair, blue eyes, and the lean, conditioned physique of the constant sportsman. He set out a tray of Scotch and soda, and we settled down beside the fireplace. The talk was general and ordinary at first, and I began to wonder why he had wanted to see me at all.

Suddenly, without previous preparation, he leaned forward in his chair and looked at me half defiantly. "There is something about me," he said, "which you seem not to have detected. Are you aware of the fact that I am a homosexual?"

As a matter of fact, I had been unaware of it. True, I had noticed that his manners were sometimes a trifle effeminate and that his voice was a bit high-pitched. There was also a blurred, opaque look in his eyes which I have sometimes noticed in homosexuals, but I had never thought of him as possibly being one. Momentarily I experienced that instinctive repulsion which most normal human males feel in the presence of this abnormality. I showed, I hope, no outward sign of it but tried instead to remember how kind and considerate this man was, and how he had never offended me or anyone I knew.

In the next instant my memory, jolted by the instant of revulsion, revealed the occasion in my youth when I had first been exposed to this aberrant phenomenon. I was spending a week in Sofia where there were then only two hotels. The better one was too expensive for me, so I took a room at the other, where prices were reasonable and where the night porter was a former Russian general. One evening I was standing by the reception desk talking with the general, when a Bulgarian officer whom I recognized as the tenant of the room next to mine came into the lobby. He was a swarthy man of middle stature, about forty years old, and under his arm he was carrying a bottle of wine. He joined our conversation for a moment and then asked if I would like to share the bottle of wine with him. Without misgiving, I followed him.

To my surprise, after we had entered his room, he locked the door. He insisted on my sitting on the bed and, after a while, placed himself by my side. This made me most self-conscious; as a youngster I was tormented by pimples, and at the moment I had a conspicuously ugly one on my nose. Suddenly the Colonel exclaimed, "I don't mind the blotch!" and kissed me on the mouth. At first I was thunderstruck, but the reaction came in a few seconds and I planted my fist under his chin. He fell backward on the bed, and I opened the door and ran into my own room, locking my own door behind me.

Since that time I had encountered plenty of homosexuals in my police work and had gradually learned to pity them. Therefore I listened carefully to the story of my architect host.

In high school he had never felt any attraction toward girls and, when he was twenty and was doing his military service, he fell in love with a boy who occupied the berth above his in the barracks. But he resisted this attraction as a kind of peculiar whim. He was a young man of good manners, and his father had been a highly placed civil servant. He was also somewhat religious. During his years at the University he felt, time and time again, the urge to have relations with other young men, but he fought against such leanings and conquered them.

After finishing his education, he was employed for a while as a rural architect. His employer had a beautiful young daughter and, in an attempt to prove himself normal, the young man one day kissed her. In that moment he knew with nauseating certainty that he could never touch a woman again. After a period of torment, prayer, and doubts, he emerged a convinced homosexual.

"But why do you tell me all this?" I asked him.

"Because I am at my wits' end!" he cried. "For two years I have been in the hands of a blackmailer. He is a nice-looking young boy, not long out of reform school, and at first it was a real love story between us. But now he is preying upon me in the most pitiless manner. He threatens to go to the District Attorney and tell the whole story if I don't give him money. Disgrace, ruin, and prison for me."

At that moment the telephone rang, and I watched my friend listen with a tortured expression on his face. "But you know I have no money at this time of day," I heard him declare. Finally, he sighed. "Well, I will meet you this evening at eight o'clock. But this is the last time I can give you anything." He hung up and turned to me. "I suppose I shall have to go to the pawnbroker with something," he said sadly. "This youngster drives me mad. I think that I shall have to kill either him or myself."

All I could do for the poor fellow was to assure him that I

would keep to myself what he had told me. Fortunately the matter solved itself in a few days; the young blackmailer was killed in a street brawl. My acquaintance could never have escaped legal punishment for the unforgivable offense of having had homosexual relations with a minor. Indeed, I know several cases of homosexuals who have been driven to suicide by blackmailers.

Without doubt, homosexuals are bad security risks. They are vulnerable not only from the legal viewpoint but also (and this is purely my personal opinion) because they are usually less balanced than normal individuals. There is the conspicuous example of Colonel Redl, Chief of the Austro-Hugarian Military Intelligence at the beginning of World War I. Redl was a homosexual and because of that the Russians had such a grip on him that they forced him to hand over the secret mobilization plans of the Hapsburg Empire. Redl was unmasked before long, yet the scandal could not be allowed to leak out at such a time. A fellow officer told Redl that his treachery was known, placed a loaded pistol on the table before him, and left the room. In a few minutes, there was a dull report, and justice had been done.

Homosexuals seem to have an almost uncanny way of spotting their own kind. Report has it that if a homosexual enters a room with a hundred unknown persons in it, at once he is able to spot among the company the one or more who might be homosexuals. In this way these deviants constitute a conspiracy by which they protect and aid each other. This grouping together has sometimes been demonstrated in an almost fantastic way. For example, in the first decade of this century, the German writer Maximilian Harden prepared an exposé of the Kaiser's entourage, proving that the high court officials and inner-circle generals were almost all homosexuals. The Kaiser himself was unaware of the abnormal tendencies of the men around him.

There has been much speculation as to the number of homosexuals existing. The first systematic attempt to ascertain such figures was made by the German scientist Magnus Hirschfeld. Before World War I he made a survey through the mails, using 3,000 students of the Charlottenburg Institute of Technology and 5,721 metal workers in a Berlin trade union, picking those categories, I suppose, because he had access to the addresses. Hirschfeld sent each of these men a double postcard, explaining what he wanted to know. The addressee was to tear off the half which was stamped, check it *Yes* or *No*, and mail it back to Hirschfeld. Of the addressees 49% answered, and the percentage of homosexuals worked out to between 2% and 3%.

Since then, many other attempts have been made to ascertain the number of homosexuals in society. On the whole, the results correspond fairly closely with the findings of Hirschfeld. In 1947 a survey was made in the United States based on Draft Board records and on Army discharges due to homosexuality. This survey revealed that 1% of the male population of the United States could be officially identified as homosexuals. These must have been blatant cases, since many homosexuals are ashamed of the fact and will not admit it. Professor Alfred C. Kinsey, in his *Sexual Behavior in the Human Male*, states that 37% of the male population in the United States has had some sort of homosexual experience between the beginning of adolescence and old age. Looking at this apparent discrepancy from a policeman's viewpoint, I think both findings may well be correct. There are so many between stages that the figure offered by Kinsey, if mutual onanism between youngsters of the same sex is included, is quite plausible. I should say that the approximate 3% reported by Hirschfeld still covers the situation.

It has often been maintained that homosexuality is an acquired vice and is the practice of old libertines, but I believe this theory is fundamentally wrong. I hold with most modern psychiatrists that in the overwhelming majority of cases homosexuality is a constitutional abnormality. Sex is established by the linkage of certain genes shortly after the fertilization of the ovum. In some individuals the personality traits of the opposite sex are predominant: the physical conformation of one sex combined with the psychological configuration of the opposite. Every human being possesses in varying degree the elements of both sexes. If there is the same degree of both male and female components in the same individual, so-called bisexuality results, depending on the influence of education, age, environment, state of mind, and so on. Individuals thus constituted may be attracted by either sex. Certain men belonging to this group, often even after a happy marriage and the rearing of several children, may in middle age show signs of homosexuality.

On the one hand, then, the congenital homosexual cannot help what he does. On the other, young people must be protected by society from the homosexual. This generates an extremely difficult question and one which is poised between two sets of valid considerations.

It is an unfortunate fact that the overt homosexual may even feel proud of his state and often regards himself as a superior person. It has been proved over and over again—for example, in the sexually immoral Germany of the twenties and more recently in Sweden and England—that when the law against homosexuals is relaxed, they no longer seek to avoid notice but, on the contrary, become a major public nuisance. This can lead to the impression that homosexuality is on the rampant increase. Yet probably there are no more basic homosexuals now than there were a hundred years ago, or two thousand years ago in ancient Rome, even though certain stories, especially in the British press, might make it appear that there are. The fact is that most people are normal and tend to find abnormality abhorrent. So the pressure for legal control, or at least a confining of the deviant within limits which appear reasonable to the majority, remains intense.

If all sexual deviation were confined to homosexuality, there would still be enough unpleasantness in the subject to last the working policeman a lifetime. Alas, there seems to be an almost infinite spectrum of abnormality, much of it even less appetizing than the tragic materials already cited. Sex is one of the mightiest of the human rivers, and by the same token it has a bewildering labyrinth of backwaters and bayous, lagoons and sinkholes. Sooner or later the working policeman is compelled to deal with most of them.

In Lyons some of Locard's other apprentices and I attempted to inform ourselves in this field. We read the works of Krafft-Ebbing and others and debated the evidence at length. This theoretical study of ours was not wasted, but there has proved to be a wide gap between the clinical considerations advanced in such specialized texts and the practical, on-the-spot contact which the policeman and the criminologist make. At least, our volunteer studies prepared us for almost anything and eliminated any element of surprise based on innocence. I cannot explore here every byway of this practical experience, but the broad topic deserves a treatment of some of the major aspects in which deviation presents itself to a policeman in the course of his working life.

In big cities everywhere there are individuals, most of them known to the police, who walk around dressed in the clothes of the opposite sex. This phenomenon, more common among men, is called transvestitism. Certainly there must be a strong homosexual trend in such people, but this is not always obvious nor the invariable rule. Other possible motives have to be considered. For example, sometimes these transvestites pose as prostitutes merely to commit robbery.

In the late twenties I encountered a case which was investigated by a friend of mine, a Berlin detective named Anuschat. Two well-to-do, middle-aged businessmen from Leipzig, in Berlin on business, on their first evening went to the *Friedrichstrasse*, which was the center of Berlin night life at the time. There they met a couple of nice-looking girls who invited them to their room. As soon as the door was bolted, the two girls turned out to be a couple of tough young gangsters who took everything of value away from the older men and then kicked them out. One of the victims, who was married, did not want to tell the police about it, because of his wife. The other, who was a bachelor, professed not to care, even though he could have complained with social impunity. Eventually, and partly to oblige his friend, the bachelor did report his loss to the police, and the gangsters were arrested.

In the Berlin of the miserable twenties, I once took part in a "control"—a sort of warning reconnaisance—carried out by the vice squad against the dance halls frequented by transvestites. In those days there were no less than three such places in Berlin, not to speak of the run-of-the-mill homosexual establishments which numbered into the dozens. The Chief of Control of the night spots in Berlin was this friend of mine, Anuschat, one of the foremost experts on small firearms. A short man with a bald head and keen, glittering eyes, Anuschat had originally been a specialist on poaching, and his position as Chief of Control illustrates admirably how the police often make wise use of men with a specialized bent of mind.

On this particular night, we entered the first of the three dance halls. Before we had got past the cloakroom we had been sold a copy of a special magazine published for transvestites who called themselves "the third sex." On the first page appeared a picture of a man who looked like a fat butcher, dressed in elaborate female attire. Underneath the picture was the caption: "*Vorbildlich Angezogene Transvestin.*" (Impeccably Dressed Transvestite). When we had found a table and had ordered beer, I looked round. Nearly everyone in the place was wearing women's clothes. Anuschat assured me that these people were all men, but I found it hard to believe him. I was especially doubtful about a young girl sitting alone at a table nearby. I scrutinized her sharply and was convinced that here, anyway, was an exception. Her delicate features, her nice hair, her pierced ears, her small hands with the pointed nails—everything bespoke her femininity. She even had pointed breasts, which showed attractively under her evening gown.

So convinced was I that here was at least one genuine girl that I made a bet with Anuschat of a bottle of champagne. He accepted the bet with a laugh, and I got up and invited the girl to dance. She assented graciously and proved an excellent dancer. We were

half across the floor before she started to speak in the gruff voice
of a young hoodlum from the suburbs. Instantly I was furious with
myself for my gullibility. With a total absence of courtesy, I thrust
my hand into the neck of the dress and fished up two sponges. The
young man was much offended and could only be pacified when I
gave him some money. When I returned, Anuschat was laughing
and I had to pay for the bottle of champagne.

The popular conception of sex terminology is often false or, at
any rate, crude. Take, for instance, the word "perversion." It comes
from the Latin, *perversus*, which means turned the wrong way,
crooked, awry. This word has caused a good deal of misunderstand-
ing because it is popularly confused with deviation and taken to
mean anything from homosexuality (a deviation) to sadism (a
perversion), not to speak of sodomy and other aberrations. But the
whole witches' garden of perversities can flourish on either normal
or homosexual soil. Putting it another way, there are perversions
of deviations. For instance, a homosexual sadist may kill a boy,
the ordinary sadist a girl. Such terrifying perversions are often the
key to the personality of a deviant and give the clue to his secret
urgings and cravings. There are, unfortunately, more perverts, including the population of deviants, than people like to believe, and
I have always felt strongly that a detective should have a thorough
understanding of problems of this sort.

Practical criminologists agree that the most vicious of all the
forms of perversion is sadism. The dictionary defines a sadist as one
who obtains sexual gratification by the infliction of pain upon others.
It is among sadists that we find the terrible killers who, in mad
blood lust, kill and mutilate. Every year in every part of the world
there are such cases, and they stir the public to such a degree that
there is a hue and cry for the incarceration or elimination of all
perverts and even deviants of every description. This is not a wise
reaction. Sadism is a special phenomenon and should not be confused with other aberrations. There are at least two sorts of sadists:
first, those who actually commit sex murders and find their sexual

satisfaction in poking around in the intestines of their victims (or, more unusually, find it only in the killing); second, the mental sadists who find some unguessable satisfaction, sexual or not, in inflicting other sorts of pain on their victims. Many of the great tyrants of history belong to the second category, but it is often difficult to say just where the borderline lies.

Even among sadists, there are many degrees. There are people who pass for years as innocent citizens but who the whole time are toying with the thought of obtaining a super-sexual satisfaction by killing, for instance, a child. Sometimes they never carry out this idea, taking their secret with them to the grave. Sometimes at last they do, and liquor often plays a role in breaking down the lifelong inhibition.

Herein lies one of the great difficulties the police experience in dealing with sex murder. It is like an unknown hand striking out of pitch blackness. Often the murderer has no previous police record and has not even exhibited any previous tendency toward violence. The number of possible suspects is therefore very much larger than in an ordinary case, and the inquiry into the crime is dauntingly complex.

One of the fathers of police science, Hans Gross, the famous Austrian criminologist, once attempted to learn how many sadists there are. He organized some research workers among his students into a team to inquire among the inmates of a large number of Austrian brothels about the habits of their customers. A curious fact came to light. The inquiry established that quite a few of the men who frequented those places enjoyed ill-treating the girls and paid special prices for doing so. One, for instance, would make a coin red-hot, place it on the upper arm of a girl, and let it stay there until it was cool. Such a man was certainly a sadist, but how could he be placed in statistics, among the unascertainable number of males who frequent houses of prostitution?

Sadism derives its name from the Marquis de Sade, a gentleman who was born in France in 1740 and whom Napoleon consigned, as an incurable madman, to the prison of Charenton. There he

died in 1814. The evil Marquis is considered literarily one of the
better French authors of the late 18th century and lately has been
regarded in some quarters as a prominent philosopher. Be that as
it may, his life was from beginning to end a scandal to his con-
temporaries. He believed in cruelty as the height of sexual satisfaction, and countless are the stories that were told of him in his
day. One characteristic anecdote recounts how the young Marquis
came to Marseilles and was gracious enough to attend a grand
ball given by the bourgeois of the city, but he found the ball dull.
To liven it up, he got hold of a quantity of Spanish Fly, which
contains a reputed aphrodisiac, the alkaloid cantharidine, which he
mixed with the wine. An hour later the affair was more like one
of the ancient Greek bacchanalia than a decent burghers' ball in
Marseilles. Laughing derisively, de Sade had to flee in the night
from the rage of the burghers.

Only a few years ago I encountered a case involving a sadist who
obtained the use of a woman's body by a business transaction on
credit. He was a twenty-five-year-old waiter, generally out of work,
who lived in a two-room flat in a suburb of Stockholm with his wife
and baby. Curiously enough he had never exhibited any sadistic
tendencies toward his wife.

This waiter was an orphan who had been adopted by a well-to-do
civil servant in southern Sweden. As he passed adolescence he developed into a young hoodlum and was eventually thrown out of
his home. So he became a waiter, settled in Stockholm, and married. The marriage was very unhappy, and on several occasions the
wife took the baby with her and went for refuge to her parents,
who lived in the country. At such times, the man stayed alone in
the flat.

One evening at a popular dance hall he met a nineteen-year-old
maidservant who turned out to be one of the stupidest girls imaginable. He induced her to follow him home, and in the flat he
told her that he was a sadist and found great pleasure in bringing
his victims as near to death as possible. But, he added, he had never
killed anyone and he always paid well for their services. His chief

pleasure was to place a naked woman in a bathtub and put her head under the water until she started to become blue in the face. He would then release her and pay her a handsome reward. But for this night, he said, he had figured out another pleasure which would not do the girl any harm. It would consist only of her undressing and lying naked on the floor. Then he was going to perform some actions which would, he promised, be by no means painful or harmful to her.

He explained further that he was a bit short of cash at the moment, having paid some large bills earlier in the day, but he was willing to give her a promissory note for three hundred crowns, as well as a bicycle which he had in another part of town. The girl swallowed this childish tale and consented.

She lay down naked on her back on the floor and the sadist, fully dressed, lay on top of her. As the girl explained later, he then started to caress her body with his right hand. After a few minutes, he stood up and she discovered that she had been cut with a razor blade in at least a score of places.

The girl's story was almost incredible, and if I had not seen her body with my own eyes, I would hardly have believed her.

The young man helped her to dress the wounds in a rough fashion, then wrote out and handed her the promissory note. Next they took the street car to the town and went to a certain house. He told the girl to wait on the sidewalk until he came back with the bicycle. She, of course, had no way of knowing that he left the house through a rear door. Finally, she went home and seems to have fallen into a sound sleep, not realizing how near she had been to destruction.

The following day, the girl did not mention the matter to anyone, but that evening her sister, who was betrothed to a young mechanic in a neighboring town, came to spend the night with her. While the two girls were undressing, the sister discovered the wounds, and the victim readily explained how they had occurred. The following day the sister told her fiancé the story, and he promptly went to the police. The girl was brought to the Police

Laboratory and photographed. The waiter was arrested and sent to a mental institution. But since there were no signs of special madness, he was released after a short while. Presumably, he is roaming around to this day.

The mirror image of sadism is masochism, where sexual satisfaction is obtained by the pervert when someone inflicts pain upon him. Ordinary cases of masochism, although they are probably just as frequent as sadism, rarely come to the attention of the authorities. Here again is that very vague boundary between natural behavior and sexual perversity. A man who kisses the body of his mistress so hard that bruises occur, or even bites her slightly, may not be a sadist. And the girl who likes those caresses may not be a masochist.

Most of the cases of masochism known to the police are the result of raids on certain shabby "massage institutes," where such practices are carried on. The Police Museum of Berlin, destroyed by the Allied bombings, had one of the most complete collections in the world pertaining to criminal sexual aberration. Much of this paraphernalia had been seized in a certain massage institute, operated in Berlin before World War I by a Countess S. In reality, the Countess was a retired prostitute who had married an elderly and destitute member of a well-known landed family of the German nobility.

Her apparatus were almost fantastic. There was a large cross on which the client was suspended in order to get a thorough thrashing, medieval torture instruments of different kinds, and of course boots, spurs, and whips. These seem to play a prominent role in the thoughts of the masochist.

Detectives sometimes say jokingly that a marriage between a sadist and a masochist must be a very happy one. But, alas, it is not always so. I have in mind a case I ran into when I was working with the Manhattan Homicide Squad in the thirties. The man, a sadist, was a Wall Street broker, thirty-five years old and with a taste for high, fast living. The woman, a masochist, was twenty-five, a pretty divorcée from somewhere in Connecticut who had come to town to have a fling at the night spots in order to forget her broken marriage. They met in a night club in Greenwich Village and soon formed a liaison. The broker, who was a bachelor, lived in a flat at a respectable midtown address but kept a studio for his debauches in the Village. There he used to ill-treat the girl in the ordinary way of a sadist, wearing boots and spurs with which he stamped on her, tearing her sides with the spurs and lashing her with a whip. The woman willingly submitted.

One night when they had been to several speak-easies, they returned to the studio and one of their sadistic episodes developed. This time, however, the sadist let himself go completely, went wild, and ill-treated the poor woman indescribably. He had, however, forgotten to draw the curtain over the window. Someone across the courtyard saw the horrible scene and alarmed the police. When the Homicide Squad arrived, the door was closed but we broke in. The man was in such a frenzy he did not even see us and had not heard the noise of the door being broken. He was blind and deaf, like a woodcock when courting. A few seconds later, he was under arrest. The woman died later in the night from the injuries she had received. The man was legally declared insane and confined in a mental hospital.

The list of sexual perversions is long and, to a normal person, disgusting. One kind, more difficult to define than most and in itself rarely criminal, is fetishism. But because of the bearing it has on the behavior of the pervert it often plays a role in criminal investigation. The word fetishism comes from the African word, *fetish*, an object of worship among savages. In sexual pathology it pertains to a sexual pleasure derived from a part of the body or wearing apparel belonging to another person.

Fetishists are a many-faceted crowd. Also, it is quite difficult to tell where natural affection for something ends and fetishism begins. The young man who cherishes the small, perfumed handkerchief of his love cannot be called a fetishist. If he starts to steal ladies' underwear from department stores or clotheslines, and if he gets sexual pleasure from surrounding himself with such articles, then he can be so labeled. A certain famous actor owned large glass-doored cabinets full of shoes. The most cherished pieces in the collection were shoes from unknown girls whom he followed, snatching a shoe from them on a staircase before running away. It is not fetishism when a young man has a strand of hair from his love and cherishes it, but it is punishable fetishism if he goes out with scissors and cuts the hair of strange girls.

Once in Lyons some light was thrown on an arson case because the arsonist was a hair fetishist. The man in question, let us call him M. Mario, had been the manager of a textile mill in an out-lying suburb, having started with the firm years earlier as an errand boy. He was about sixty, a small man with a bald head and a some-what straggly, graying beard. He was a bachelor but had a house-keeper who lived with him in a company-owned house which was situated quite near the mill. He had few friends; indeed he was a recluse, living only for his books. Almost the entire second floor of his house had been converted into a huge library where there were thousands of valuable volumes, and he had quite a reputation as a bibliophile. It is an essential part of the story that he himself had paid out of his salary for all the expensive mahogany fixtures of the library, which included hundreds of shelves. He had also added a magnificent English-style fireplace to the room, even though the building was not his own.

In his later years, M. Mario had grown a bit peculiar. More and more rarely was he seen in his office at the mill, and the business of the company was left to take care of itself. He spent all his days and nights in his beloved library, peering with short-sighted eyes into some ancient volume. After several warnings and much dis-cussion, he was fired. He did not receive a pension, because the Board said that he was well-off and had enough money for his old age. He was given a month to clear out of the company house. He was not even allowed to take with him the fixtures from his library or the fireplace, since they were built into the house. This must have grieved him enormously. He bought a small villa in a neighboring town, and within three weeks all his possessions were moved except the furniture in his bedroom and the books in the library. Meanwhile he continued to live in the half-empty company house until he could arrange for the transporting of his books.

Late one night, M. Mario summoned the fire department. He declared afterwards that he had been sleeping and had been awakened by the fire at about two o'clock. No one remembered how he was dressed when the firemen arrived, and no one even looked to see if his bed had been used or not. The library was burning, and by the time the firemen arrived with their apparatus the conflagration had turned into what is called a smoldering fire. This kind of fire occurs in rooms where there is not enough fresh air for the fire to blaze, and is characterized by the slow creeping of the fire along the surfaces of the walls and ceiling. Paint and residues in the wood are completely consumed, the room is filled with the nauseating black smoke of tar products which settles as a brown, gummy film on the cold windowpanes. Firemen dread those smoldering fires because, if they break a window to thrust a hose inside the room, an explosion is likely to occur as the fresh air streams in.

The fire was extinguished, but the once beautiful library was by then a pitiful sight. Furniture, books, and bookshelves had been hurled by the powerful streams of water into one big heap.

The circumstances of the fire were certainly suspicious. We spent several days in the room, cleaning it carefully and examining every piece of debris. We replaced all the shelves and books, a painstaking job which was possible only because parts of shelves were not charred and the books could be replaced with the aid of markings. We were able also to replace a large radio in its former position beside the fireplace, because its legs had left a clear mark on the charred floor. About two feet from the corner of the radio, there was a deeply burned crevice in the wooden floor, and it seemed likely that this was the place the fire had originated. The top of the radio cabinet was charred except for a broad stripe which ran diagonally from the corner across the top. The width of this stripe corresponded exactly to the width of the bookshelves.

Next, we examined all the bookshelves and found one which was charred on one side only, the other side showing a protective marking corresponding exactly to the stripe on the radio cabinet. It seemed probable, then, that at the outbreak of the fire, this bookshelf had been lying on top of the radio, protruding a few feet out from it, its end exactly over the crevice in the floor where we assumed the fire had begun. When the bookshelf was microanalyzed, traces of stearin—an ester of animal and vegetable fats— were found on the end which had been over the crevice, suggesting that there had been a couple of candles as part of some time-fuse device.

We had now gone far enough to be able to arrest M. Mario, who indignantly denied having made any attempt at arson. Against him, however, there was the evidence of the not-yet-reconstructed device, as well as his grievance against the mill company, and the curious fact that we had found the remains of very few valuable books but only penny novels, catalogs, and old magazines.

While going through the drawers in the writing desk in the library, I came upon dozens of postcards with photographs of the busts of women. Neatly gummed to each picture was natural hair, arranged in elaborate coiffeurs in many styles. I had not known until then that such things were manufactured and sold to hair fetishists. These particular cards were indeed masterpieces and must have been expensive. In the desk there were also other photographs of women, and on these M. Mario had drawn intricate hair adornments. There was, then, a strong suspicion that M. Mario was a hair fetishist, although this detail of his private life did not at first seem to have any bearing on the case.

Nevertheless, it was all-important to establish whether M. Mario had been asleep in bed when the fire broke out. In this connection we got to thinking about his weakness for hair, which, with luck, might lead us somewhere. We imaged that a hair fetishist would prefer women with plenty of nice hair. If M. Mario had been out that evening with a woman, he would logically have been with someone of that kind. And so we began searching the neighborhood for such a woman.

We had almost no expectation of success, but we did indeed find the woman. She was a beautician who lived not far from the mill. A Junoesque creature of about fifty, she had luxuriant hair which had never been cut; it was arranged in innumerable locks and curls around her head. She must have spent several hours a day dressing it. This woman readily admitted she was M. Mario's mistress, that he had spent the evening in question with her, and that he had left her about two o'clock in the morning. M. Mario could not, then, have been asleep when the fire began.

When these findings were brought to M. Mario's attention, he used his ripped-up shirt to hang himself in his cell.

27

VOLUNTARY EXIT

Of all the crimes of violence, self-murder is one of the most terrible. My Catholic friends have told me that the Roman Church classifies suicide as a mortal sin because it signifies despair of the divine mercy of God. There is much logic in this. If a person has no right to deprive another human being of life, how can he assume the privilege of ending his own existence? Yet a great many people every year decide for themselves; in the year 1952 there were more than 16,000 suicides in the United States alone. Most of these cases must have involved some police work, and not a few of them a great deal. Every policeman encounters case after case in the course of his working life, but seldom is he able to become hardened against the horror and pity of this crime.

One aspect of self-destruction is especially pitiful. Age is no bar to it; a man or woman having only a few more years to go, or perhaps even only a few more months, often cannot wait for a natural end. Soon after I had returned from New York to my native country, I came upon a case which illustrated the elements which seem to impel old people to anticipate their natural date of death. In many rural districts of Sweden, especially in the north, farming is a hard and demanding occupation; it calls for strength and great vitality. Therefore an ancient custom developed whereby a man would hand over his farm to his heir even before death, receiving in return a kind of mortgage under which the younger man agreed to provide a house, firewood, milk, potatoes and similar foods, and sometimes even subsistence money for the duration of the life of the elder and the elder's wife. Such agreements were legalized in a court proceeding and had binding force upon the new owner of the farm, whether a relative or some other person. In some instances, these contracts worked a considerable hardship on the new owner of the farm. The retired farmer or his wife, or both of them, might live to extreme old age and gradually become an intolerable burden. Sometimes, especially when the farm had been bound over to a stranger, the old people were treated harshly, and even in cases where the holdings had passed into the hands of a son, instances of cruelty were not rare.

Not very long ago, in country districts, stories were told to illustrate this situation. Timeless is the account of the young farmer who, after some years of paying these old-age benefits to his own father, one winter evening went to the old man in his seat by the fire.

"You old goat!" the young man shouted. "I can't stand seeing you round the house any more!" He picked up his sire and carried him to the door.

The old man began to weep. "I said the same thing to my own father when I carried him out of the house fifty years ago."

In a case which came to my attention, a distant relative had contracted for a farm from an old man of about eighty-five, a widower. The old man was to live in a couple of rooms in the farmhouse, and for a time the arrangement worked out tolerably. Then one day he went with his successor to the general store in a neighboring village to purchase some tobacco out of the slender living allowance the new farmer gave him under the contract. It is easy enough to picture the younger man driving the gig and brandishing the whip to get more speed out of his horse, tearing along the road unmindful of the thin little oldster at his side.

At the store there were, as usual, many people. The young man pushed forward and made his purchases with bravado, but the old fellow had to wait in line. After a while the new farmer became impatient. He threw his own parcels into the gig, turned his horse around, and drove off, leaving the old man to make his way home on foot the whole ten miles.

Hours later, when the old fellow finally got back to the farm, the afternoon sun was almost setting. He trudged wearily into the house, went to his room, and returned outdoors with his ancient double-barreled shotgun. Seating himself in the high grass behind the red barn and leaning back against the wall, he placed the barrel of the shotgun against his heart and pressed the trigger with his walking stick.

Looking down at the old man's body, I reflected that very likely nothing would have deterred him from his act, once he had resolved upon it. Years earlier in Lyons, we had the case of a young man, a promising musician who had an unhappy love affair on which he had spent too much money. He was being hounded by his creditors, and whichever way he turned it seemed to him there was nothing worth living for. He tried to drown himself in the Rhone River, but the police managed to fish him out at the last moment. He was taken to a hospital where he spent several weeks recuperating, but the moment he was released he went home and hanged himself. That time the police did not arrive in time.

The urge to self-destruction seems strongest in Nordic peoples, who also have the highest percentage of insanity. A French statistician years ago conducted a survey of suicides in northern Europe, using a four-year span on which to base his study. Saxony was far and away the leader in this melancholy tabulation; 392 people per million killed themselves each year in that small area. He found Denmark second with 251, Switzerland third with 239, and so on down to Ireland, where in spite of the sorrows not only of Deirdre but of the whole Irish people oppressed by the Sassenach, only 17 people per million killed themselves each year. Innumerable studies have been made since that time, but the general patterns seem to hold true. It is as true today as three quarters of a century ago that more men than women kill themselves, that more unemployed men than employed men do so, that nearly half of the women who commit the act are having their monthly periods at the time, and so on. The vast amount of work that research investigators have done on this subject indicates that, even more than a murder, a suicide is an implied criticism of human society.

It would be reassuring to report that evidence suggests the suicide rate is partly due to the tensions or strains of the twentieth century. Yet the figures do not bear out this hypothesis. Between 1912 and 1930 the suicide rate in twenty representative countries of the Western world did increase, but only slightly, although the first date falls before the horror of World War I, the latter after the onset of the depression in most Western countries.

Fifteen years ago an American sociologist, Professor Bailey of Yale, studied 10,000 suicide cases in his country and abroad. He found that the age decade of thirty to forty was the commonest for suicide, and that the ratio of men to women in the group was three and a half to one. In America, he found, despondency was the commonest cause. Shooting, poisoning, hanging, and drowning were the favorite methods.

Among such studies, a number have dealt with the occupation or profession of the suicide himself, and in the case of men, soldiering stands high on the list. In my early youth I remember a close friend, an older man who was an officer serving as instructor in a military college. He attained the critical age of fifty without being promoted from Captain to Major; this meant that regulations forced him to retire. He was devoted to his profession and his retirement, as it developed, was a mortal blow. One evening shortly before his retirement there was a formal dinner at the house of the Superintendent of the college. All the officers were in fulldress uniform, and the candles in the chandeliers of the old mansion spread light over the gala scene. It was noticed that this friend of mine drank heavily before he returned to the bungalow in which he lived as a bachelor. When his orderly knocked on the door the next morning, there was no response.

The orderly, detecting a strange odor, forced an entry and found the Captain sitting in his chair unconscious. A big fire had been lighted in the stove and then the draft had been closed. Kerosene had been poured over all the upholstered furniture, which he then set on fire. Probably the officer had lost consciousness soon afterward, but, having a strong constitution, he had not died from the combustion gases. The furniture was damaged, but the fire had not spread. The orderly ran for the doctor, and the Captain was put to bed, the orderly at his side to watch his movements.

A couple of hours later, the Captain awakened. He must have felt very ill, but he swallowed the contents of the carafe of water at his bedside, got up, slung his greatcoat over his shoulders, put on a pair of slippers, and took his service pistol from the table. The terrified orderly tried to stop him but did not dare to lay hands on an officer, especially one who was a veritable giant, so he ran for help. Before the sentry returned, the Captain had walked to the nearby park, seated himself on a bench, and put a bullet through his brain.

Another thing which suicide cases teach the policeman is that human beings often display a tortuous and torturing inefficiency. It would be reasonable to suppose that once the decision had been reached, the personal judge who had condemned himself would at least recommend a humanitarian and quick way of executing the sentence. But even here the evidence is against the logicality of those people who defend suicide as a permissible decision where there is a societal custom to sanction the act. Of course there is something ritualistic about some few forms of suicide. The Roman, in his warm-water bath with the opened artery and the drowsy descent into death, is one example. Perhaps the nearest equivalent to that today is the overdose of sleeping pills. Far more frequent in Oriental psychologies is the pattern of the Japanese ceremony of hara-kiri, the disembowelling, so to speak, of oneself as an act of protest, with the slow, lingering, and pain-filled death which generally follows. In such cases, the pain itself appears to be part of the act.

Most suicides, though, are not ritual, and frequently they are unbelievably clumsy. Often and often I have wanted to disbelieve the testimony of my own eyes as I have stood over the anguished body of a suicide who chose some hideously painful and protracted method of doing away with himself. The policeman with a heart wants, at such times, to cry out, "Poor devil! Why, with so much water and rope available in this world, did you try this clumsy and long-drawn-out way?"

Some of these protractedly painful ways are selected because of ignorance. In ancient days in China it used to be believed that gold was a mortal poison. A wife, childless and thereby disgraced, would swallow a gold ring and fling herself down an abandoned well, only to die in pain and terror days or even weeks later. Modern Europeans, especially women, seem equally vulnerable to superstitious ignorance, particularly in the case of what we used to call contemptuously in our police laboratory the "housemaid's poisons." This category included everything dangerous which is used in household work, such as lye, creosol, concentrated hydrochloric acid, chlorine compounds, and the like. Only a person with abysmal ignorance of the mechanics of her body and the action of these chemicals could dream of swallowing a pint of any such stuff to achieve death, for no death ensues (at least not soon), only horrible burns of the gullet and the stomach. In most such cases death comes in the end, but often only after indescribable agonies. In some cases, surgery may succeed in patching up the damage. For instance, the gullet can be replaced by a metal pipe, so that at long last the intended suicide can walk out of the ward, probably no wiser, but tragically and permanently disabled.

The ignorance of the average person concerning his own anatomy is peculiarly well demonstrated in the effort to commit suicide with a razor or a knife. It is not unusual to find suicidal cuts in the most unlikely places. In some cases the subconscious intention may not have been firm, but in many others the intention could not be doubted. I remember a woman who slashed her thighs several times with a razor blade. I have seen cases where people made superficial slashes on the stomach and even at the temples.

There is more difference than a mere gulf of time between such a person and the Roman who elegantly and mildly opened his main artery at the wrist while taking a hot bath.

Some nearly unbelievable suicides have been committed by people who can be described only as lunatics. One case of this kind was that of Therese Colombard, the widow of an Italian road-worker. About sixty years old, she lived alone in a broken-down hut, earning a meager living as a newspaper vendor. The neighbors knew little about her, but it was said that she was prone to brood over religious matters and that she was habitually gloomy.

Exactly what brought her to her terrible decision will never be known. One day when she did not appear at the newspaper office where she fetched her papers, another newspaper vendor was asked to look for her. He went to her shed and knocked on the door. There was no reply and the door was locked, so he went his way. A couple of days later the neighbors called the police, fearing that Signora Colombard was sick.

A young patrolman, sent to have a look at the place, succeeded in opening the door. What he saw filled him with horror. Inside the small dark, dirty shed was a large, old-fashioned cook stove. The lid to the firebox was open and the old woman was kneeling before it, her hands clasped. Her head was in the actual firebox, totally carbonized, and even a part of her dress had burned. The young officer ran to his precinct station to report the awful sight, and we at the police laboratory were summoned. Obviously the woman had lighted a fierce fire, put her head into the firebox, and burned herself slowly to death.

This method of suicide is perhaps the most violent imaginable, since the effort of will involved seems to me almost inconceivable. But it contains the element common to many forms of self-destruction—the fury directed against the body. This is so violent that it seems as if the suicide meant to cause even his body to be destroyed. My years in Scandinavian police work taught me that this obliterating plan is not rare. Numerous cases of dynamite suicide in Stockholm and rural Sweden suggested that the will was directed toward total obliteration rather than the mere termination of life.

Most of these cases could perhaps be explained occupationally. The self-selected victims were generally construction workers or miners with access to dynamite and familiarity with its results. In such cases, I can only say that the suicide cared nothing at all for those who had to deal with the aftermath of his act. I once had to investigate a case in which a quarryman had killed himself with dynamite in a small shed. When I entered the place, its entire interior—what was left of it—was literally painted with blood, fragments of bone, and hair. One detail has never left my memory—a single eye, plastered to the roof and looking down on the indescribable scene below.

This quarryman had been a periodic drinker, going on sprees at unpredictable intervals. At such times he trumpeted abroad his contempt for religion of the accepted kind and reverted to a fanatical belief in the ancient Norse gods of Odin and Thor. This was in the days before the Nazis did their publicizing of these ancient deities, so our friend was something of a pioneer in the field. At any rate, when he departed for his Valhalla no mead was available, but outside the hut we found an empty bottle of gin and a jar of pickled anchovies.

In such cases there seemed to be two general techniques. In one, the dynamite stick is placed on top of the head, but this method results in the obliteration only of the head. By placing the stick in the mouth, the suicide atomizes the neck and part of the chest also.

Sometimes the circumstances vary. Not long ago a gentleman walking along a street in Stockholm took a stick of dynamite out of his pocket, along with a percussion cap and fuse, fitted the fuse carefully into the cap, stuck the cap into the dynamite stick and, putting the whole thing into his mouth like a cigar, lighted it. The surrounding pedestrians saw what he was about. In a flash, the street was empty and the neighboring shopkeepers were hiding under their counters. After a couple of minutes, the dynamite exploded and the gentleman was no more. He, too was an alcoholic, and had an unhappy marriage. In addition he was a braggart who liked to show off. This final occasion was his most dramatic performance.

There seems to be something in the atmosphere of Scandinavia which induces the use of dynamite. The Nazi High Commissioner of occupied Norway, a brutal and treacherous bank clerk from the Rhineland, Terboven by name, used it when he chose death instead of execution after the collapse of the Nazis. But as he was High Commissioner and so a Very Important Person, he used an entire barrel of dynamite. He had the barrel brought into a bomb shelter and lighted the fuse, which is said to have burned for twenty minutes before the explosion occurred. All this while, Terboven was sitting on the barrel calmly reading *Mein Kampf*, with the dead body of a friend, a German Police General who had shot himself a few hours previously, at his side.

After the explosion, there was very little left of Terboven, but identification was established by one of his arms. He had previously broken an arm while skiing, and the fracture had been X-rayed. Another X-ray, taken of the arm found in the bomb shelter, matched a negative in the files of the hospital where he had been treated.

The inexperienced detective is frequently tempted to wonder whether a suicide which he is investigating may not, after all, be a murder. This temptation is a form of optimism because the idea that the corpse is the result of self-execution is repellent. Why it should be preferable to think that someone else has done the killing is not clear; perhaps it is because, in the presence of a person dead by violence, it is consoling to hope the author of that violence may be punished.

As years passed, though, I found myself troubled by an equally disturbing question: Is this a simple suicide or an accident resulting from a subtler form of aberration than the urge to kill oneself? Enough has been said in preceding chapters to suggest that there is an almost infinite catalog of the ways in which abnormal members of society seek sexual gratification. It seems to be true that there are a few people who find a pleasure that I can only describe as sexual in bringing themselves as close as possible to the verge of death and then drawing back at the last moment.

One difficulty with this form of gratification is that it is sometimes fatal. We had such a case in Lyons. A teen-age schoolboy tied himself up in an almost unbelievable manner, with both arms and legs immobile. Then he lay on the floor, his head in a noose of hanging rope, and his neck raised only a few inches from the floor. Undoubtedly, it was his intention to retract his head from the noose after he had experienced the morbid sensation of strangulation. Unfortunately he had not calculated on the fact that there need be only a few pounds' pressure on the windpipe to cause unconsciousness. This is because the two main arteries which carry blood to the brain are situated at each side of the gullet; if they are squeezed, no more blood is carried to the brain. With his body trussed, the boy could not free himself from the noose. Strangulation set in, and in a few minutes he was dead.

There are many other such cases on record, the most notorious being that of a young university student in England who, in the mid-thirties, was found dead in his room in almost the same manner as the French schoolboy. The English lad's parents could not believe he had engineered the situation himself and thought the death a result of a cruel student hoax. But Sir Bernard Spilsbury, the famous London pathologist, demonstrated that all the complicated knots and tightening-up could indeed have been done by the student himself.

There is even on record the case of a man who built a faithful copy of a guillotine, and took some sort of curious pleasure in putting his head under it while he fumbled with the handle. One day he fumbled too much; the blade came down and chopped his head off.

No policeman is willing to let a case of murder remain camouflaged as suicide, yet there are times when one cannot be sure which crime has been committed. In every big city this problem comes up frequently. Suicides often travel to an unfamiliar part of the world to execute sentence upon themselves, but the murder of a transient is also bitterly familiar to the investigating detective.

The story often goes something like this: The preceding evening a man has arrived at a hotel. There is nothing unusual about him. He is assigned a room and goes to it—happily, as far as can be known. Next morning the maid knocks at the door. There is no answer, and she cannot enter by means of her passkey. Perhaps she assumes that the guest has locked the door from the inside and left the key cross-wise so that it cannot be pushed out. This is an old precaution on the part of travelers who imagine that a skeleton key cannot be used under such circumstances. (In reality this precaution simply paves the way for hotel thieves who may use a special pair of pliers to turn the key from the outside, thereby avoiding the use of a skeleton key.)

The maid calls the manager, who gains access to the room. At a glance he sees that the man on the bed is dead. Then the police are summoned, and the investigation starts.

The scene itself always leaves many questions in the mind of the investigator. The door was closed from the inside. Does this prove that the man closed it himself? Decidedly not, since a door can be locked from the outside with the key inside, either with that special pair of pliers or with a piece of string running through the crack. So with his magnifying glass the detective examines the key for marks of pliers. Likewise he takes a close look at the crack to see if there are any marks from a string on the paint.

The dead man is lying, fully dressed, with a hole in his temple. The area surrounding the entrance to the bullet wound shows some burns and powder grains. This means that the shot was fired at close range. But someone who knew the dead man well could have been close and shot him with the gun muzzle pressed against the skin. (Once in Lyons a young university professor was shot by a girl undergraduate. They had been intimate and the professor had broken off the relations. The girl asked to see him for the last time, and they went to a park. There the girl said she wanted to give him a last kiss and, while doing so, took a pistol out of her handbag, pressed it against the back of his head, and shot him dead while he was still kissing her. That particular girl was from Corsica.)

To return to the hotel room: One hand is still clasping the pistol. Certainly, but it is easy to arrange the fingers of a newly-dead person around a pistol butt in a natural manner. Not many hours later, rigor mortis will set in and the stiff fingers will hold their position. Very well; on the writing desk is a portable typewriter, and in it a farewell letter. Such a letter would ease the task of the investigator if it were hand-written and could be compared with the handwriting of the deceased. Typewritten it is worth nothing.

Well, but if a shot was fired, why did not the sound alarm the guests in the adjoining rooms? Unfortunately a small pistol does not make a loud report, and in a busy hotel there are so many noises that the sound of a shot is likely to go unnoticed.

All these facts have to be carefully weighed. Sometimes the decision is reached on the basis of corollary evidence. Often there is a plausible reason for suicide, and that turns the scales. For instance, the dead man may prove to be bankrupt or to have had some incurable disease. He may have been facing a jail term, or he may have been driven to his deed by that inexplicable urge for self-destruction which, in many cases, is constitutional and follows families for generations. Whatever the geneticists may think about it, suicide does seem to run in families. A look into the deceased's family history is often useful. But, after all, in every investigation of suicide there are factors of uncertainty. Nothing is a hundred-percent certain in this world, not even a verdict of suicide.

The question of how well a sleeping person can hear a shot or a similar sound is often puzzling. It complicates gunshot-suicide investigations time and again. There was a case in Sweden in the thirties when the safe in a small country post office was blown up with dynamite. The burglars had to repeat the explosion because the first blast did not open the door of the safe. While all this was going on, the postmaster and his family of four were snoring away peacefully upstairs, in the far from sound-proof setting of a frame house.

In 1940 I came across the champion sleeper of my experience when I was called to investigate a suicide in Stockholm. A young civil engineer of a noble family, here called Ankarblad, had graduated from the Institute of Technology. His father, a colonel, more or less coerced him into marrying a patrician girl, and he lived with her unhappily for ten years, having two children. Then he moved to a rented room, and divorce proceedings were instituted. His wife and children remained in their suburban villa.

Soon after he left his wife, Ankarblad met a beautiful model who was employed in a big department store. This girl shared with another model a two-room-and-kitchenette flat, where Ankarblad often spent his nights. Perhaps judgment on him might be suspended in spite of those circumstances. Ankarblad's father was stern, and the families on both sides were upset about the divorce, and the young man was also disturbed about the custody of the children and the alimony.

Ankarblad belonged to a prominent fraternal order, and one evening he was scheduled to receive a high degree in the lodge. Dressed carefully in his tails, a black overcoat with white scarf, and a top hat, he went to the meeting, received his degree, and had a gay evening. Just before leaving, he was invited to have "one for the road" by a superior in his firm. This man said afterwards that he did not detect the slightest thing out of the ordinary about Ankarblad, who was very merry. Indeed, the witness said he had even offered Ankarblad a promotion.

About one o'clock in the morning Ankarblad said his good-bys and went straight to the girls' flat. The model's girl friend, when we interrogated her later, said that she did not hear him arrive;

this was credible since he had a key to the door and she was sleeping. In the morning, on her way out to work, she noticed his top hat and overcoat hanging in the closet and did not, for reasons of discretion, disturb her girl friend. When she came back in the afternoon, the top hat and the coat were still hanging there. Puzzled she opened the door to her friend's room and discovered the couple lying dead on the bed.

When we arrived on the scene nothing had been moved. The young couple were lying naked, close to each other. Each had a shot in the heart, and these shots had been fired with a large-caliber Army pistol which was lying at the side of the bed. Obviously Ankarblad had shot the girl first and then himself. No one will ever know if the girl agreed to accompany Ankarblad in death, but she was said to be a sentimental creature; it is possible that Ankarblad's divorce troubles and his remorse over his two children whom he loved had affected her also. There had been no struggle. The whole room was neat and in order, and Ankarblad had arranged his tails, his starched shirt, and his underwear in precise order on a chair, with the insignia of the lodge at the top of the pile.

The mysterious thing was why the roommate had not heard the shooting. The two rooms of the flat were separated by only a thin partition, and a .45-caliber pistol fired in a small room makes noise enough to wake all but the dead. Yet the girl insisted she had heard nothing.

It interested us to learn at what time the couple had died. A detective went round to the neighbors, asking them for information. He had no success until he arrived at the flat just below. The commercial traveler who rented it was away, but his wife was home and opened the door. When asked if she had heard any shots in the night, she exclaimed at once, "Yes, we heard them both. It must have been around three o'clock." Then she blushed and quickly corrected herself, saying, "I mean I heard it."

The detective had caught the slip of the tongue and pressed her for a fuller explanation. The woman was no hardened criminal, and after a few minutes she confessed that a police sergeant from a neighboring town had spent the night with her. The couple had awakened about three o'clock on hearing two shots from above. The woman had told the policeman to get up and see what it was all about, but he, a married man, feared to be identified as an adulterer. His case was reported to his Police Commissioner, who was very angry about it, taking the position that a policeman is always a policeman, apparently even when committing adultery. Under this theory, a policeman must never place himself in a situation in which he cannot act at any moment to protect law and order.

On occasion a genuine suicide is disguised as a homicide by relatives or friends of the deceased or by the deceased himself. The reasons are various and not always easy to fathom. The family may not like having a suicide's skeleton in the family closet, or sometimes the victim pretends to be murdered in order to defraud an insurance company.

In Hapsburg Austria, there was the classic episode of the man who planned to shoot himself. He took out a large life-insurance policy in order to protect his family, but he discovered when he read the clauses in fine print that the policy absolved the insurance company in case of suicide. Therefore, he went one evening to an inn of bad repute. There he flashed large sums of money, bragged, and drank wine with some hoodlums who were sitting at the inn tables. Finally he went out into the night and down to a wooden bridge which crossed a river. Halting in the middle of the bridge, he attached a string to the butt of his revolver and tied a large stone to the other end of the string. He left the stone dangling over the outside rail of the bridge. Putting the pistol muzzle to his head, he shot himself to death. As soon as the revolver was released from his grip, it snapped over the rail and disappeared into the river.

Next morning the body was found, and the first assumption was that he had been killed and robbed. In the course of the police investigation the hoodlums from the inn were arrested, and it looked very dark for them. But an ingenious policeman examined the bridge carefully and found a dent on the handrail where something hard had banged against the wood. It was the disappearing revolver that had made this mark. This discovery led to the river's being searched, and in due course the revolver, with string and stone attached, was found.

Another strange aspect of many suicides is the suddenness with which the self-destructive tendency develops. Not many years ago, there was a detective in Stockholm who was apparently a happy man. His name was Blaggett and he lived with his wife and their fourteen-year-old son, who adored his father. Blaggett was a real merrymaker, a special devotee of that sort of humor called practical joking.

For example, we had on the staff another detective named Johansson who was a nice, mild chap but a bit absent-minded. He belonged properly to the municipal force but was, by a special agreement with the city authorities, serving with my National Institute, as were several other detectives. Each of these city detectives carried a card with his photograph. This identification entitled him to free trips on city-owned trolleys and buses. When the ticket collector asked for the fare, the man would show his card. Now, Blaggett had observed that Johansson, when he was going home in the afternoon, generally traveled on the crowded front platform of the tram. When the ticket collector rattled the door, he would take the card out of his pocket and hold it aloft.

On this small trait Blaggett established his plot. One day he removed the card from Johansson's pocket, pasted the photograph of a nude woman (which had probably been confiscated somewhere) on each side of the card, and replaced it in Johansson's pocket. That evening some of the conspirators, headed by Blaggett, boarded the same trolley as Johansson, went to the front platform, and started a lively conversation with their victim. When the ticket collector rattled the door and stuck his head inside, Johansson took the card out of his pocket and held it over his shoulder.

A howl of rage from the ticket collector followed. Poor Johansson thought that he must have displayed the wrong side of the card and turned it over, revealing the picture of the other nude woman. The collector stopped the car, and it took a good deal of argument to prevent him from kicking Johansson out on the street.

Blaggett spent his summers with his small family in a log cabin which he owned on one of the skerries in the archipelago off Stockholm. He could commute from the island easily enough and did so with every evidence of enjoyment. But one July evening he came home as usual, had dinner, and left for a stroll. After a quarter of an hour, his son followed along the same path and almost bumped into his father's body, which was swinging from a tree.

Afterwards some of Blaggett's friends maintained that he had really been a most unhappy man. His wife, the stories went, used to tease him about his ugliness, which seemed to be a weak spot in his personal armor. These same friends said that he had hidden his domestic troubles under the mask of the merry joker. Perhaps. It is easy enough to build up stories after the event. All I know for certain is that many suicides are unpredictable in advance, even, I suspect, by psychiatrists.

Once in a very long time an incident occurs in which the attempt to use apparent suicide as a cloak for actual murder takes an ingenious turn away from the more usual pattern. The most remarkable of these cases which I can recall took place in Bavaria; I heard about it from a friend of mine who was in police work there. It happened in the early 1930's.

In a Bavarian village lived a woman who owned and ran a grocery store. She was married to a wisp of a man, generally esteemed a characterless fellow with no force, a sort of "little man who wasn't there" person. So great was the wife's contempt for her husband that she quite openly kept a lover, a young miner, whose hobby was the practice of hypnotism. He was as familiar with the husband as he was intimate with the wife; to the practice of cuckoldry he added the special fillip of hypnotic experiment on his victim, whose milk-toast nature seemed to make him the ideal subject. The husband came so much under the influence of this pickaxe-and-shovel Svengali that the younger man needed only to fix him with his eye, wave a hand, and say, "Sleep!" Promptly the husband would fall into a deep hypnotic trance, which stopped the clock as far as he was concerned and allowed the lovers an indefinite amount of trouble-free privacy.

Ideal as this situation should have been for the pair of them, it began to pall after a while. They talked the matter over and decided that the husband must go. In view of the esteem in which he was held in the village and his utterly passive nature, they decided to allow him to commit suicide—with a certain amount of assistance. One evening, while the three of them were sitting in the house, the lover put the husband into hypnotic sleep. Then he fastened a large, strong hook into the frame of a doorway. To this he knotted a length of stout electric cord with a running noose at the end of it. Underneath the noose he stationed a chair and led the entranced husband gently to it. Lifting him up onto the chair, standing him up on the seat, and adjusting the noose around his neck, the miner commanded his victim to walk. The husband walked off the chair all right, but the knot of the noose was not well tied and it came apart. The older man fell with a thud to the floor and awakened. The embarrassed lover tried to explain away the whole thing as a practical joke, but complaisance had reached its limit. The husband went to the police and denounced the couple. Both the lover and the wife were arrested and confessed.

Several times in the thirties there occurred on the Continent, especially in Germany, cases in which an attempt was made to defraud insurance companies by trying to pass off homicides as accidents. As then practiced, the racket was carried out by the owner of an automobile, who would go shopping for a victim among hitchhikers. When he found one with approximately his own coloring and stature, he would pick the man up and, at a convenient time, kill him. Next he would dress the body in his own clothes, complete with watch and other personal belongings. Most often the murderer would then drive to some place where there was a deep embankment at one side of the road, put the body at the wheel and cause the car to plunge to the bottom of the declivity, following on foot to set fire to the car. Of course, he would previously have taken out heavy insurance on his own life, and the beneficiary was usually either his wife or some accomplice. The killer then proceeded to start life anew under another name. Thanks to the efforts of the police, a number of these creatures were tried and executed, and the racket abated.

All these variations on the theme of self-murder, and murder disguised as self-destruction, do not remove the essential quality of suicide—a lonely and despairing act, usually committed by a human being who feels abandoned by life or by his God, and who can see no valid reason for continuing to live. Sometimes, as I have said earlier, there is an element of more than private protest in the act. One such instance embodies all the pity and tragedy implicit in the other such cases I have investigated.

It happened in the year 1940, after the outbreak of the Second World War but before the attack on Pearl Harbor. One day I was notified of the suicide of a man. His name shocked me when I saw it on the telephone-message memorandum, for I knew him well and liked him deeply. My first reaction was probably a good deal like that of a surgeon who is told he has to operate on his own wife. Nevertheless, it was my job to go, and with a heavy heart I set out for the hotel where my friend's body had been found.

Driving through the streets toward the scene, I recalled the time, eight or ten years earlier, when we had first met. In those days I was often asked to dine at the house of Ragip Raif Bey, the Turkish Minister to Sweden and a vigorous and strikingly original man. The company often included the Russian Minister, the famous Madame Kollontay, as well as other diplomats, and my friend who was then Minister to Sweden from one of the small states on the Baltic. He was a cultivated gentleman, urbane, quiet, and thoroughly human. He was also (a point which would endear him to any Swede) a deep patriot. He loved his country, its people, and its culture—a man of the world devoted to the small and precious part of it which he had the honor to represent. All of us were fond of him.

The world history which followed upon those days is familiar to all of us. The Russian behemoth gulped down my friend's little state almost without pausing to chew. One by one, and with obvious reluctance, the nations of Europe recognized the *fait accompli*. To the honor of the United States be it said that to this day the conquest of those three small nations has never been admitted diplomatically, and for this my friend was grateful in a wistful and despairing way. We used to talk it over once in a while. He recognized that his state and its two equally defenseless small neighbors were now part of a Communist empire. As time passed, he seemed to be at least partially resigned to this bitter fact. Underneath, though, he gradually came to feel that since he was deprived of the object of his deepest love, his native land, there was no further point in living.

Had he been Japanese, he would have killed himself on the doorstep of the Russian Legation. But I found him—found his body—in his modest hotel room. There he was, dressed in pajamas, lying on his bed, his small beard neatly trimmed as usual. His round, kindly little face was already colorless and his body was stiff. I was glad that his eyes were closed. The whole room was neat and all his affairs, including this last one, were in order. On the table beside his bed was an empty bottle of potent barbiturate pills and a hand-written letter: "I cannot bear to go on living, now that my country has ceased to exist."

The letter went on to express his wish to be buried at the side of his parents in a remote Baltic churchyard, but even this last testament to his love for his native land could not be honored in the midst of a world war.

POLICEMAN'S WORLD

28

THE DENT IN THE NECK

My years under Maître Locard had given me something more than the techniques, practical and intellectual, by which a specific crime should be approached. This broader philosophy had in it three main strands, and it is these to which I should like to devote the last portion of this chronicle. First, there was the concept of criminology as a science—a new science, less than a hundred years old, but still an applied science of great value to society. Second, the notion that crime is not communal, or national, but an aspect of humanity as a whole and as such is often international. This conception was reflected in the International Criminal Police Commission, to which I had belonged before the Second World War and with which I was associated even more closely when it was revived after that conflict. In this respect I found myself far differently situated from my father, the redoubtable Pehr Söderman, whose service as Sheriff had hardly ever forced him to think or act beyond the bounds of the district for which he was responsible.

The third of these categories was the future. If criminology, as a science, was to be no more than the apprehension of persons who had already committed a crime, increasingly it seemed to me, as the years passed, that here was a kind of hopeless treadmill with the police, by definition, always one step behind the criminal. That step, of course, would be the crime itself—the act of violence which brought the police into the scene.

Those of us who studied police science under Locard gradually assimilated a good deal of the history of our profession. Like most sciences, it was built on the work of men who had preceded not only us but our masters. The approach to any crime, even as far back as the early 1920's, was not all practice. There was a constellation of theories behind what we did, and these theories had come into being under the inspiration of a series of brilliant minds. Many of them had been formed in that most remarkable of all Christian centuries, the nineteenth.

All through the eighteenth century, criminology had been nearly entirely a matter of knowledge of criminals considered singly and as individuals. A great policeman like Vidoq was a man who knew his criminals, their haunts, and their individual peculiarities. Detection as a scientific art was undreamt of in today's sense of the term. Identification, technical steps of investigation, and the whole modern panoply of the science of criminology were unknown. The science of criminology, a term which I use in a somewhat narrower sense than is sometimes employed, is just under a hundred years old. Excluding the wider fields of what we now call penology, abnormal psychology, certain fields of sociology, and other techniques which are sometimes broadly lumped under the term "criminology," the study of the criminal himself, his heritage, his physical and mental defects, his specifically criminal psychology, and his treatment began with a young Italian physician named Cesare Lombroso in the 1860's. One of the great political events of the nineteenth century was the initiating cause of a relatively minor episode which in turn resulted in Lombroso's becoming the founder of a science.

In 1864 the peninsula of Italy was united, with the aid of France, into a single nation. Up till then the land was infested with brigands who profited because the country was divided into many sovereign states. Thus, if the Papal State became too hot for a brigand, he simply "took a walk" into the Kingdom of Sardinia, or the Kingdom of Naples or, perhaps, the Grand Duchy of Tuscany. For hundreds of years, brigandage had plagued the Italian countryside, and literary tradition had even established a romantic conception of the robber. But, despite sentimental fiction, which often depicted the brigand as a kind of Mediterranean Robin Hood stealing from the rich in order to give to the poor, in most cases he was nothing more glamorous than a dangerous enemy of all society. The brigand almost always operated on a local, or area basis, and there were scores of regions which were virtually dominated by these rogues.

The new Italian government determined to stamp out existing brigandage and establish the authority of law and order. This was an immediate necessity if the unified country was to have any sort of cohesion and peace within its borders. Squads and units of various sorts were organized from existing police and army groups and sent out to bring in the brigands, dead or alive.

One of these numerous task forces was ordered to apprehend a certain Villella who held forth in the province of Calabria and, like many of his colleagues, specialized in highway robbery. Attached to this police group was its assigned doctor, the young physician, Cesare Lombroso. Villella was caught and thoroughly hanged. Lombroso, who was among other things somewhat of a comparative anatomist, felt that it would be interesting to discover if Villella's skull differed in any physical way from that of his fellow men. He detached Villella's head, cleaned and preserved it, and brought it back to the medical school at Pavia, where he occupied what would today be called the chair of psychiatry when not on leave of absence for such public services as the Villella expedition.

The story goes that one day Lombroso was examining this collector's item and noticed something which had never before been recorded in connection with a human skull. There was a small dent on the inside of one of the bones at the nape of Villella's neck. This dent had hitherto been observed only in the bony processes of gorillas.

To understand what followed, it is important to remember that it was in this era that Darwin's theory of the development of species was making its victorious way throughout the scientific and intellectual world. It was strongly supported by the corollary theory of microgenesis. According to the latter, just as the human individual, during the months it is in the womb as an embryo, develops through the various evolutionary stages from egg to lower vertebrate and finally to homo sapiens, so man must, over an enormous period of time, have developed from a one-cell organism through ever more complex species before culminating in his present form.

Generalizing from Darwin's theories and citing the evidence of Villella's skull, Lombroso advanced the theory that the habitual and incurable offender was a savage sprung from the womb before developing all the way to homo sapiens. This "fact" explained the criminal's maladjustment to society and his savage conduct. To substantiate his theory, Lombroso set about examining the inmates of the Italian prisons. And what did he discover! The worst criminals, he found, had skulls resembling those of apes, with protruding cheek bones, ears the whole lobe of which was often joined to the skin, heavy jaws, excessively long arms, a preternatural nimbleness, and a remarkable capacity for moving the toes. Further, Lombroso noted that such criminals were excessively tattooed. He proceeded to make a study of tattooing, which supported his theory; only savages normally adorned themselves in such fashion. The habitual criminal, Lombroso concluded, was born to his destiny, and thereafter driven to it by unconquerable, biologically-supported antisocial tendencies.

It is difficult now to imagine the impact of Lombroso's theories on the then-prevailing ideas of the origin of crime. Heretofore, the accepted belief was that man had a free choice between good and evil and that punishment was to be meted out accordingly. The influence of Lombroso's theories on penal reformists in the last decades of the nineteenth century was enormous, and his creed was influential even as far afield as the speculations of the positivists, a school of philosophers who held that knowledge was empirical and had to be based exclusively on the data provided by the physical or "positive" sciences.

But Lombroso was not accepted universally. He had a number of English and American critics who accused him of having been inexact in his measurements and observations and of having tried to shape his data to fit his theories. One of his most formidable adversaries was the famous Professor Jean-Alexandre-Eugène Lacassagne, a French criminologist who was Locard's own teacher. Lacassagne contended that environment was the most important factor in creating a criminal, and it was he who coined the phrase: "Every society has the criminals it merits."

And so eventually Lombroso and the science he had created, which he had called "criminal anthropometry," fell into disrepute. Yet its influence has never entirely died out, and even today his critics must award him the historical honor of being the pioneer in applying scientific methods to the study of criminals.

And what about today? Do we now know much more about criminals than Lombroso did, or Lacassagne, or the others who fought in the campaigns of the nineteenth century? Probably not, though thousands of volumes have been written on criminals and criminology in the past fifty years. True, the importance of heredity is now accepted, even though it is not pictured in the crude terms of Cesare Lombroso. In parallel measure, the enormous influence of environment is admitted, just as Lacassagne argued. Nevertheless, there is still no definitive answer as to why a particular individual becomes (or is born) an habitual criminal.

It is important to make a distinction between that curse of modern society, the habitual criminal, and what may be termed the chance offender. My old friend Robert Heindl, the German criminologist whom I shall have more to say about later, defines the chance offender as being a man who never *looks* for occasions to commit a crime. In his heart, he abhors crime. He does not like the habitual criminal and does not seek his society. The chance offender is a person who commits a crime under the impulsion of financial need, sexual drive such as love or hate, or revenge, or from rage or fear. Afterward he shows repentance for his crime, confesses when he is apprehended, and, after his punishment, becomes once more a law-abiding citizen unless or until his character is not strong enough to resist a new temptation. The true chance offender may have a relapse into criminality, but even several such backslidings do not make him an habitual offender.

The true habitual offender may also commit a crime by impulse or momentary aberration, but the difference is that mostly he *looks* for criminal chances as systematically as a salesman looks for buyers. He fights no battle within himself. Business is business. He sees in crime a profession—or at least a way of life—like any other. He may, at the start of his course, have been a chance offender but, constituted as he is, he has only to go to prison to have all his bad instincts stimulated and confirmed by the cheap-fiction romance, the debauchery, and the easily-gained wealth and free life of that obscure world of crime which he may have only partly known before his sentence. He does not stop to count costs; he muses very little on the drawbacks of the life of crime. A dissipated interlude of a few days or even weeks is paid for by years inside penitentiary walls. Such an offender almost always passes the greater part of his adult life in prison, and his death, inside the walls or out, is generally as wretched as his life has been poor and cheerless.

The habitual offender—the kind of criminal Lombroso and Lacassagne studied and of whom Heindl was speaking indirectly when he described the chance offender—is not ordinarily of high intelligence. More often than not, his intelligence quotient is below average. The small fry of his ugly world are often caught by the police simply because of their inability to vary their methods of work. If one of these characters began his life of crime by climbing through a window, having unfastened the latch with the aid of a hook, he will generally continue doing so as long as he lives. His mind is similar to that of the old circus horse who trots round and round the ring without the wish or capacity to make a break. If another of this fraternity found on his first burglary that some marmalade in the kitchen tasted good, he will continue to look for marmalade in every house he burglarizes. This adherence to pattern is sometimes almost past belief. In large cities, for example, certain criminals will steal overcoats only from schools, others only from dentists' offices. Still others specialize in burglarizing the house of unmarried schoolteachers who are known to be away during the day, and so on.

Habitual offenders have their special vanities. too. A safe burglar, for instance, will be greatly offended if asked whether he is a pickpocket; a holdup man resents being confused with a con-man who prides himself on the fleecing of elderly spinsters. At times, this vanity may reach almost heroic proportions. Locard told me he once had to visit a condemned man who was to be executed a few days later. Locard informed him that his picture had been in all the papers and that there had been newspaper headlines about his crime.

"Then I must make a fine show when I walk to the guillotine," the man replied.

A working policeman comes to see habitual criminals as something more than, or different from, cases of personality derangement. To him these offenders appear beyond the reach of any mental science so far developed. Meantime, society must be protected, and the policeman is not paid to be a theoretical psychologist or a social reformer.

It may seem paradoxical, but police have very little to do with practical penology and human rehabilitation. A criminal passes only a brief fraction of his life in the hands of the police. The rest of it is divided between social workers and prison personnel.

To get a criminal behind bars is the job of the police and, specifically, of detectives. Everything that pertains to the routine work of detectives—methods of interrogation, ways of tracing fugitives, systems of keeping files, methods of trailing, and so on—comes under the heading of police tactics, just as the broad study of the techniques for apprehending and convicting criminals comes under the heading of police science, or as the French call it, *technique policière.*

Police tactics involves the bulk of detective work. It too has its history, a much older one than that of police science, although most of it is lost in time. Little has been preserved on how the Assyrians, the Cretans, the ancient Greeks and the Egyptians apprehended and interrogated their offenders. It is reasonable to assume that their methods were crude and the subsequent sentences severe. Much more is known about the Romans, but there are few surviving details describing the work of the lictors, as the attendants to magistrates were called. Their duties included the seizure and scourging of criminals. Nevertheless, the criminal investigative procedure which gave birth to modern detective methods is fairly ancient. It was called the inquisitorial system (not to be confused with the Holy Inquisition) and was in practice for hundreds of years in most countries of the Continent. In fact, it is said to be one of the factors which led to the French Revolution.

Under the inquisitorial system, the court consisted of a lawyer, generally called the inquisitor, who was at once judge, prosecutor, and chief of detectives. When the inquisitor learned of a crime, he sent his court officers out to fetch the criminal, then interrogated him, took the testimony of witnesses under oath and, in minor cases, pronounced the sentence. In cases where a life might be forfeited—and there were many such in those days—the inquisitor made up a dossier and sent it to the superior court, which consisted of at least three lawyers. These men made their rulings from the inquisitorial record alone and never saw the prisoner.

All hearings were held in secret; this practice led, after the French Revolution, to a reform called the accusatorial procedure, in which a prosecuting attorney spoke publicly to the court in the name of the people and where, at least theoretically, the prosecutor and defendant had equal standing, even if, for reasons of security, the defendant himself sometimes had to be kept locked up. The American institution of bail does not exist on the Continent and is regarded there as an unfair and undemocratic practice which puts the wealthy in a more favorable position than the poor.

To return to the inquisitorial system, the written records in serious cases had to be of a high standard because they were the only source of information for the higher court. So, even in those days, clarity and exactness of expression were highly valued. I have myself read several such records dating from the end of the eighteenth and the beginning of the nineteenth centuries, for this system did not disappear in certain regions (notably southern Germany) before the middle of the nineteenth century. Some of those old records can be regarded as pieces of a fine art now lost. I remember, for instance, the inquisitorial records of a case of poison murder in Bavaria in 1810. There were seven suspects, and the summing up of the pros and cons for each one was masterful yet extremely brief.

It is fair to assume that the inquisitors were often men of a high standard. At least, the last of them was: the famous Hugo von Jagemann, pioneer of modern investigating methods. Von Jagemann was born in Baden, Germany, in 1805 and died in 1853. He came from an old family of judges and inquisitors, and there were centuries of family experience with human behavior and the ways of criminals behind him when, at the age of twenty-six, he published his now classic textbook on legal investigations. What von Jagemann expounds in his book about individual human characters— the shy people, the pretentious ones, the impudent, the stupid, the children, be they suspects or witnesses—is timeless truth. He describes how to make arrests, how the locking-up will influence the mentality of the prisoner, how to trail suspects, and how to examine scenes. Making due allowance for changed modes of transportation, the astonishing fact is that there is not much difference between detective work in von Jagemann's day and the present. But there is logic behind the similarity; human beings are exactly the same, and he described them superbly. No wonder the spirit of von Jagemann is still embodied in every textbook on police tactics.

It is painful to admit that some of this underlying police wisdom derived from the use of official torture cellars. Until the French Revolution, in most parts of the Continent, torture was regarded as a perfectly legal means of obtaining evidence. To the shame of humanity thousands and thousands of people, up to the end of the eighteenth century, suffered indescribable agonies at the hands of official torturers and under the sanctioning direction of learned judges. This black chapter in the history of justice was ended before von Jagemann started his career, and yet, coming from a family such as his, he must have been keenly aware of it.

Police science could not fully develop until the natural sciences had attained sufficient maturity. Although man had discovered the fundamental laws of nature and had accumulated considerable knowledge about his environment, it was not until the Industrial Revolution that these scientific principles were fully utilized. Previous to 1850, microscopes, scales, and analytic methods in general had not been sufficiently perfected to suit the exacting needs of justice.

Those decades in the middle of the nineteenth century were a milestone in the progress of civilization comparable to no other. A man born at the beginning of the nineteenth century and dying at the end of it was brought up, as a child, in a world not essentially different from the middle ages. Before he died, railroads had connected distant parts of the world, steamships had conquered the sailing vessel, modern industry with its mass production was a fact, the fundamentals of the radio were known, the first automobiles were running, and even the first airplane was trying to lift itself from the earth's surface.

This panorama of change was reflected in the development of police techniques. Their expansion and refinement had a corresponding effect upon criminality. Before 1818, police science could not with certainty identify the presence in the human body of the most common of all poisons, arsenic. Not until about 1840 was it possible to determine whether a dark stain was blood, paint, or just spit from a tobacco-chewer. Not until 1890 could it be decided whether a blood stain was human or animal, and the blood grouping tests which were to become so important in criminal cases had no application in practice.

Police science everywhere started with methods of identifying human beings. Around the anthropometrical and, later, the fingerprint bureaus, gradually evolved laboratories to compare the markings on burglars' tools, to analyze stains, to identify bullets and cartridges, to examine questioned documents, footprints, hairs, and all kinds of traces. These developments were not viewed as godsends by the working police; an overwhelming majority of detectives were not much interested in "scientific stuff," and it is chiefly in the last few decades that police science has become universally recognized by the police themselves. Not long ago, for instance, most large cities had no police laboratory and had to call in private experts to fill some special need.

Instead of being a public and official service, police science in the first fifty years of its existence was chiefly carried on by private individuals. They were few, particularly if only those with the necessary scientific background are counted. A good proportion of them were chemists who maintained commercial laboratories for analytic work and who had taken a liking to detective problems.

The two fathers of police science—the Frenchman, Alphonse Bertillon, and the Austrian, Hans Gross—were, in their two ways, self-taught. Enough has already been said of Bertillon, that narrowgauge genius of identification who in the 1880's started a *Bureau d'Identité* in the Sûreté of Paris, the first such bureau in the world, and who lived until 1914. Hans Gross, who died in 1915, laid the foundations, to a greater or less extent, for the remaining major aspects of police science. Gross was a professor of penal law at the University of Graz in Austria and had in his youth been a judge. His educational background was purely legal, but for decades with unparalleled diligence he unearthed everything which might be useful in police work. The outcome of this self-imposed labor was a brilliant manual first published in the early 1890's which has since appeared in numerous revised editions. It has been translated into many languages and for many years was regarded as a sort of Bible for detectives.

The generation which followed Bertillon and Gross produced two stars of the first magnitude, the Frenchman, Edmond Locard, and the Swiss, Rudolph Archibald Reiss. Scientific photography was added to the resources of police science by Reiss, a man who was a great connoisseur of the methods of burglars and con-men and who was regarded in his day as the leading expert in bill forgeries. Reiss must have been an extraordinary man. The story was that he was the child of a liaison between a reigning German prince and a beautiful Jewish girl. The expectant mother was sent off to Switzerland, and a comfortable fortune was settled on her. However it was, young Reiss received an extensive education at the University of Lausanne and became a doctor of chemistry and physics. With his own money he later founded there a University Institute for police science, which still exists.

Although of German descent and half-Jewish, he was reputed to be violently anti-German and at the same time anti-Semitic. His two sole interests were his science and tobacco. It is said he smoked at least two yards of cigars a day; he was also the only police scientist who ever looked like Sherlock Holmes. If one of those old-fashioned deer-stalking caps had been placed on his head, it would have been easy to imagine him walking out of the famous fictional house in Baker Street.

After the first Balkan War in 1912, the Serbians requested an international committee to investigate the atrocities committed by the Bulgarians in the Serbian part of Macedonia, and Reiss as a member of that committee acquired a great love for the Serbian people. When World War I broke out in 1914, he gave most of his fortune to the Serbian Red Cross, went to Serbia, and even fought with the Serbians against the Germans. Finally he accompanied old King Peter when that monarch was compelled to leave his country.

After the war, when Peter became the first King of the new nation of Yugoslavia, Reiss followed him, bought a house in Belgrade, and lived there until his death in 1928. He was given the empty title of Director of the Laboratory of the National Bank of Yugoslavia, which carried some salary. Once a week the King came around to play cards at Reiss's house, but it still remains a mystery why this genius buried himself in Belgrade. One spring morning in 1928, while he was taking his usual morning walk, he met a neighbor, with whom he was having a controversy about the boundaries of their gardens. The two men quarreled, and in the heat of argument, Reiss lifted his walking stick to strike the man. At that instant he dropped dead of a heart attack.

I had never met this odd, great man, but I had corresponded with him. Several years later, when chance brought me to Belgrade, I visited the cemetery and left some flowers on his grave.

The three leading police scientists in Germany during this period were Robert Heindl, Rudolph Jeserich, and Karl Popp. Robert Heindl was a lawyer, but even so he occupied a central position in police science because he was the editor of the famous *Archives of Criminology*, a journal which Hans Gross had founded. Through this editorship Heindl was in constant touch with the leading criminologists of Europe.

In the mid 1920's, while passing through Berlin, I made Heindl's acquaintance. Though only about fifty, he had already become a figure of great reverence to the German police because he was the man who introduced fingerprinting to Germany. Heindl had finished his law studies in the early part of the century and, though a Bavarian, had become the head of the Detective Division in Dresden, the capital of Saxony. Before then, however, he had made a world-wide voyage, including stops at many obscure places in the tropics, to study the penal colonies of France and other countries. On this macabre subject he published an interesting book. His *magnum opus*, however, was his encyclopedic work on fingerprinting, still the most comprehensive study of its kind.

At the start of World War I, Heindl was transferred to the Ministry of Foreign Affairs in order to inaugurate for Germany an organization comparable to the British Secret Service. After the collapse of the Kaiser's Germany, Heindl continued on the payroll of the Foreign Office, but was employed by the Weimar Republic to write a law to unify the German police forces, which up to then had operated on a sectional basis.

Heindl led an ideal life. He was a bachelor, and his large suburban house was maintained by a devoted housekeeper named Gertrud, who provided excellent meals and kept the beer at the right temperature. Heindl had become one of the foremost collectors of the engravings of the great medieval artist Albrecht Dürer. He was also surrounded by thousands of books, and he kept up a lively correspondence with scientists and prominent policemen all over the world. Next to Edmond Locard, there was no one who influenced me so greatly in my professional career. Often we sat till late at night discussing criminology and human relations and, as the foaming beer sank low in the glasses, I profited more than I realized then from his friendly advice and profound knowledge.

In addition to his other attributes, there was a broad humanity about the man. I never heard an unkind word about any colleague pass his lips, although he must have been in an excellent position to know the weaknesses and foibles of his compeers. At most, in lieu of comment, he would relate a humorous anecdote about the man in question.

Once he told me a story about Rudolph Reiss. When Heindl was serving as head of the Detective Division in Dresden, Reiss paid him an unexpected visit. The police of the capitals of Europe had been alerted by the French Sûreté because a counterfeiter of French bills had fled, presumably to Germany, on the eve of arrest. Heindl had received a telegram from Paris advising that it was likely the escapee had gone to Dresden. Heindl himself went to the railway station at the crack of dawn to greet the inspector sent from the Sûreté. Out of the train stepped not one but two men. The second was the famous Reiss himself, then acting as expert on forgery for the French National Bank. At the last minute he had decided to accompany the inspector. Heindl was pleased to make the acquaintance of the world's leading specialist in the detection of forgeries and, next to Bertillon, in the technical description of criminals. In this latter field Reiss had published an elaborate study.

After breakfast, Reiss and the inspector asked Heindl to assemble all his detectives so that Professor Reiss might give the group a complete description of the counterfeiter. While Reiss, with great detail, was describing the escapee, one of the local Dresden detectives, a veteran plainclothesman who was not over-bright and had never been promoted, tried to speak. His fellow detectives hushed him, and Reiss managed to get off his eloquent speech without interruption.

After Reiss finished, Heindl went over to the old plainclothesman and sternly demanded an explanation for his impolite action.

"But sir, I have already caught the man," the old fellow whispered in a hoarse voice. He claimed to have apprehended the escapee in the street, with nothing to go on but the first vague description sent out from Paris, in the half hour while the three luminaries of criminology were breakfasting.

Doubting the old detective's report, Heindl and the two visitors ran down to the detention cellar. When they opened the door of the cell, they found the counterfeiter sitting on a bench. When he saw Reiss and the inspector, he began to laugh and could not stop for several minutes. Eventually he was able to explain the joke: all the way from Paris to Dresden he had been traveling in the same compartment; he had even eaten at the same table with them in the dining car!

This ability to recognize persons from a description, displayed by the run-of-the-mill experienced detective, is not unusual. It does not necessarily mean that the detective is especially bright or fitted for promotion to a higher post. On the contrary, many detectives who have the intellectual capacity required to lead a large investigation or head a department may lack this peculiar flair. Nevertheless, the number of arrests made by a Detective Division is closely related to the number of detectives who possess the ability to visualize a criminal from his description.

On the eve of the Nazi era, Heindl's position became precarious. He had never been politically active, but his cosmopolitan and liberal mind was not of the type to be appreciated in the Third Reich. Nevertheless, he was still regarded as the greatest living German policeman, and when Goering assumed power and organized the Secret Government Police (which was soon to become the notorious Gestapo), he tried to engage Heindl as the first Chief. But Heindl, in personal horror, fled to his native Bavaria, where he remained stubbornly in exile in a house he had inherited from his father, in the Alps not far from Munich. There he feigned illness until the end of the war, forgotten even by the Nazis. When the Americans arrived in Munich, they dug him out of his books and papers in this lonely mountain retreat and made him the head of the Bavarian Criminal Police. It is said that they were able to trace him through a drawing and a footnote about him in a book which Inspector John J. O'Connell, my New York colleague, and I had written in 1935.

Heindl organized the post-Hitler Bavarian Criminal Police, and was its Chief for a few years. When he was nearly seventy, he retired again. "This is the third time I have retired," he said with a twinkle in his eyes. And now he lives again in his mountain villa (where I have visited him several times), and he has even recovered some of his Albrecht Dürers from Berlin, where they had been hidden. Best of all, Gertrud, that faithful housekeeper, is sharing his fate again. She had stayed in Berlin to take care of his house until the end of the war, had suffered some sad and violent experiences at the hands of the Russians, but managed to keep her spirit intact.

The second of the great German criminologists of this period was Rudolph Jeserich. Just as Heindl's fame rested on introducing the technique of fingerprinting, Jeserich's was founded on working out methods of applying spectrographic analysis to police work.

In his researches he had made contributions to a number of allied fields, such as the technical description of the shape of blood-stains.

The last of the triumvirate, Karl Popp of Frankfurt, came into police science by reason of his skill as an expert in another field. He was the leading commercial chemist in southern Germany and earned his living as a specialist in the analysis of tobacco. From time to time he was consulted by the police, and his interest developed into an enthusiasm for police science. This led to his becoming the German authority in forensic chemistry.

Like so many other criminologists, he might be said to have posed for the composite photograph out of which Conan Doyle constructed the image of Sherlock Holmes. Whether he ever identified the ash of a Trichinopoli cigar I do not know, but Popp was the first to analyze ashes and other residues in cases of suspected arson in order to ascertain the presence of inflammable oils. I first met him in Brussels before World War II. He was then over eighty but still vigorous. That evening he consumed a dinner consisting of snipe roasted in brandy at our table, and all the appropriate side dishes, washed down with several bottles of good wine. Black coffee and Kirsch followed, and Popp relished the entire meal.

The last years of this fine old gentleman's life were full of trouble. His only son, who was supposed to inherit the laboratory, made the political mistake of marrying a Jewish girl. In the middle 1930's in Germany this was regarded as a crime against the Third Reich, and yet the young man refused to divorce his wife. Popp himself pulled every possible string to save his daughter-in-law— and succeeded, as far as I know. The experience embittered him. He was filled with disgust for the regime and retired into the Black Forest to live out what days remained to him. This he was able to do because of a matrimonial gambit of his own.

A long-standing friend of his was an elderly widow who owned a large German automobile factory. She had also inherited a hunting lodge in the Black Forest. The old couple were *simpatico*, and both detested the Nazis. So together they spent their last years in that lodge, hunting deer and reading classic philosophy. Both of them died at the beginning of World War II.

In Amsterdam Mynheer van Ledden Hulsebosch was one of the most colorful criminologists on the Continent. The bridge of his big, protruding nose was conspicuously dark blue because of an incident in line of duty. One night he was routed out by the police to examine the scene of a crime. No car being available, he was being transported in the side car of a motorcycle. Along the route, some excavating had been in process, and the lamp to mark the danger had gone out. The two policemen on the motorcycle and van Ledden in the side car were precipitated headfirst into the hole. No one was hurt, but there was coal dust in the bottom of the hole, and it was rubbed by the impact so violently into van Ledden's nose that a regular tattooing occurred.

"I am too old for plastic surgery, and anyway this gives me an occasion to tell the story every time I meet a new person," van Ledden used to say. "I never before met with so much sympathy."

The van Leddens had been apothecaries for several generations, for two hundred years living in a narrow Dutch brick house with the pharmacy on the ground floor and the living quarters upstairs. It was a charming place which still contained much chemist's paraphernalia from bygone days. The last apothecary of the family was van Ledden's father, a man who had every day for thirty years analyzed his own excrement and written a large treatise on the subject. So it could be said that the present van Ledden came naturally by his analytic talents.

In his youth van Ledden studied criminology at the famous University Institute founded by Reiss in Lausanne, Switzerland, where he and Locard became friends. Eventually Locard sent me to spend a few weeks in van Ledden's Netherlands laboratory. He was a consulting criminologist with no official status though constantly employed by the police and courts. In spite of having experienced much sorrow in his personal life, he was a gay person. In many ways he was a most old-fashioned chemist, paying no great attention to the refined methods of physics and chemistry which were then becoming so successfully used in police science. But this lack was fully compensated for by van Ledden's ingenuity. I have rarely seen a man with so much practical sense coupled to human sagacity.

One case which he solved in a simple but masterly manner involved a not-too-intelligent young maid servant in Amsterdam who fell in with an apprentice draftsman. She was happy because he spoke of marrying her some day, but when one day she told him she was pregnant he accused her of carelessness. He then recommended an abortion and said that he could arrange the matter at a certain clinic.

A few days later, he called on her at her employer's house while she was serving dinner. She went to open the door when the bell rang and explained that she would not be free for another hour. The man said he was in a hurry because he was on his way to the clinic to talk about the abortion.

"You know," he told her, "it is the law that no one who is the father of a child can ask for an abortion, so you will have to write a few lines saying that I am not the father. It's a mere formality," he added. "You know as well as I that I am the father."

The stupid girl believed him. There was no table in the entrance hall, but the boy held a slip of paper against the wall, thrust a pen into the girl's hand, and dictated: "I herewith declare that Marius van der Gelden is not the father of my child." And the girl, hearing impatient voices from the dining room, scribbled her full name, Juliana Fransen, underneath.

This was the last she saw of the young man. All her attempts to get in touch with him were fruitless, since he had changed lodgings and had even left his job. When she had to confess her plight to her mistress, fortunately she was sent by that kind lady to a maternity home. The official guardian appointed for the infant set out to track down the father. As the law required, the young man was summoned to appear at the city hall, where he was interrogated. He calmly produced the slip of paper written out by the girl.

The guardian was at first too stunned to speak. "Is it your habit to get declarations of this sort from the young ladies of your acquaintance?" he finally managed to ask.

The young man shrugged his shoulders. "Not as a rule. But in this case I saw that the girl had become pregnant. I knew I was not the father of the child, so I thought it wise to have her testify to this effect."

The guardian considered such an unheard-of precaution a bit too forethoughtful and took the young man with him to a police station. There the seducer was closely interrogated as to the circumstances under which the girl was alleged to have given him such a remarkable certificate of absolution. Willingly, and with many details, he described how he had visited the girl in the evening, how they had talked the thing over in a friendly way, and how she had confessed that he was not the father of the coming child. Then she had written the certificate, or so the draftsman claimed.

The guardian referred his problem to the authorities, and the case was turned over to van Ledden, who affirmed that the certificate was undoubtedly in the girl's handwriting and asked that the youth be interrogated once more by the police. This time, with much circumlocution, he was asked in what position the girl had been while writing the certificate.

"Why," he said at once, "she was sitting across from me at the table."

This response was his undoing. Van Ledden had already noticed a salient fact about the note: in each of the letters the dark area of ink was concentrated in the lower section of the written characters. The upper parts were pale by contrast. He made several experiments which showed that, when a person wrote with ink on paper in a vertical position, the ink before it dried tended to flow to the lower parts of each letter.

By now, van Ledden concluded that the girl's version of the origin of the exculpating note was true, and this view was in due course taken also by the Civil Court, which decided that the young draftsman was the child's father and must pay for its support.

The most peculiar of European criminologists in the twenties and thirties was, without a shade of doubt, Herr Gustav Kogel. He was not a criminologist in the exact meaning of the term, but as a professor of physics at the Polytechnic Institute in Karlsruhe he had done more than any other man to introduce the use of ultraviolet light to police science. Kogel was the twelfth son of a Bavarian blacksmith. Soon after his birth, his mother vowed that he should take orders and dedicated him to the Augustines. When he was eleven years old the monks came for him, and he was sent to study in an Augustinian monastery in Brazil. At twenty, he presented himself for the dreaded Magister's Examinations.

What a strange situation! Imagine this young, highly intelligent German lad who knew no other form of life than that lived within the walls of a monastery. For him, under the instruction he had received, the planet Earth was immovable, the sun circling around it. His conception of the world was, in fact, wholly Aristotelian. For the examination he had even to memorize verbatim the four books of Aristotle. The texts of the four famous books, in the original Greek, lay on the table in front of his examiners. After a short prayer in Latin, one of the monks put his finger between the leaves and opened the particular volume at the spot thus selected by chance. The young scholar was asked to recite the contents of that page. Nothing this side of China could approach such a test. In old China the books of Confucius would have been used, but the idea was the same.

Kogel passed the test with honors and graduated. Immediately a new and fearfully strange world was opened to his eyes. He was now admitted to the library of the order, where hitherto forbidden books were to be found. With a mind as gifted and intelligent as his, it is difficult to imagine what the impact of that library must have been. The first volume he took down from a shelf, he once told me, was a work by Ernst Haeckel, the German biologist who explored many of the implications of the Darwinian theory.

Kogel was never able to breach the gap between what he had

been taught before his graduation and what he read afterward. His intelligence was that of a natural scientist, and a brilliant one, quite irreconcilable with the thought of the Order in which he had been consecrated. He told me that he could never forgive the Fathers for the deception under which they had compelled him to live for so many years, though outwardly he remained an obedient son of the Church.

His unusual gifts were eventually brought to the attention of Rome and he was sent there to complete his studies under the auspices of the Church. By the time he earned his doctorate in physics he was more than slightly known in the scientific world for his specialized studies in optics. For several years he had a part-time job as secretary to Cardinal Rampolla, the then Secretary of State to the Pope.

Eventually Kogel felt compelled to leave the Church. He returned to Germany, where he married and sired a large family and became a professor of physics. He invented a new method of blueprinting which was said to have made him a millionaire, although of this he gave little social evidence. He was jokingly accused by his colleagues of never having paid for a glass of beer for himself if he could avoid it.

These, then, were some of the minds which shaped the science of police work in the years when I was a student and a young practicing criminologist. Like all other policemen, I owe a debt of professional gratitude to them and to many who came later. The scientific aspects of criminology have now become both numerous and highly technical, and there is no place here to discuss the many practitioners of police science who succeeded in turning a profession based on special knowledge and flair into one operating on provable fact.

Yet such advances were by themselves incomplete. All of us were aware that the sharing of knowledge and skills, as they developed in the inventive minds among us, was not enough. The protection of society from criminality calls for more than technical knowledge, no matter how ingenious. Long before I said farewell to Locard and Lyons, I had grasped the fact that the old Socialist slogan—"Workers of the World, Unite!"—applied also to policemen who cared about making their work more useful.

29

PRESENT AND FUTURE

So much for the story of criminology past. The future
has always been as much a part of my personal life as the past or
present. As I sat behind my desk in Stockholm year after year and
did what I could to make the National Institute of Technical Police as fine a tool for the protection of society as I could, my conviction grew that the most important crimes to solve are not those
which have already taken place, but those yet to be committed.

The true solution to a future crime is to make sure it never happens. In this respect, future crimes are not dissimilar to past crimes
—a certain percentage of them will inevitably go unsolved. That
is, they will take place no matter what is done to forestall them.
Homicidal maniacs will continue to exist until the science of the
mind is developed past any point which can reasonably be
imagined now. There will always be pyromaniacs and sadists and
a whole gallery of malefactors. It would be impractical to pose the
question of how every crime can be prevented. "Only when the
millennium has arrived" is the answer to that one. Rather, the
question which occurs over and over to working criminologists is
how to keep the number of future crimes down to the irreducible
minimum.

Whether or not it is justifiable to think of crime as a mental
disease, it is useless to regard it as analogous to a physical con-

tagion. There is no way of inoculating newborn infants with a serum guaranteed to immunize them against all future criminal tendencies. The basic human drives of sex, hunger, greed, hate, and their companions in the subconscious mind are bound to produce violence century after century. All working policemen know this bitter fact. Furthermore, their day-by-day experience with crime tends to make them impatient with what they sometimes think of as sentimentality. The safeguards that society sets up to protect the innocent and the rights of individuals, even criminals, often generate a sense of frustration and occasionally anger in the police breast. While it is understandable that some people feel a greater sympathy with the criminal than with his victims and believe that society should devote its primary effort to the restoration of the lost lamb to the flock, the policeman feels that it is his duty to protect the flock. He has no quarrel with ideals or with the safeguards intended to embody them, but his working life has given him a highly pragmatic philosophy in regard to the protection of the public.

There is no human type which grows up into being a policeman, any more than there is a doctor type, or a bus driver ordained in the cradle. There are as many different kinds of policemen as there are citizens. Some are more intelligent than the average, and some are below the median line. Some are brave, some are not. Some are diligent and devoted, others are lazy. But the life of a policeman is no bed of roses, and there are few who remain in the profession lacking a substantial drive toward hard work carefully performed.

In speculating on the problem of future crime, most criminologists would subscribe to the proposition that since a life of crime often starts young, with juvenile delinquency, the best opportunity to rehabilitate the potential or actual criminal is in his early years. The role of the understanding judge, the older, wiser man or woman, is of paramount importance at this stage. In the light of experience it seems debatable whether the regular police court or even the special juvenile court is the right place to take care of young offenders. Eventually, perhaps, all delinquents under the age of sixteen, or even seventeen, may be placed in the hands of public-welfare agencies, if only such agencies can be provided with the means and personnel to do a wise and effective job.

It must immediately be added that these agencies should not be responsible for the criminal aspects of an investigation. Welfare agencies are not equipped to determine the facts and patterns of cases. In my own country there is a law which forbids the sending of very young people to the penitentiary, and such a provision is wise and humane; what is foolish about the law is that it compels the police to keep their hands entirely off such cases.

A few years ago, in Sweden, a boy of fourteen was suspected of having killed a small girl. He was committed to the care and supervision of welfare agencies while the police were compelled to stand by and do nothing, not even investigate the case. The reported circumstances did suggest that the boy was guilty, but the agency's handling of the matter was inefficient and inconclusive. The argument here is not that the boy should have been sent to prison; far from it. The point is that it is vital to be as sure as possible, in a factual way, that the boy and not some undetected other person was truly guilty. In different words, society has a stake both in the future of that particular boy and in its own future safety. No law which forbids investigation and the interrogation of offenders, young or old, is a wise law.

To see the face of a young offender behind bars has always disturbed me. My observation is that the first brutal contact with jail, inmates, and the whole ugly pattern of prison life makes a lasting impression on a sensitive boy or girl, and too often it confirms the youngster in a criminal pattern which might have been erased. The company of confirmed criminals is not the best rehabilitating agent imaginable for young and impressionable minds.

Juvenile delinquency is one of the great problems of present-day society, and it is the fault of us parents, teachers, policemen, and professional students of the human mind that no solution has yet been found. It is common to the whole civilized world today; I should be surprised if it does not exist even behind the Iron Curtain, although the Communists do not release such statistics.

One current theory to explain the rise of juvenile delinquency is that the nature of the present age induces it. The argument runs that the aftermaths of great wars tend to destroy standards and weaken the sense of security so important to children, with recklessness and looseness of morals as a logical consequence. But this explanation does not seem to cover the present-day situation satisfactorily. In Sweden, for example, where there has been no recent war experience, juvenile delinquency is a current problem, even though not of the same magnitude as in the United States. And of course, even in the United States juvenile delinquents of today have not had actual war experience. It is, moreover, significant that the frightening effects of war have not resulted in the same rate of juvenile delinquency in combat-ravaged West Germany and France as in the prosperous United States.

The assembling of gangs has also been given as an important factor in causing a juvenile to become delinquent. But all boys like and need to belong to a group of similar age, sex, and environment. It is thus a boy expresses his solidarity with youngsters of mutual interests, as well as his distrust of adults. The danger of a gang is that one bad seed in the packet may transform the whole group into a more or less criminal organization.

An old friend of mine, who is today a middle-aged civil engineer and the highly respected director of a big company, told me that once, when he was thirteen, he nearly became a criminal. Up to that moment his criminal activities had been confined to filching sugar and cakes from the kitchen. Two or three times he stole several crowns from his father's trousers, while his father was asleep, in order to buy cookies and cigarettes. He was ashamed of this pocket-picking but consoled himself with the thought that his father had so much money that the thefts did not matter. The truth was, however, that his father was a poor man, and the boy must have known subconsciously that this self-excuse was not valid.

In his class in school there was one boy who was two years

older than the rest. He was also bigger and stronger, he frequently bullied the smaller boys, and he was therefore looked upon with awe and respect by his juniors, including my friend. These two became close companions, and the older boy confided that he was accustomed to augment his pocket money by stealing from suburban houses. He asked my friend to go with him on his next expedition and, bedazzled by the aura of maturity and manliness the older youth displayed, the thirteen-year-old agreed.

Next evening the pair went out to a suburb of the small city where they lived and began knocking at doors. The technique was that if anyone answered, they would ask innocently for a person who did not live there. After a few such trials, they came to a house where the door was open and no one was in. A woman's bag was hanging in the hallway. The boys opened it and found several crowns inside. It was the older boy who did the stealing while my friend watched, but he was delighted to share in this adventure and had no moral hesitation in doing so.

Shortly afterward, the older boy was arrested and confessed everything, including my friend's participation in one of his thefts. Then, for the first time, with the impact of the police interrogation and his mother's sobs, the boy understood the wrong he had done.

Now, my friend was obviously of good character, for he never went astray again. But certainly there are thousands of juvenile delinquents with the same childish lack of judgment, the same admiration for the gang leader, the same delight in adventure, although perhaps not endowed with the home surroundings and up-bringing he had. How are such boys to be put straight before they become criminals? This is a sorely difficult question to answer.

In the United States, the second-generation pattern was thirty years ago considered a major cause for juvenile delinquency, and it is true that when I worked with the New York Police Department in 1934 I saw several cases of young gangsters who were excellent illustrations of this theory. The father and mother of such a teen-age gangster might be God-fearing people who had brought the potential hoodlum to the United States as a child. The family generally lived in one of the slum areas, and the father worked hard as a manual laborer. Neither he nor his wife learned English fluently; at home and with the neighbors they spoke their native language. Such a boy grew up in the streets, went through elementary school, and, by the time he became a teen-ager, felt himself a full-fledged American, even to the point of speaking slang. The relations between parents and child were not close; even the cementing contact which a common language affords was lacking.

The idea of getting rich quickly and without work can haunt such a youngster, and those subtle brakes which come into evidence in most human beings when evil thoughts arise were either too weak or absent entirely. Paternal authority was not sufficiently operative; for instance, the example of the father as a peaceable and philosophical but poor laborer was not the central fact in the young boy's mind and even the morality taught by the Church had not taken root. Competing with these good influences was the glamour of crime, endorsed by cheap magazines and bad movies. One day, the boy might become a member of a neighborhood gang, and another member might get hold of a pistol somewhere. He might take a pair of youngsters with him on their first stick-up.

Sooner or later, and sometimes on the first such foray, disaster descended. I remember an evening when I had been out to dinner and was returning to the Manhattan Homicide Squad about eight in the evening. In those days Homicide had its headquarters on the top floor of one of the precinct police stations. To get up there it was necessary to go through the police station itself. As I was walking through, I noticed some policemen with a pair of boys who might have been as old as sixteen. Curious, I went over to the group and asked what was going on.

"These young punks tried to stick up a cigar store," one of the policemen told me. "They was three of them, but the one with the gun beat it and O'Toole, here, couldn't catch him. We're just after askin' those young gentlemen who their friend with the rod was."

Although the officer was seventy and past retirement age, the shortage of policemen had enabled him to stay in uniform and continue walking his beat. He had stepped into the corner store to buy his after-dinner cigar at the very moment when the three gang members were holding up the place. Single-handed, the undaunted old man arrested two of the young hoodlums, but the third, who was armed, escaped.

The interrogation was naturally concentrated upon the weaker of the two youngsters, who soon broke and answered all the police questions. This was unusual because as a rule these gang members are more afraid of one another than of the police, the fate of the "squealer" being well known. Anyway, a radio car went immediately to the place where the third youth lived and caught him, his topcoat still on, in his parents' home. When taken to the station house and searched, he was found still carrying the gun. This particular trio all proved to be the sons of immigrants, living in cold-water tenements. Since the passage by the United States government of the immigration restriction acts of the 1920's, such second-generation problems are becoming a thing of the past in America but, while the particular generation which those three boys belonged to was still young, its plight pointed up two of the essential factors in the field of juvenile delinquency: deterioration of the relationship between parents and children, and the discomforts of the home.

Respect for and obedience to parents is being negated by many aspects of contemporary life. Individualism is supplanting the old sense that each member of a family owes loyalty and warmth to the other members. The focus of attention is no longer on the affairs of the family as a unit; the members rely on outside rather than family stimuli for their entertainment. Radio, television, comic strips, movies, and the insistent advertising pressures from a thousand sources appeal to the individual's self-interest rather than to a dedication to the family group.

I am not maintaining that these various media teach immorality.

In every tale of crime on radio or television, the villain is caught and receives his come-uppance. A life of sin is not made to seem attractive. Justice and decency usually triumph. The point, it seems to me, is that the cumulative impact of all these aspects of contemporary life is unfortunate, particularly in the case of uneducated people. And almost all people are uneducated. It is too much, perhaps, to call the average person simple-minded, but he is certainly more naïve than the skilled professionals for whom his pocketbook is the target.

The ordinary man today seems to find very little leisure in which to ponder his problems. How profitable is it to be the proud owner of a car, a refrigerator, and a television set, if you lose something of your own identity? In past generations, the family was a world in itself, leaving lifelong impressions of solidarity upon its members. The small, closed circle around the domestic hearth hardly exists any more.

Respect for all elders has dwindled, often with the encouragement of foolish fathers and mothers who enjoy being "comrades" on an "equal footing" with their children. It is open to doubt that any normal child enjoys that sort of equality. The adult is someone who cannot by definition be merely the equal of a child in thought or experience. A child admires adults as superiors, or detests them.

Admittedly it is not easy to inspire respect in children. Most people are not trained psychologists, at least not in their homes. For the average man and woman it is impossible to build up respect without the support of tradition and the high walls around family life.

A child's mind is sensitive. The drinking father who makes scenes at home, or a parent who constantly scolds or who is eccentric can throw the child out of equilibrium, deprive him of the mental comfort and tranquillity which he needs. The worst harm can be caused by the family in which a child is not curbed. Most children are hungry for the world around and beyond them; they want to grasp everything they can reach. Discipline ought to come into play, and it is just here that many parents fail. The home is a proving ground for the outside world, the first community where the child has to learn to live with his fellowmen, to be considerate, to recognize certain limits in behavior over which he may not step.

In thus writing outside my professional field, I shall probably incur criticism. Policemen are not experts in child care and guidance, but they are exposed to thousands of cases of tragic violence and human disaster; it is natural to warn the present generation that the next one is headed for trouble. If every child in every family could learn that there are limits to the liberty allowed any single person, and that society has rights the transgression of which will be painful to the transgressor, police work would be a far lighter burden, not only on the force itself, but on the taxpayer, the educator, and the whole human family.

Baffled by the pressures operating against the family, parents seem to turn to the school for help. In this they have perhaps been somewhat encouraged by a sector of the professional teaching class which has tended to believe that education can accomplish more than it is reasonable to expect. No school can build upon foundations which have not been laid in preschool years. The purpose of schools is not rehabilitation or crime prevention or group psychiatry. Schools exist essentially to hand on the race's store of wisdom, knowledge, and skills. It is not wise or fair to expect them to make up for the lack of the home as the primary human experience of children, or to suppose that the second grade, or the fifth, can become an improvement on the family itself.

Modern educators seem often not to appreciate that a child's world, even his school world, should not be a game, even in the early stages, but rather a preparation for the hard and serious business of adult life. Self-expression, for instance, is not necessarily the first prerequisite of the good life. If a child has been taught to think first of himself and what he personally wants to do, if he has had no responsibilities or duties at home and has been given whatever his little heart desires, how can he be expected at some future date suddenly to assume duties and responsibilities and live off only what he can earn?

Parents should not send a six- or seven-year-old to school and say to the school, "Here! Take over this human being and make a man out of him." It is too late for that. At six or seven his character is already molded. The average school can only take what it has been given and ten or twelve years later turn it out, for better or worse, to the adult world of work and opportunity. Possibly a teacher in a small country school can now and then do something to build a mature human entity, but this is certainly not the case in the educational factories found in large cities. And how many teachers can be expected to have that force of personality, that indescribable quality which is found only in masters of men?

There is, besides, the daunting fact that a certain number of children in the school population do not fit into the schools as they are constituted for the majority. The working policeman, in his interrogations of delinquents, soon learns to recognize these cases. Quite a number of boys and girls in each school generation are either psychotics or behavior problems so extremely advanced that no ordinary school can deal with them. They are not susceptible to a civilizing influence designed for the average child. In the United States—at least in some parts of it—there are school psychiatrists who are supposed to recognize such cases and make provisions for special handling. The policeman would say that this is all to the good. The rest of the youngsters ought not to be exposed for a single unnecessary day to the impact of the wayward and aberrant. Several European countries are also making this effort to segregate unassimilable children.

Even assuming that tests and observations reveal every potential enemy of society, what ought to be done with these discards from the general, educable group? Should they be sent to institutions? Well, institutions differ, but there are not many equipped to make the necessary discriminations. The record shows that psychotics of one degree or another are mixed indiscriminately with youngsters who are merely disturbed and maladjusted, or perhaps almost normal. The almost-good tends to be corrupted by the incurably bad.

Most thoughtful people believe with the working policeman that the number of children committed to institutions ought to be kept to a minimum. This is not to minimize the work of such remarkable places as the George Junior Republics or Boys' Town. But even these shining examples are not homes. They are institutions in which the morale of the place substitutes for the morale of a family. In future, it might be wise to explore further the wider use of foster homes. Even if foster parents are highly paid, or receive special exemptions, the ultimate cost to society might well be less than an increasing use of institutions—even the best.

In discussing such matters, every man speaks from his personal experience. One example does not prove a point, but the following example may serve to show the trouble with the institutional solution. The man I have in mind is now in his early thirties. He currently owns a small machine shop, is self-supporting, and to all outward appearances is living a life that society can accept. At least, he is no trouble to the police. But that is not the whole of it. After a few minutes' talk with him, it becomes apparent to anyone that there is something frighteningly wrong.

This man never knew his parents; his father had been a drunkard and his mother a prostitute. In his infancy he was turned over to a welfare agency, and he grew up in institutions. In all, he once told me, he had lived in some fifteen different charitable homes. He remained maladjusted, sensitive, and difficult. No one liked him, no one cared especially about him; so he lived under a cold star all through his childhood and adolescence. He learned a mechanic's trade and at twenty was turned out to take care of himself. After he had been on his own for a month, he took part in a hold-up, robbing an old man of his wallet. For that he was sent to prison for a short time. As soon as he was out, he committed a new hold-up, but this time, on the advice of psychiatrists, the court sent him for a time to a mental institution. After that he started to make a bare living in his machine shop, an embittered and lonely man who will pay all his life for the sins committed against him by a well-meaning society.

One more thing needs to be said, unpopular though it may be. I have come to the conclusion that the fundamental moralities, as taught by the Christian and Jewish faiths, are a lifelong asset. It is necessary for every child to know that thou shalt not steal and thou shalt not kill, because God does not like it. These simple and fundamental precepts for a humane society have not been pounded into the heads of the young who come under police scrutiny. I have come to believe that every child needs Sunday school and church, where the fundamentals of a religion are taught even when they are slighted at home. The foundations of Western civilization are built upon religion.

While society waits on a rebirth of the family pattern and a reappraisal of the value of religion, what is to be done with the juvenile delinquents today, the immediate products of background deficiencies? Shall the police be asked to take care of them? The affirmative answer is not too implausible.

By this I do not mean that a Police Athletic League or a Police Boys' Club is the answer. The individual case ought to be dealt with by enlightened humanity as circumstances indicate. But there is an area of police contribution which is being overlooked.

Society is not getting so much as it might out of its police, and particularly out of its detective forces. A working detective in his official rounds observes a great deal that never gets into any official report. He can observe, or guess at, situations in which a future crime is more than probable, but he is powerless to take any kind of official action to forestall it. The good men on the force are keenly aware of this. They inaugurate clubs and activities designed to salvage youngsters who are visibly on the verge of criminality. Their resources of time, energy, and money are always limited, but the existence of police-sponsored welfare activities is proof of the further contribution that might be made by these men devoted to the widest implications of their work.

Most of the detectives and uniformed officers would like to do more to prevent future crime. Wider educational opportunities, including a richer background in juvenile psychology and the underlying causes of the criminal drive, would be welcomed by most of them. They would, indeed, like to be more fully partners of the rest of society than they are today.

As long as the average citizen enters a police station with a defensive chip on his shoulder, a feeling of hostility unlike the sensation with which he would enter some other welfare agency, there is certainly something wrong. A policeman does not enjoy the sensation of being looked upon as the enemy of the very people who hire him to protect them. Particularly in the case of children, he would welcome the opportunity to work a cure before the damage is irreparable and society finds itself with another candidate for a police dossier on its hands.

What about the criminals who have progressed beyond the stage of juvenile delinquency and have become hardened in their role as enemies of society? The present reliance in most countries is on incarceration. This serves temporarily, at least, as a protection to society, but the percentage of rehabilitation thus achieved is not impressive in view of the cost to the taxpayers. Putting a man or woman in prison is not an answer but only a postponement of the problem, because a penitentiary term seldom makes a convict into a useful member of society. It has been bitterly said that if reform schools are the high schools of crime, penitentiaries are its colleges.

As long as there is no present substitute for prisons, the youthful offender should be given several chances, at the discretion of a judge, before he is sent to prison for the first time. Thereafter, prison terms should be uniform in length for every sort of crime. By this I mean that there should be a punishment number I for first-time offenders, a punishment number II (longer) for second-time offenders, and there could also be a punishment number III. But that third one ought to be the end, for society's sake. After it, any person who gets into trouble with the law and so proves to be an incurable, habitual offender, ought to be taken away from society and put in a safe place permanently.

Such a place should not be a conventional prison or even an Alcatraz. At such a stage in the relation between society and the criminal, there is no further point to revenge or punishment. There is no need to torment incurable criminals. Before the First World War the Australians experimented with something of the system I suggest here. In an oasis in one of their vast deserts they established a settlement for criminals from which there was no chance of escaping. Here the incurables could live a reasonably decent life, working in shops and at agriculture, wearing ordinary clothes, buying newspapers, beer, and tobacco at their discretion.

Any proposal to deal with incurable criminals by exile and penal colonies sounds like turning back the clock. It must also be admitted that there is the possibility of police abuse and the certainty that for criminals so exiled there would be inequities. The American concern for the rights of the individual is vital. But one individual right which is endangered a thousand times a day in our society is the right of the law-abiding person to be free from criminal molestation and intimidation. Life as it is lived by decent people ought to be free of this hazard.

Perhaps there is a way of arriving at a solution such as this penal-colony one within the framework of individual justice. The grand-jury system suggests such a possibility. A special jury might find that a person, giving repeated evidence of preferring to prey upon society rather than joining and working with it, could have a larger measure of freedom in a place of exile than inside the walls of a penitentiary. In such a light it might appear just and humane to establish him in such an isolated spot.

Such criminal communities are merely future projections. Meantime, criminals are present every day in every country; every day they victimize innocent people—killing some, robbing others, poisoning the lives and happiness of others, destroying property, and carrying on guerrilla warfare. Day by day, year by year, they purloin tangible things like money and lives, and intangibles like confidence in the safety of society. With this situation the police must deal.

What sort of police force might cope with today's criminals in such a way as to diminish tomorrow's in number and cost? Well, there are two phrases which sum up the present police situation. The first is a corollary of Lacassagne's comment: "Every society has the kind of police it deserves." The other, suggested earlier in this chapter, is: "There is something wrong with the police as long as any citizen, guilty or innocent, enters a police station feeling different from the way he would feel if he were entering some other welfare agency." These two statements deserve a great deal of consideration.

Leaving out technical details chiefly concerned with criminal investigation, traffic control, or the filing of data, no essential improvement has been made in the concept of a police force since the first one was set up a hundred years ago. Except for high officials, police the world over have a doubtful social standing. Members of all forces are inadequately paid, even in the United States. In 1956 a rookie who entered the New York police force received only $4000 his first year and a raise of $250 for the second year. For this sum he risked his life, had to cope with any situation which arose on his beat, and lived a closely-supervised life. It is surprising that there are any candidates at all, much less any good enough for promotion. Yet in other countries the salary scale is even worse. The pay of French, German, and Italian policemen is low beyond belief. A German police captain today receives a monthly salary of about $100. Any ordinary German chauffeur is far better paid. But the most outrageous case in my experience was in Israel, where, a short time ago, the Inspector General of Police received a salary smaller than that of the driver of his official car.

Unbelievably, in spite of such salaries, able and devoted police officers are still recruited. There are many devoted young people among the police. Apparently once a man gets the taste for police work, and especially detective work, he cannot quit. The multitude of problems, their variety and scope, the spectrum of humanity in its most naked terms, the excitement of the hunt— all these attract men of the highest caliber. The type of man on the force does not require to be changed, but the system under which they are expected to do their work ought to be improved. No intelligent policeman ever resisted efforts to raise his standards, professionally or educationally.

This is a scientific age. Society spends billions on educating children and develops complicated machines to ease the burden of the working man. When a person is ill, all the resources of modern science are at his disposal. But when a crime is committed, the offender is not dealt with by the same kind of highly trained professional who might remove his appendix. Instead, in most countries, the whole pattern of his life is probed by a man with little more than a grammar-school or high-school education. This investigating officer may be a human being of the utmost worth, and, if he has been long in his calling, a man also of wide human sympathies. But there exists in him, all the same, a vast area of incomprehension. The best policeman in the world cannot exceed his own limitations.

In some countries the police profession is now attracting more highly educated men. Today's slowly improving pay scales have a good deal to do with that. Whatever the reason, it is a step in the right and inevitable direction. The educational prerequisites of the police of tomorrow must be materially raised. I would advocate a college education at least for every detective. If detectives are drawn exclusively from the uniformed police, as is the practice in the United States and many other countries, a college education ought to be necessary for the uniformed police as well. Postgraduate courses in police science, sociology, and general criminology ought to be an essential corollary to promotion. Increased and adequate salaries are also necessary.

Society demands such background of schoolteachers. Why should it not expect as much from the experts to whom it entrusts the maintenance of law, order, and the assurance of personal safety?

30

AN END AND A BEGINNING

My retirement from the National Institute of Technical Police was not a resignation from the world of criminology. It was a step I had thought about for a long time, and in the final pages of this chapter I shall have something more to say about that. Meantime, the night train for Oslo and the 1953 annual meeting of the International Criminal Police Commission.

Whenever I am scheduled to go off on such a trip, my wife has a custom of packing my suitcase for me. This is charming, and I would not forego that loving service for the world, but in a family such as ours it takes a little extra time to honor it in the observance. This time our son, aged seven, and our daughter, three, had joined the committee which saw to it that I left the house fully packed and equipped. Joyfully they helped my wife by investigating all possible bureau drawers and the bedroom closet. They piled crumpled shirts and unmated socks on the bed, and located many weeks' supply of ties—some of which I had mercifully forgotten. It took some while to make tactful order out of this happy chaos.

Late in the evening, the sturdy old Nash set out for the station, carrying me and rather more baggage than I required. I settled back in the seat, for there was a great deal to think over.

First the convention. In it, and in the Commission itself, I believed wholeheartedly. Even before going to study under Maître

Locard, I had begun to realize that crime is not merely communal, or even national. As the reader already knows, while wandering through the Near and Far East, I had visited the police bureaus of many countries, not only because I earned some of my expenses as traveling correspondent for the *Swedish Police Journal*, but also because the subject held a fascination for my father's son. Later, at Lyons, the international flavor of the group studying under Locard reinforced the lesson that crime is a world-wide phenomenon which in many cases can best be coped with by cooperation across national boundaries.

This conviction was of course shared by Locard, who heartily approved anyone's interest in international police affairs. His sponsorship was partly responsible for my becoming an assistant editor of *La Revue Internale de Criminalistique*, a magazine published in Lyons to further the dissemination of technical information in the field. In the following year, 1930, I undertook the editorship of the *Nordic Journal of Police Science*, published in Stockholm. These two posts, the publication of several books and monographs, a good deal of teaching and lecturing, and the acceptance of various invitations from Israel, Estonia, Ireland, Germany, and other countries to do advisory work, seemed to me a necessary part of any criminologist's work.

Of all these activities, as I stood on the threshold of a new life and bade adieu to the career of a civil servant, my connection with the International Police Commission appeared the most meaningful. I looked forward with anticipation to the meeting scheduled to commence on the morrow.

The old Nash came to a halt at the Sodertalje station. In a few minutes the headlight of the train for Oslo came down the track, piercing the darkness with a cone of yellow. I swung aboard, bag and baggage, and in a minute we were rolling along through the night. But I was not sleepy; my mind unreeled a hundred recollections of men I should see next day, and of men whom I would never see again. In particular, I was eager to talk with the delegates from Germany; only two years before I had assisted in reorganizing the police system of that country, and I wanted to learn how it was working out.

Any police officer who operates in a small European nation will from time to time find himself compelled to take business trips to other countries on the Continent. The International Police Commission had always played a most useful part—and still plays it—in familiarizing each of us with his opposite number in other countries. We could do business together on a basis of mutual trust. During the war most of these valuable connections were interrupted and when, in 1946, in connection with a journey to Switzerland, I had had occasion to go to Cologne, I was hopeful that I could do something to reinstate some useful working relationships.

The moment I crossed the German frontier I found myself in the midst of privation and hunger such as I had not seen this side of the Near and Far East. The German people were living on a handful of calories per capita, and they were gray, tired, almost sluggish. It was hard to believe that this had once been a bustling, energetic nation with an almost fanatical devotion to productive work.

When I reached Cologne I managed to locate, among several pre-war friends and connections, the man who had been Attorney General in the Weimar Republic and a banker and his wife who had spent the last eighteen months of the war hiding out from the Gestapo in a workman's attic. They and all my other friends were as haggard and exhausted as the rest of the Germans. I could not help being moved, and was impelled to take a day off from official business to go into one of the workers' districts of the city, with a policeman for guide.

What I saw there made an even more pitiful impression; I felt a kind of sick despair. In family after family mothers were surrounded by their half-starved children, crying over their empty cooking pots and waiting the return of their husbands, who had no jobs and were foraging in outlying farms for a few potatoes.

The eyes of the children were large and hollow with hunger, and their little, thin faces reflected their mothers' bleak hopelessness. Everywhere I went, in Cologne and elsewhere, I saw suffering. For me, the worst was what the children endured.

My occupation is that of policeman, not social worker, but the Germany of 1946, and particularly the children of that country, would have challenged the conscience of any human being. I determined to try to do a little something about it. It would not be easy; in those days the victors had not begun to forgive the vanquished, and even to many neutrals the very children of the country were looked upon as "vipers' offspring." But with the help of a wonderful woman, a Swedish countess named Ebba Bonde, a plan was worked out to salvage some of the children.

The essence of the scheme was to bring German children from the worker families of the Ruhr to Sweden, there to stay in individual private homes for periods of at least six months. This would give them a chance to recover from the effects of malnutrition and, equally important, an opportunity to see what a peaceful, normal world was like. It seemed to us that no better propaganda for a different and better future could be imagined. Eventually all the difficulties and red tape were cleared away, and we succeeded in bringing into Sweden some seven hundred kids ranging in age from five to twelve. Practically the whole cost of the venture was borne by Countess Bonde, as unselfish and courageous a philanthropist as I have ever known.

The experiment worked out so well that both of us wished it might have been attempted on a much larger scale. The parents of the children were grateful and happy; the youngsters themselves returned to their homes with a priceless heritage of health and a new look of hope and liveliness in their faces. It was a rich experience for me as well; I felt that I had been doing something positive for a change. Adding good citizens to society is more rewarding than abstracting bad ones.

This work with the children had brought me into touch with many leaders of the new Germany, particularly in the political, social, and religious areas. It was no doubt they who in 1951 secured for me an invitation to go to Germany as consultant on the organization of a Federal Police for West Germany. Dr. Robert Lehr, Minister of the Interior in the first Adenauer administration, officially extended the invitation, and the Swedish government was generous enough to grant me a leave of absence.

The next eight months were among the most interesting of my professional life. In addition to laying the groundwork for the new police force, it was part of my mission to work out a network of police connections with other European countries. Situated in the heart of Europe, Germany can not hope to have effective police services without such a series of liaisons.

The Germany of 1951 was very different from the one I had seen five years earlier. It was bustling with energy and the will to work. Houses were going up, factories were under construction, and even shipbuilding was once more under way. There was good food in the stores, and gallons of good German beer were spilling out of the breweries. In spite of the unemployed, of whom there were still many, and the gnawing problem of the refugees, there was hope and confidence in the air. Here was a country in which something useful could certainly be accomplished.

The very day I arrived in Germany, I went to the Federal Ministry of the Interior and paid my compliments to Dr. Lehr. The first Adenauer cabinet was sometimes called "the cabinet of old men," and Lehr was at that time nearly seventy. The son of a Prussian general, he had made a brilliant career, ending in the mayoralty of Düsseldorf, an office from which the Nazis had ousted him. He was typical of the fine, old-school German, and his administrative experience was a great asset when he became Minister of the Interior. That day I also met Ritter von Lex, the Under Secretary of State, Hans Egedi, Director of the Security Section of the Ministry, and Dr. Max Hagemann, preliminary head of the proposed detective division.

Lex, who was to become one of my best friends in Germany, was a blond Bavarian in his middle fifties. In the First World War he had fought in the Bavarian army, lost a leg, and for bravery on the battlefield been elevated to the nobility by the King of Bavaria. He was a lawyer by training and had behind him a distinguished career as a civil servant. Even so, he might not have attained his present position if he had not been a Bavarian. Bavaria still maintains the role of a semi-independent country within the boundaries of the Federal Republic, and no important decision can be made without the consent of the Bavarians. They also demand quite openly to have representation in all ministries. No German federal government can be conceived without the Bavarians in an important role.

Egedi, by contrast with Lex, was a typical Prussian high-ranking civil servant of the old school. He had been one of the leaders of the Christian-Democrat Party in the East Zone until he, his wife, and children were compelled to flee for their lives.

Dr. Hagemann, the head of the future detective division, was an old acquaintance of mine. He had been a prosecuting attorney in Berlin in the twenties, for a short time head of the Detective Division of that city, and then judge of the Administrative Court of Germany through the tumultuous Nazi years clear to the end of the war. Being a liberal of the Weimar stamp, he had certainly met with difficulties, but his mild and scholarly nature saved him. He was a considerable scholar in criminology, had written several papers in the field, and had a reputation not only in the learned world of Germany but also with the police, being one of the few experts still remaining who had held a major post in the police of pre-Nazi days.

After I had seen the Minister and the leading lights of the security section, I was ushered to the third floor of the building, which was occupied by a staff already working on different police projects. Here I was assigned a small, neat room with the usual office paraphernalia and a telephone which could be connected with the reception room. There was even a card on the door with my name neatly lettered on it. A Mercedes car with a chauffeur was put at my service. On my desk lay printed copies of two laws just passed by the German parliament, one creating a federal detective division (*Bundeskriminal-amt*), with limited executive powers, the other a Bureau to safeguard the constitution (*Bundes-amt für Verfassungsschütz*). My advisory capacities were supposed to be employed chiefly in connection with these two agencies.

When I was alone, I leaned back in my desk chair and let my thoughts run back over what I knew of the German police.

My first connection with it dated back to 1923. On passing through Berlin on a vacation trip to Germany, I had braced myself and gone to see a certain Herr Hoppe, then chief of detectives of Berlin. He was a characteristic Prussian official surviving from the Kaiser's time, with his narrow trousers, his shaved head, starched collar, and even a pincenez. I am not certain whether Hoppe was a professional criminologist, but he knew how to run a big police force and keep his men in order; for a man in his position, that is more important than to know about criminals. He retired a few years later, and it speaks well for him that Berlin has never since had such a tough and good chief of detectives. Whatever may have attracted him to me, after our first discussion he threw the doors of his department open, and, to my delight, I was allowed to walk around everywhere with an inspector as guide. I indulged myself particularly in the famous museum, where I studied all the cases of the last decades.

So Chief Hoppe had given me my first insight into the organizational difficulties of German police work, which in the days of the Kaiser was more fragmented than in any other country I know about. The question of jurisdiction, for instance, was enormously intricate because of the independence at the level of police work of each of the duchies, kingdoms, and princedoms which made up the German federation. Every one of them had its own autonomous police force. On the national level, the Berlin police theoretically operated on an equal and cooperative level with each of the other forces, and to augment the national interest a kind of parliament called the German Police Commission, to which each state sent delegates and which met frequently to iron out common problems.

This system worked better than might have been expected; the policemen of the Kaiser's day looked upon one another as professional colleagues and fellow practitioners of a specialty, and they helped out one another to an extraordinary degree.

Traditional German police organization, from the Kaiser's day to the present, differed from the American and British systems in another respect also. The division between police work and detective work was sharp. Men were either uniformed officers or they were detectives, but they did not cross the border between the two. This difference was accentuated by a double system of possible careers; if a man had no more than a grammar-school education he could not hope to rise above a sort of warrant-officer rank. If he had more education or had received some special training, he might be taken into police work in a higher bracket and be given a three-year introduction to his field in work with various police squads, attendance at police school, and a sort of internship for a third year. This had worked well in the years before the First World War, when cadets from many German noble families or families of means entered the field for love of the work itself.

Although the first world war, the years of the Weimar Republic, the bloody interlude of Hitler and a second great war had altered this original pattern in many respects, the basic thinking which underlay the two new laws on my desk had its roots solidly in tradition. The problem was to take the natural German way of thinking about police work and develop a program which would go with the grain of the native wood instead of against it.

This is not the place to detail what my German colleagues and I attempted to create. The system we worked out seems to be standing the test of practical experience. The natural genius of the Germans for making even imperfect organizations operate effectively is a tremendous national asset; it will not be long before the companion talent for research and analysis will make German criminology and police tactics the equal of any in the world.

On the final night of my stay in the country we celebrated the conclusion of our labors with a party, at which I was the host.

Heads of ministries and their wives, a general who was a good friend of mine, several young Silesian noblemen, and a number of attractive young ladies, excellent dancers all, attended. It was essentially a decorous party, but toward morning the young Silesians began a series of Russian dances, which they performed as expertly as any Cossacks of the Don. This performance did not receive the critical attention the papers might well have awarded it, except for the leading Communist sheet, which somehow or other had got wind of the affair and reported it with considerable malice, winding up with the statement: "Revolver Harry (this was my sobriquet in the Communist press) bathed his guests in champagne."

The memory of that remarkable party was my last conscious thought before I drifted off to sleep on the train for Oslo.

For almost twenty years I worked for the International Criminal Police Commission, beginning as an expert on forged passports and other documents. From the start I felt sentimental about the organization which was—and is—the only realistic, effective intergovernmental organization of its kind in the world. The Commission began in 1923 as the more or less personal enterprise of Dr. Hans Schober, then Police Commissioner of Vienna, who was later to become Chancellor of Austria. It was a natural moment in history for such a development. After the dismemberment of the Austro-Hungarian Empire, confusion and misery reigned in postwar central Europe. All the new states carved out of the old Empire proudly started printing their own banknotes. The situation was made to order for forgers, check swindlers, and black-market dealers of all kinds. Since each of the new states demanded complete autonomy, and because there was little or no collaboration among the various new national police forces, it was easy for criminals to move freely.

This was the situation which induced Hans Schober to summon some of his police acquaintances of Central Europe to a conference in Vienna. There it was decided to found the International Crim-

inal Police Commission. The organization was to have its headquarters in Vienna, and the police commissioner of Vienna was
automatically to act as president. Membership was on a national
rather than individual basis, and each country which joined paid
a contribution in proportion to the number of its inhabitants. Soon
practically every European government except Russia had joined.
By World War II almost every civilized nation, including the
United States, was a member.

The Commission was not an international workaday police force,
since no state allowed detectives from another state or organization to work within its own boundaries. Rather, the Commission
served as a center of information about international criminals. It
also had another very important purpose. It undertook the responsibility of asking its members for quick arrests of criminals, pending
extradition. Extradition, as policemen have sorrowful occasion to
know, is a diplomatic and legal business which often drags along
for several months or even years. But in order to extradite there
must at least be an arrested person, and this was what the Commission could furnish. Avoiding the slow, diplomatic channels, it
could, upon a bona fide demand from the police of one of its member states, ask the police in all the other member states to search
for and arrest the criminal in question. Bona fide, since the Commission has always avoided dealing with crimes which have a political, racial, or religious aspect. It deals solely with ordinary criminals. There are enough of these.

A few years after its formation, the Commission was already
proving indispensable. The bureau in Vienna was organized into
departments dealing with such subjects as international search war-
rants, the International *Police Gazette*, forged documents, the
drug traffic, and so on. The delegates, generally the chiefs of
police, met annually in a convention held in some European capital. As these gatherings were sponsored by the Government of the
host nation and city, the particular minister of the interior was
generally the specific host, so the conventions were gay and festive
occasions, with much display and pageantry. But they served a

more important purpose than to furnish opportunity for talk and eating at banquets. They fostered personal relationships between the police chiefs, and this is all-important. If Herr Banzinger, chief of the Federal Police of Switzerland in Berne, received a telegram from Police Chief Mustapha Pasha in Cairo asking him to arrest a certain Spaniard called Ramón Gonzales for having committed a fraud in Egypt, Herr Banzinger would know that Mustapha Pasha was a thoroughly reliable person, that he need not worry about whether Gonzales was being accused of some special sort of crime for which he could not also be arrested in Switzerland, and that he could be certain the Egyptian authorities would eventually ask for his extradition.

What Churchill called "the gathering storm," that storm which almost brought Europe to an end, could be scented in the business of the Commission, closely related as it was with governmental affairs. The 1935 convention in Copenhagen provided a forecast of what was to happen.

That year the German delegate was a giant of a young man, very dapper in his Police General's light-green uniform, accompanied by an aide-de-camp. His name was Daluege. The last time I saw anything of him was in a photograph in which he was dangling, face distorted, from a gallows in Prague. In that ill-fated country he had been the last Protector of the Reich. But in 1935 he was young, gay, and an arrant Nazi. He took a liking to me and I accepted his invitation to dine one evening. When I asked how he had become the head of the German police (which he was in the days before Himmler), he replied laughingly, "My chief qualification for the job is that I have been in almost every cell in the Moabit prison in Berlin."

Daluege then offered to bet that he could drink me under the table. Another of his qualifications, perhaps? I hadn't accepted such a challenge since I was a very young man, but he was so insolent and overbearing that I became foolishly angry and agreed. It was a regrettable decision. Our bout went on for hours. Finally, the big German general slid under the table, where he was picked up by his aide-de-camp and taken home. I must confess I was not much better off myself, thereby illustrating the well-known adage that in all wars both sides are losers.

Daluege had arrived at Copenhagen in an enormous Mercedes sports car of the "Gauleiter" type. The Commission took a day off to go in buses to visit an ancient castle outside the city. We were followed by Daluege in his wonderful car, which he parked in front of the castle. Sir Norman Kendal, the Chief of Scotland Yard's famous CID, went up to it, took a close look, and asked in his fragile, old-man's voice, "How many horsepower has it?"

"Two hundred," answered Daluege proudly.

"I don't think I need so many," Sir Norman observed.

Daluege never returned to our convention. He was replaced by Arthur Nebe and Carlos Zindel, who headed the Prussian and later the German Criminal Investigation Department. Both were professional policemen, both were very mild Nazis, and even that Nazism wore off in due time. They and I were to become very close personal friends and I have always lamented their terrible ends. Nebe was involved in the plot against Hitler in 1944 and was slowly strangled to death by piano wire, after having been severely tortured. His offense was considered even greater because of his position as Lieutenant-General of the SS. Gay and cultivated Carlos Zindel left Berlin just before the collapse of the Third Reich and headed for the south in his car, which was filled to the brim with the documents of the Commission. When he reported to French Headquarters in Stuttgart to give himself up, he was badly treated, kicked out, and told to return in the afternoon. His dignity mortally injured, he went to a park and swallowed a capsule of potassium cyanide.

At two of the Conventions before the war, Germany was also represented by Count Helldorf, at that time Police Commissioner of Potsdam and later of Berlin. He was the type of Prussian Junker who makes the rest of humanity furious. For one thing, he was a homosexual and was always accompanied by a preternaturally good-looking young police captain, who was described as his aide-de-camp. Helldorf chiefly owed his career to the strength of his being a pronounced anti-Semite, and he had been instrumental in the burning of the synagogues.

My clearest memory of Count Helldorf goes back to a night in a Yugoslav coastguard cutter in the Dalmatian Bay. There was a terrible storm and most of the members of the Convention were seasick. The chief of police of Montenegro, Count Helldorf, and myself, had the good fortune not to be, so we assembled in the Captain's cabin and were drinking wine. We were talking about Communism. The Montenegran, oddly enough, showed some tolerance, saying that food and shelter were the best medicine against Communism.

"I know only one good medicine," snarled Helldorf. "That's the firing squad."

During the war, even before Stalingrad, Helldorf turned anti-Hitler. I could hardly believe my ears when he told me that after he had taken part in the first offensive against Russia he was so horrified by the massacres of the Jews and the Bolsheviks, that he went almost mad.

"I see my mistake," he said, "and I am going to put myself voluntarily before an Allied court martial."

He never got the opportunity. With Nebe and many others after the July attempt to assassinate Hitler, he was arrested and hanged. This brawling, supercilious creature at least died as a man. I have been told that on his way to the scaffold he uttered curses against Hitler in a loud voice, using the vocabulary of a medieval mercenary, which he certainly might well have been in a different incarnation.

At international conventions, even of such specific and limited a kind as ours, there are always some strange individuals. This was especially true before the war. Out of politeness the Commission did not refuse to receive, for example, former delegates who came from far away, even if they were no longer in office.

I remember especially one man who in the late twenties had been Commissioner of Police of the large port of Constanza in

Rumania. He had lost his job through some local political up-
heaval but continued to attend the annual conventions, claiming
that he was one of the founders of the Commission. He looked
like a caricature of a pre-1914 German, with shaved head, stiff
collar up to his ears, a huge tie-pin, and the conventional gold-
rimmed pincenez. Among ourselves, we maintained that he came
to the conventions chiefly to eat and drink; his Gargantuan appetite was insatiable. At the 1935 convention in Copenhagen he arrived as usual. When it was over, he walked over to gentle Eigil
Thune-Jacobsen (then chief of the state police of Denmark and
later, when the little country was occupied by the Germans, a very
unhappy Minister of Justice) and explained that he had expected
a remittance from Rumania which had not arrived and asked for
a loan of a few hundred crowns. He was accommodated unob-
trusively, but the Dane did not hear from the Rumanian until
the convention in Yugoslavia a year later. There the innocent hosts
quartered him and Thune-Jacobsen in the same hotel in Belgrade.
A meeting was inevitable. The Dane said nothing, but remorse
evidently gnawed at the Rumanian, for on the second evening he
appeared in the Dane's room, apologized, and asked him to accept
part payment in neckties. "Whereupon," said Thune-Jacobsen
laughingly when he told me the story, "he produced a dozen of the
most awful-looking green-and-red ties I ever saw." And all the leading criminal investigators in Europe, when they finally heard the
story, were unable to explain why the man's token payment was
neckties alone. The store where he obtained them must have
stocked socks and shirts as well, but perhaps he did not know
Thune-Jacobsen's size.

In 1938, the Commission nearly collapsed. That was just after
the *Anschluss*, which reduced Vienna from the capital of a sovereign state to a mere German provincial town. The police commissioner of Vienna had remained the automatic president of the
Commission since 1923. After the *Anschluss*, the Nazis disposed
of the highly respected Skubl, who had become police commissioner of Vienna after Schober's death. In Skubl's place the Nazis

appointed Steinhausl, a former Austrian police official who was a Nazi; at the time of the *Anschluss* he had been released from the penitentiary after several years' incarceration. Steinhausl was even then in bad condition and died of tuberculosis a year later. But in 1938 the Western Powers, especially France and Britain, were not pleased with a Nazi provincial police chief as the automatic head of an international police organization.

There was a feeling of great tension when the Commission convened in Bucharest, just after the *Anschluss*. This was to be the last pre-war international convention, and it was probably very fitting that it was held in Rumania. In the light of the drab, colorless, and frightened world of today, it is almost unbelievable how life was lived on the pre-war Continent, and especially in the Balkans. Today I have trouble convincing myself that such an interlude was true.

In Rumania the hospitality was lavish, to use an understatement. Since such a show was staged for police chiefs, what must have been done for visiting royalty? First we all spent a week in Bucharest. Then there was a second week on the royal yacht, going slowly down the Danube to the Black Sea. I imagine this trip was arranged by our benevolent and astute host, Beanu, the head of King Carol's secret police, with the idea of escaping the tense proceedings of the Commission in the city. Several times events had come near to open disaster, for the patience of many of us was tested to the utmost in that first week.

Beanu was the very model of a Balkan gentleman, in gray cutaway and light gray trousers, gray top hat, and the whole ensemble climaxed by a meticulously-pointed mustache. He was always kind, always smiling, and full of savoir faire. He was also loyal. When his king and Mme. Lupescu had to flee their country, he went with them. He must have been present at that terrible moment when the royal train was stopped at the frontier station and General Marinescu, the hated chief of the Rumanian police, was pulled down from the train by a mob and torn to pieces. But perhaps Beanu has come at last into quiet waters. There is a report that he is now

living as a chicken farmer in California. If it is true, I heartily wish
him a peaceful old age.

The reconciliation among the 1938 convention's contending
parties, which Beanu hoped for, pretty well came about on the
trip in the royal yacht, and how could it have been otherwise? At
every meal Russian caviar was served in unlimited quantities.
Champagne flowed from breakfast until late at night, beautiful
gypsy singers sang melodious Transylvanian songs at all times. A
bar, stocked to provide all the drinks of the entire world, was
open free of charge twenty-four hours a day, and two orchestras
played within earshot. In the evenings, when we arrived at small
fishing towns, all the fishermen were out in their boats. Hundreds
of them surrounded the ship, and in each boat there was a paper
lantern and a man playing a mandolin. The effect of this on a
dark night, to one standing on a ship's bridge overlooking the black
waters of the Danube, was enchanting.

After a few days, one fell into a sort of agreeable madness. For
my part, I was flirting with Maria Tarasana, the famous gypsy
singer, with the Chief of Police of Hungary as my rival. Maria
told us both that she would favor the one who danced the best
Wallachian folk dances, so he and I spent several delightful nights
trying to learn those difficult solo dances under her supervision.
But clear up to the end of the voyage she was never able to decide
which of us was the better dancer.

General Marinescu, the all-powerful police chief of Rumania,
occupied a suite of the best staterooms on the ship. He looked like
a fat old pirate, which without doubt he was. He was accompanied
by a beautiful young secretary who lived in his suite, probably to
be always at hand for dictation. A haggard young man, who was
quartered somewhere down below in the neighborhood of the
keel, was to be seen every day, circling around the General's suite.
He was obviously neither a delegate, a Rumanian police official,
or a member of the crew. A curious delegate one day asked him
what he was doing on the ship.

"I am the secretary's husband," he replied.

For my part, I spent as much time as I could with the Rumanian police officials on board, especially with the man in charge of the King's bodyguard. With the truly Rumanian unfettered mind, he used to tell me fantastic and indiscreet stories about the royal family. He also impressed upon me how much the Rumanians disliked the Germans and how they had introduced a new law forbidding Rumanian officials to marry girls from the German part of Transylvania. This was for the purpose of keeping the Rumanian race pure.

Finally the yacht sailed out in the Black Sea and we all took part in the sturgeon-fishing and had still more caviar. Then we steamed up the Danube again to a railroad station and took a train to Bucharest. That was certainly a fabulous voyage, about as far removed from the normal tenor of a policeman's life as I can imagine.

The delegates of the Commission took leave of each other with promises to meet in Berlin the following year. Mighty Gross-Deutschland was to be the host next time. At least, the situation had been glossed over, and the members were agreed to have the Commission work for another year under the old system. What might have happened in 1939 is anybody's guess. The convention in Berlin never was held because Hitler was already invading Poland. Most of the delegates on that incredible cruise of 1938 were never to see one another again.

In 1941, when the war was going full blast, I got a letter from Heydrich, Chief of Police of all Germany—later assassinated in Czechoslovakia—announcing that since the police of Germany was now unified and since he was the chief Police Commissioner of Vienna, it was logical that he should take over the presidency. Almost all Europe was either occupied or Fascist, and the western powers, for obvious reasons, could not be asked to a convention, so the result of this fiat was foreordained. In Sweden, we could only shrug our shoulders. Heydrich became president and the

Commission moved to Berlin, taking the unhappy Austrian Bureau officials with it. There it stayed until the end of the war, magnificently housed in a huge villa seized from some wealthy non-Aryan. The house was located in Wannsee, a fashionable suburb, and later won its greatest fame from the fact that at the end of the war, when the headquarters of the Gestapo in Berlin had been bombed by the Allies, Kaltenbrunner, by then president, made it his headquarters for a while. It was here he met Count Bernadotte when the Count attempted to negotiate the fate of the inmates of the concentration camps.

In the immediate postwar hysteria it was said that the Nazis had used the Commission for their own purposes. I don't think that this is fair. As far as I can judge, they kept up its outward seeming, at least, for the sake of vanity, and scrupulously avoided mixing any politics into its remaining activities. Many times, by the intercession of the Commission, it was possible for us neutrals to help colleagues caught in the fearful destiny which overtook so many leading Continental policemen during the war.

When the war was over, the Commission had, by force of history and by attrition, ceased to exist. There was no parliamentary way to bring the dead to life. The Russians were in Wannsee and Kaltenbrunner had been hanged in Nuremburg. So, in 1946, I started to correspond with M. Florence Louwage in Brussels, an old friend and former chief of the Belgian CID. He was the only prominent member of the old Commission who had come untainted out of the ordeal, and he was now head of the Belgian political police. In the old Commission he had been a permanent reporter. Soon he and I were agreed on renewing the Commission, and we asked all the former member states to send delegates to Brussels for this purpose.

On arriving at Brussels, where I had been so many times before the war, it struck me that the life of the city had changed considerably. In this connection the term "life" has a special meaning for a policeman, who learns from bitter experience to look at his environment with a somewhat skeptical eye. What he likes to see is order—a solid, definable kind of order in which the pattern of society can be expected to produce the minimum constabulary difficulty. In this aspect, Brussels was not so satisfactory as I had remembered it. In a country not noted for the rapidity of its changes, there were thousands of new establishments, many of them not of the sort to gladden the policeman's heart. Most conspicuous were the hundreds of new, small night spots combined with miniature brothels everywhere in the center of the city. These obviously were catering to the many American soldiers still in Brussels.

The first evening, when I was returning from a party, I dropped into one of the new cafés near the hotel to have a glass of beer. The place was gay and crowded, the kind of place and evening to be found only in the aftermath of a great war. While I was sitting looking the establishment over, in came an American soldier. I judged him to be of Scandinavian, German, or possibly Irish descent, a blond giant, gloriously drunk. He was carrying every conceivable weapon, from hand grenades to a sub-machine gun, and was obviously in search of sympathy, as well as company. He went from table to table telling the frightened guests, "I American soldier, I good soldier, I killed many Japanese," using that childish English which many Americans think foreigners are best able to understand. But the guests of the café stared, hypnotized, at his huge hands and at his grenades. Not one invited him to join the party. After a while he left, presumably to resume his hunt for understanding elsewhere. Without doubt he ended the evening in the custody of the formidable M.P.'s who patrolled the streets. Personally I could not avoid a feeling of compassion for him while breathing a heartfelt sigh of relief. Hand grenades have always made me nervous.

Next day, when we assembled in the Palais de Justice, there was a surprisingly large attendance, but few familiar faces. Many of the delegates were in uniform and many others were certainly picturesque. Instead of the intelligent, learned, and popular Nagler, who had attended so many conventions before the war and was now reported lost in the turmoil of the German Occupation, Poland was sending a colonel and a major, both former Partisans and now police officers. The colonel was more than seven feet tall and the major just about five feet. I never saw a paid who better matched the popular conception of Don Quixote and Sancho Panza.

It was unanimously decided to revitalize the Commission, but with two important changes: the Secretariat General and the International Bureau were to have their permanent sites in Paris, and the President was to be elected for a period of five years and could reside anywhere. The new Board was to consist of the President, the Secretary General who of necessity had to be French, and three Reporters General. M. Louwage of Brussels was elected president. The astute and broad-minded Louis Ducloux, the head of the Detective Division of the Sûreté, became Secretary General, and the Reporters General were Ronald Howe, head of the CID of Scotland Yard, Colonel Werner Müller, head of the police of Berne, and myself. We were all old friends who knew and trusted one another, and we set out to make the best of the new pattern.

Under the benevolent and generous protection of the French Government, the Commission proceeded to grow rapidly. Today, about fifty different states are members, among them all the leading Asiatic ones. From its huge radio station in Paris, the Commission is in daily contact with the national bureaus in most member states. The number of arrests attributable to the performance of the Commission is rapidly growing, the files on international criminals are now fully reconstructed and, if there exists a nucleus for a future world police, it is certainly in the Commission.

In 1946, when we began to reconstruct the files of the old Commission, we were not quite sure they would be of use. It was hard to believe that the steamroller of war, which had gone back and forth over the Continent in the intervening years, had left any of the prewar galaxy of international swindlers, forgers, and con men still operative. To our surprise, however, many of the old, familiar characters turned up again, starting their remembered tricks, apparently none the worse—nor more skillful—for their war experiences. The only difference was that now they had graying temples and were hard to recognize from their prewar photographs.

In prewar days, the new Communist satellite states had all been members of the Commission. Although in 1946 they did turn up with representatives in Brussels, they quickly disappeared when they saw that there was nothing for them to gain by cooperating. I cannot say that this surprised me. Officially, there is no crime (as the word is used elsewhere) in any Communist country. I remember a night I spent in 1931 with Professor Esrim, the penal doctrinarian of the Soviet world. I was studying the Russian police system, and he told me that when the Communist state was finally built in all its splendor, there would be no crime any more because all crimes had their roots in the capitalist system.

"But what about sex crimes?" I objected. "Do you think that homosexuality, for instance, has anything to do with capitalism?"

"Most certainly," the little professor in the Russian blouse answered condescendingly. "Homosexuality is a direct outcome of the rotten and perverted capitalist system."

With this official view the Russian-dominated small countries had to agree, and they rapidly ceased to cooperate with the Commission. The last to disappear was Czechoslovakia. And now, for several years, the Commission has had no members from the other side of the Iron Curtain.

These memories and a hundred others had been going through my mind on the night ride to Oslo. In the morning, the train came to the Norwegian frontier, and there were the inevitable formalities with the police and the customs. The long story of the relations between Sweden and Norway—in which the Swedes have often been at fault—has no place here, but I could not help thinking how unfortunate it was that two peoples who are perhaps closer than any other two peoples on earth should require these hindrances to human interchange. The very convention to which

I was going surely proved that the need for nations to work together was greater than the need for separateness. One thing that I and the other delegates had certainly learned through long years was that crime knows no boundaries. Only the Communists, who would not be present, clung to the idea that it is impossible to cooperate with someone unless that someone believes exactly as they believe, and the even less sensible idea that trouble (and crime is one of society's troubles) can be isolated and kept behind some kind of pale.

Still, there was a measure of hope in the fact that the police of the rest of the world had managed to learn this rudimentary lesson, at least, and had set up a means of dealing with the kind of human trouble which they were partly responsible for preventing. Even though I was leaving the life of a working policeman behind me, I had no intention of forgetting the things that service in my curious profession had taught me. If crime is an endemic disease of society, there are still ways of coping with it on a basis larger than any one country can provide. That is the mission of the International Criminal Police Commission.

At the railway station in Oslo, Police Commissioner Kristian Welhaven was waiting. I knew that he was about to retire, having reached the age of seventy. Even now, it is hard to think of the police department of Oslo without Commissioner Welhaven. He is one of those Vikings who are still produced in Norway, high of stature, lofty of morals, and a master of men. In the Occupation, he was arrested by the Germans and put to hard labor in a concentration camp because he would not relinquish the principles of legality which had governed his life. After a couple of years he was sent to Germany and kept for several months in a cell deep in the cellar of the Gestapo house in Berlin. Finally we managed, with the International Criminal Police Commission as intermediary, to have him banished to a village in Bavaria, where he was joined by his wife. There he remained until the end of the war.

The day was fearfully hot. High temperatures are not rare in Oslo, which is situated at the bottom of a natural cauldron, with

high mountains surrounding it. Still, it was rather surprising to hear
a few days later that the Syrian delegate had had a heat stroke.

The convention was held in the main building of the University,
a comparatively small house flanked by statues of two of its famous 19th-century professors and quite near the comely small
castle of the King. The usual eloquent opening addresses, this time
by the Norwegian Minister of Justice and the president of our
Commission, were delivered, and then we settled down to work.
From my seat on the dais at the side of the president, I could
overlook all the delegates. Their places were marked with the flags
of their nations. What a contrast to the prewar Commission, which
was almost entirely a Continental affair! Today I could see the
slightly-built Burmese in their peculiar caps and silk shirts, husky
Indians, the mild and smiling Japanese, a fiery Filipino colonel
straight from the Korean war, and many other non-Europeans.
It was a heartening sight, an assembly created by a profession and
brought together without benefit of diplomats.

A whole week raced by with discussions and drafting of resolu-
tions. No time was wasted in speeches. At our conventions there
are no lectures, and contributors' papers are not read but only explained and given in resumé by their authors. All papers have to be
in the hands of the secretariat a couple of months in advance.
They are then printed and sent out in advance to the delegates.
This procedure saves a lot of time, especially at a bilingual convention where every sentence has to be translated back and forth
in French and English.

On the last evening of the week, the Norwegian Government
gave a farewell banquet at the Akershus, the medieval castle of
Oslo. The Akershus is unique. It is almost the only medieval building still standing in a city which for centuries has had practically
nothing but frame buildings, and which has been ravaged many
times by fire. Even the Castle did not wholly escape. It was formerly partly in ruins, but has been reverently restored in the last
twenty years. That night the wonderful big banquet hall was lit by
a log fire and candles, and a herald in medieval costume blew a

trumpet before and after every speech. It is easy to understand why
this magnificent place is dear to the hearts of all Norwegians.

I left the banquet finally to catch the evening train for Sweden,
eager for the fields of swaying wheat, for the skies above my little
lake, for my library with the many books that I had never had
time to read carefully.